THE
LOST
ORCHARD

A French chef rediscovers
a great British food heritage

Stories and recipes
by

RAYMOND
BLANC

First published in 2019 by Headline Home
An imprint of Headline Publishing Group

4

Hardback ISBN 978 1 4722 67580
eISBN 978 1 4722 67573

Text with Sheila Keating
Publishing Director: Lindsey Evans
Senior Editor: Kate Miles
Copy Editor: Kay Halsey
Proofreaders: Sarah Coward and Margaret Gilbey
Index: Caroline Wilding

SOURCES

Scott's Orchardist (2nd Edition), 1872
Robert Hogg, *The Fruit Manual*, first published 1884, and *The Herefordshire Pomona*, first published 1878
Joan Morgan, *The New Book of Apples*, 2002, and *The Book of Pears*, 2015
Sue Clifford and Angela King, *The Apple Source Book*, 1991
Barrie E. Juniper and David J. Mabberley, *The Story of the Apple*, 2006
Christopher Stocks, *Forgotten Fruits*, 2008
William Lauche, *Deutsche Pomologie*, 1883
Edward Bunyard, *The Anatomy of Dessert*, 1929
William Forsyth, *A Treatise on the Culture and Management of Fruit Trees*, 1802
John Worlidge, *Vinetum Britannicum, Or a Treatise of Cider*, 1678
Various editions of *The Gardeners' Chronicle* and *The Practical Gardener*

And the websites of orchard groups all around the country, who do inspiring and important work researching old
varieties, encouraging the swapping of information, spreading the word about grafting courses and 'Apple Days' etc.

Typeset by CC Book Production
Printed and Bound in Great Britain by Clays Ltd, Elcograf S.p.A.

HEADLINE PUBLISHING GROUP
An Hachette UK Company
Carmelite House
50 Victoria Embankment
London EC4Y 0DZ

www.headline.co.uk
www.hachette.co.uk

THE

LOST
ORCHARD

'With much appreciation to our wonderful garden team, led by Anne Marie Owens, at Belmond Le Manoir aux Quat'Saisons.

Also, much gratitude to my expert friends and partners, who have supported me in making my heritage orchard dream a reality.'

Raymond Blanc

'I have long admired and supported Raymond's passion and commitment to organic values, his love of gardens and his celebration of the craft and knowledge of both the chef and the gardener and the way these two are intertwined. Beyond the twelve gardens at Belmond Le Manoir aux Quat'Saisons, he has now created a wonderful heritage orchard, an important contribution to reminding us all of the wonderful varieties of fruits that we may be losing, evoking a time when apples, plums or cherries were connected with a local village, town or county, and could be again . . .'

Sue Biggs, CBE
Director General of the Royal Horticultural Society

CONTENTS

CONTENTS

CONTENTS

INTRODUCTION

LE MANOIR

This is the story of not one, but two orchards: an English orchard and a French orchard, but intertwined. At Belmond Le Manoir aux Quat'Saisons, an old English house in Oxfordshire with a French heart and vision, our two cultures constantly enrich each other: the British flag next to the French flag, petanque next to croquet on the lawn . . . and so we have our two orchards, planted in different phases and for different reasons, but united in the spirit of rediscovery and celebration.

The orchard – or orchards – is the latest chapter in the story of our magical organic gardens, which are the beating heart of everything that we do at Le Manoir. The twelve gardens are the canvas on which our gastronomy and our values are written by people who are in love with what they do. Each garden adds its own layer of beauty, fantasy and emotion, from the wildflower garden to the mysterious valley of mushrooms, but equally they are all part of one vision, of an entire sustainable ecosystem. For so long I had dreamed of enriching this ensemble with an orchard filled with thousands of fruit trees, and finally that dream has become a reality.

The English orchard was all about bringing back some of the wonderful heritage varieties of apples and pears and other fruits that had been lost or forgotten. Fruit gardens have been a huge part of British culture since medieval times. Serene and often secluded inside their protective stone walls, they evoked the Garden of Paradise, perfect for quiet religious contemplation – or secret romantic trysts. Shakespeare set his famous balcony scene in *Romeo and Juliet* in the Capulets' orchard, whose high walls Romeo had cleared 'with love's light wings'. Yet since 1950 England has lost 57 per cent of its traditional orchard area and, shockingly, by 1997 in our county of Oxfordshire alone, around 90 per cent of orchard acres had been destroyed or abandoned.

Let me paint a picture for you that still haunts me. It is of thousands and thousands of dusky purple plums, fallen on the ground and lying unharvested and unwanted, in an abandoned orchard in the Vale of Evesham. I saw this for myself while filming there for a TV programme. Once, this vale was lit up with the glorious colours of Victoria plums, Yellow Egg plums and Purple Pershores, but since the Second World War 80 per cent of plum orchards have been lost.

And where are the hundreds of diverse and fascinating varieties of apples whose rich and complex flavours the Victorians celebrated like fine wines? Our choice has been whittled down by the supermarkets to a mere handful, mostly imported, and selected for their bright colour, uniform shape and sweetness.

And so to my beloved French orchard, which is about a different kind of rediscovery, of the fruits and flavours that are in my heart from my childhood spent in the gardens, hills and forests of Franche-Comté in Eastern France. I wanted to find the apples, pears, apricots, mirabelles, cherries and peaches that my grandfather and my father grew and my grandmother and mother cooked and bottled and preserved to feed our family of five children, and I wanted to bring them to Oxfordshire. *Terroir* – the local conditions, soil and climate – is so important, no matter whether you are growing flowers, vegetables or fruit, but I wanted to push the boundaries and find out which of my treasured fruits it might be possible to grow in our local soil and climate. Or would this end in disaster?

Of course you cannot just create a magnificent orchard on a grand scale overnight. It is not easy, I promise you. I had to fight for my orchard! Of all my projects this was the biggest and most complex, and it demanded an incredible amount of hard work, money and research, and above all the help of my knowledgeable friends and my gardeners, led by my wonderful, long-suffering Anne Marie. I am a chef who loves art, gardens, music, design, food, of course – too many things! But I accept that I know only so much in these other areas and so in order to create a truly special experience for our guests, not just good, but sublime, I needed help to make the dream become reality.

Gathering the right knowledge and preparing the groundwork took the best part of five years and mountains of documents. Everything begins with the health of the soil. That is the foundation of all organic growing, and the purity of my orchard had to be sacred. It must be free of any pesticides and herbicides to give the healthiest fruit to our guests. First we had to establish the kind of soil we had in this part of the gardens, its structure, what minerals it contained. And it was bad news. The first samples were full of clay, and as we know very well, clay retains water, which is not good for fruit trees. Equally it was missing a number of minerals. So now we had to drain it completely, then plough and enrich this clay with potassium and potash before we could even plant the first tree.

Next came the story of the borehole. I wanted to find enough water for all the fruit and vegetables at Le Manoir; I hoped to bottle our own pure water for our guests, and I even dreamed of discovering pure spa water for a future project. Of course life rarely turns out the way you expect it to. Instead what we found was a high level of iron, so my dream was doomed, but this very expensive borehole still allows us to irrigate each of our trees and all of our gardens.

We also had to consider the wind direction and the exposure of the trees. It is a very English thing to do, but we must talk about the weather. The orchard is at the bottom of a slope and, as cold air is heavier than warm, frosts and mists travel down through it. Just this year we lost my apricots and peaches to frost and I was disconsolate. And more and more we will have to confront the newer challenge of climate change. In one spot in the gardens it could be 22 degrees where it had been –1 degree the week before.

An orchard has so many enemies. Viruses and diseases, not to mention creatures: airborne, burrowing, furry, cute, they can attack from anywhere. The deer, who wander everywhere in Oxfordshire, can eat the tender shoots of a tree and kill about fifty in a night, while the rabbits gnaw away at the bark of young trees. And then there are the foxes, who can jump up to 1.8 metres, and will eat dozens of the chickens at a time. These chickens will soon be scuttling through the orchards, so we had to put up two-metre fencing around and through the orchard to try to keep the foxes out.

And, of course, the great project is not yet finished. We still have so much more to do. As I write we are planting more varieties to replace some that haven't coped with the vagaries of the weather. Beauty and structure are crucial (see page 148), and so the orchard will soon be surrounded by fruit hedges and cane fruits, from blackcurrants to Glen Doll Scottish raspberries, and Burgundian blackcurrants, which we will use to make our jams. More lavender paths, which will blaze blue and purple in the summer and turn silver grey in winter, will attract the bees from the bee village, which is yet another story (see page 246)! And I am already planning the next adventures:

a farm, with a farm shop to sell our fruit and vegetables, and a vine-yard, so that we can produce our own wine – a long-standing dream.

I am a happy man when I see our guests wandering through the gardens, chatting with our gardeners and enjoying the fruits of our orchards, be it a plum or apricot compote for their breakfast or a *paquet surprise* with plump, spiced cherries. And I smile when I see a waiter explaining the variety of apples in our fruit bowls. But the orchard is also part of a much bigger picture that is to do with the huge questions we face about the kind of agriculture we will have and what kind of food we will be eating tomorrow. It is about reconnecting with our food, growing more of it locally and with fewer, or no, chemicals. If we could restore our lost orchards and replant the diversity of apples, pears, plums and cherries associated with our own regions and communities, then we could help support our small shops and markets. This in turn could help the farmers, growers and craftsmen to keep their businesses and the villages to hold on to their pubs and their post offices.

And in a small way you too can help. Even if you have a small garden, a backyard or a balcony, you can plant a heritage fruit tree. It is easy to train an apple, apricot or pear tree against a wall, or grow one in a container (see page 262). It will be a joy to behold and a source of lasting pleasure. Imagine picking your own fresh fruit and making your own compotes, tarts, jams and preserves (see the recipes section from page 267 onwards). I urge you to do it. In fact I beg you to do it.

A LITTLE HELP FROM MY FRIENDS

An orchard on the scale of ours requires a phenomenal amount of expertise in the planning, and then it demands constant love and care to keep it healthy and fruitful.

Of course our orchard would make no sense commercially, as today most fruits are grown and graded for size, shape, colour and flavour uniformity according to the demands of the supermarkets. As consumers we have been convinced to buy by looking at what is attractive on the outside, not what is inside. And what is inside many modern fruits is often a monotonous sweetness at the expense of the complexity of flavour of some older, heritage varieties. What is more, it is a huge challenge to grow fruit without chemicals. We accept that we will not match the volumes of a conventional orchard, but I believe that it is right to avoid spraying our trees, or using even the permitted 'organic' pesticides, as I don't want these to go into the soil – or my chickens!

So I am indebted to the many wonderful friends, craftsmen, academics and gardeners who pooled their knowledge into this huge project. Without them my dream would have stayed just a dream. All of us are in love with the drama and romance of growing, grafting and sharing good food, and in our very different ways we are all seeking those special moments when you might just touch excellence.

There are no adequate words to thank my lovely Anne Marie, who began as a young apprentice and has had to keep up with this demanding dreamer of a Frenchman for thirty-five years. Twelve gardens on, when I said, 'Anne Marie, we are going to create a wonderful orchard filled with thousands of trees', she just smiled – a smile I know very well – in her serene way and gave me that look that says, 'Oh my God, here we go again.' But deep inside she understands the big dream of creating excellence for each of our guests. And so the research began.

On a beautiful summer's day we visited the RHS orchard at Wisley together. This extraordinary orchard has over 1,300 different fruit cultivars, including almost 700 apples, 175 pears and 100 plums, many trained in espaliers and fan shapes. There are collections of cider apples and also cultivars that are disease-resistant and grown organically, so these were a huge inspiration. We learned so much about varieties and techniques from the gardeners who shared their knowledge and enthusiasm in that typically generous way of people who work with plants and the soil.

And when we visited Brogdale Farm, home of the National Fruit Collection, I was similarly blown away. Imagine, 150 acres of orchard, with 2,200 different varieties of apple, 550 varieties of pear, 337 varieties of plum and 285 different varieties of cherries! I have been so touched by the support we have continually received from Brogdale, and by their extraordinary generosity when some of our trees failed, and they immediately offered to replace them.

In search of a template for our orchard I was prepared to venture to every corner of France, as well as the UK. On one momentous occasion in October I borrowed a small plane and its captain from a friend in order to fly off with Anne Marie to a mythical place whose owner is one of the greatest fruit growers in the world. His name is Arnaud Delbard and his grandfather, Georges, was a rose specialist who first began breeding fruit trees on the family's farm in Malicorne in 1935. Following on from his father, Henri, Arnaud has taken the Delbard Nursery to new heights, using innovative scientific methods to develop superb, delicious fruits with great resistance to disease, and introducing more than fifty new varieties to the market, always with beauty, flavour and respect for the environment at the heart of his work. These fruits connect so well with our own organic ethos at Le Manoir aux Quat'Saisons.

I wanted to visit Monsieur Delbard in his very beautiful *verger* (fruit garden), which is over eighty years old, not only to discuss varieties that might enjoy the climate of Oxfordshire, but to see in practice the principle of growing fruit trees *en espalier*, in a 'double palmette' and in columns.

Flying through a storm in this little plane was an experience neither of us will forget, especially Anne Marie, who likes to have her feet planted firmly in the Oxfordshire soil, preferably at Le Manoir. But we landed safely in Malicorne, deep in the quiet of this remote part of the French countryside, where we had arranged to meet William Sibley (see opposite), and he introduced us to Arnaud Delbard and his papa. In a very French way we enjoyed a wonderful long meal with good wine and I felt so privileged to share this private moment with such great craftsmen. Following this lovely gathering of new friends around the table, Monsieur Delbard took us to see the treasured fruit gardens, which were extraordinary. The large gates opened up onto his life's work. The old, sculptured trees in their neat rows were heavy with perfectly formed fruit: it was such a resplendent sight. Despite its age, the orchard was positively breathing good health. As we wandered through this beautiful place, images of what my own orchard could be like began to form in my mind.

We came away armed with a tremendous amount of information about which varieties could grow in England, as Monsieur Delbard had planted some vergers here, and I even had my own rose named after me!

Will Sibley has been a great friend and a tower of strength for twenty years and his generous help and advice have been crucial to the creation of the orchard and the fruits we chose to grow. For many years Will was a trustee and then chairman of the trustees of East Malling, the biggest centre of fruit science in Britain, which has been responsible for the development of most modern varieties of fruit in this country. Always searching and researching requires such patience, knowledge and commitment – for it can take years to create a single new variety that satisfies the many demands of looks, resistance to disease, reliability and, most of all, flavour.

With Will I travelled many times to France, especially to the apricot regions to see where the best fruits grow and which might do well grown organically in the cooler and wetter climate of Oxfordshire. The first ones we chose were grown around Nîmes and planted before we even began work on the orchard. They grace the old stone walls at the entrance to Le Manoir aux Quat'Saisons and almost every year for over a decade they have produced hundreds and hundreds of beautiful sweet orange- and pink-flushed fruit (see page 218). And Will has been integral to the job of selecting the fruits for what we call our 'taste and textures' section of the orchard, in which we grow the varieties specifically for use in our kitchens.

One of the fine fruits he has championed is the Avalon Pride peach, which is the only variety that doesn't suffer from peach leaf curl, and he tells a wonderful story of its discovery. It was first noticed in the 1960s in a forest in British Colombia by a British woman called Margaret Proud. She had moved there with her father, who was a keen gardener, and she knew that leaf curl was a problem for peaches, and so she was amazed to see that this tree had perfect leaves. She took some buds and grafted them, and one of them grew in her garden.

Some time later Margaret moved to Washington State, and on the day she was due to leave, a bear came into the garden and destroyed

11

the tree! Will promises me this story is true. However, she managed to salvage some pieces of wood and took them to a grower called Sam Benowitz at Raintree Nursery, who propagated the tree, and Margaret named the variety Avalon Pride after the house she grew up in in England. Sam Benowitz suggested that he send a sample to Will so that he could look after it and promote it for her, and it is now probably the best-selling peach in the world: yellow-fleshed and gorgeous. And soon to be in our orchard!

In my insatiable quest for knowledge, I enlisted the help and advice of Dr David Pennell, former director of Brogdale, home of the National Fruit Collection, who became an invaluable support and source of information throughout the difficult and demanding job of planning and planting an organic orchard through its different phases. David perfectly understood my goal of combining flavour, heritage and beauty through a combination of fruits mainly from Britain and France.

One of the most charming orchards I had the good fortune to visit belongs to the wonderful Dr Barrie Juniper, academic and author of *The Story of the Apple* (2006). Such a lovely man. His hidden sanctuary must be one of the oldest and beautifully natural, even scruffy, apple orchards in England, and he proudly introduced me to so many venerable varieties, and mostly in French!

I have always understood the influence that terroir can have on a fruit or vegetable, and I wanted to discover more of the history and culture of fruit and orchards around Britain, especially the fruits that had traditionally been grown locally to Le Manoir – many of which were almost lost. So I am indebted to Marcus Roberts, founder of the Mid-Shires Orchard Group, who assisted me with our project from the start: a man who is totally dedicated to encouraging people to set up community and heritage orchards, teaching traditional skills, researching and seeking out old varieties, and grafting them and distributing them around our surrounding counties to ensure they avoid extinction. He also advises historic properties on conserving and planting orchards. When we decided to taste over one hundred different varieties of heritage apple to determine their profile for use in the kitchen, Marcus scoured nurseries and old orchards in private gardens around our region to find the finest samples. Many of the traditional varieties are now planted in our orchard and appear in this book.

I love to teach, and to see young chefs and gardeners alike developing their craft, so it was a joy to me to watch the development of one of our gardeners, James Dewhurst. A quiet young man, as we began to plant the orchard I could see his enthusiasm and interest grow. He couldn't spend enough time there, learning about growing, grafting, cultivars, rootstocks. Even though he has now moved on he still returns every so often to help keep the orchard looking beautiful and healthy. When you have people like this on your team, you are truly blessed.

Two extraordinary, generous friends, the best in their field, planted my French orchard with varieties grown in my beloved Franche-Comté. I was first introduced to Henri Xavier Guillaume and his brother, Pierre-Marie, by the mayor of my village, as their world-famous viticultural nursery in Charcenne is only about twenty miles from my home.

The Guillaume family have been grafting vines since 1895, at a time when Franche-Comté, along with wine regions throughout France, was rebuilding its vineyards after the phylloxera crisis. Xavier is a genius *vigneron*, who looks after the rootstock and the vines of some of the most famous vineyards in the world, such as Domaine de la Romanée-Conti, Château Margaux and Louis Roederer. The

Guillaume family also supply the seedlings for Taittinger and the Louis Pommery project, as well as helping and advising winemakers at more than a hundred British vineyards, such as Nyetimber and Chapel Down, and our neighbours, Hundred Hills Vineyard in Henley-on-Thames, who make excellent wines. And Pierre-Marie is a well-known agronomist who concentrates on research and genetic selection. Together they make a formidable team, and in the true tradition of great nursery families, Pierre-Marie's son, François, is also a knowledgeable craftsman.

Already I am working with Xavier and Pierre-Marie on the next magical chapter of the Anglo–French story at Le Manoir: our own vineyard. We will grow Pinot Noir, Pinot Meunier, some Chardonnay and the 'must-have' grape from my home, Savagnin, which is most famous for Vin Jaune, and I hope that our new friends from the magnificent Hundred Hills will help us to vinify our own wine!

APPLES

Once upon a time on a summer's day, the Royal Horticultural Society, with William Sibley, organised a tasting of heritage apples at Le Manoir. It was the memorable day I discovered what I regard as the world's greatest apple, the Cox's Orange Pippin (see page 84) (though for many years I thought it was a Queen Cox, until Will corrected me!). And it was pivotal to the birth of this wonderful project: the creation of a beautiful orchard that would acknowledge and glorify the magnificent old apples that were once grown around Britain, as well as some from France – many of which are so nearly lost to us.

Each one of these apples has a story to tell, so for me the orchard project and the writing of this book has been a magical adventure into a world of discovery. Sometimes the fascination begins with a strange or amusing name. It seems that even centuries ago many of the old nurserymen knew that an evocative or clever name could help market their new varieties. How elegant must an apple be that is called Faerie Queene or Ballerina? How romantic the Leicestershire apple Marriage Maker, which has pink flesh and, if you are lucky, when you cut it in half shows a perfect white heart.

But how unfortunate the apple that is called Duck's Bill or Eynsham Dumpling! Sometimes life is cruel.

An apple might be known by many alternative names in different regions of England, let alone abroad (a muddle that the Victorian pomologists tried to resolve). And sometimes names become mangled in translation. There is a rare Yorkshire apple called the Sykehouse Russet, which was thought to be lost, but was rediscovered in 1999 by a retired canon from West Sussex. According to the great expert and writer Robert Hogg (see page 20), at the turn of the nineteenth century the German pomologist August Friedrich Adrian Diel translated it as the 'English Hospital Reinette', thinking that Syke was an old way of spelling 'sick' and not the name of a Yorkshire village.

What should I make of the Gloucestershire apples Arlingham Schoolboys or Old Tankard; the Devonshire Slack-ma-girdle, and more curious still: Hen's Turd? And who was Charles Ross (see page 65) or Annie Elizabeth (see page 30)?

Some great stars of the apple world have been discovered as seedlings growing in cottage gardens, on rubbish heaps, or under the protective walls of stately homes. Others are the results of experiments by connoisseurs, amateur horticulturalists, or the great Victorian nurserymen and women who made it their life's work to discover, graft and propagate the finest apples of their day, detailing them in beautifully illustrated catalogues, or *Orchardists*.

Some varieties still bear the names of the farm workers, clergymen or seedsmen who found or raised them, but sometimes, frustratingly, an apple's history is simply lost in the mists of time. Some of these beautiful old treasures, whose names have been long forgotten, may still exist in people's gardens, or in hedgerows, or the scruffy long grass of an abandoned orchard, which is why orchard groups all around the country are keenly identifying, seeking out and re-establishing as many as possible of these old heritage fruits.

These days, when the emphasis is on modern varieties, it is hard to imagine stumbling across the new Cox's Orange Pippin or Blenheim Orange (see page 42) growing in a hedgerow, but it could still happen. Marcus Roberts told me of a seedling discovered in a hedge by the co-founder of the Mid-Shires Orchard Group, Andy Howard, which was unlike any variety he knew. It was a striking, large, conical apple that was quite flavoursome and juiced fantastically well. He and Marcus grafted it, named it the Deddington Pippin, and distributed it around the area. So next time you are walking along the country lanes keep an eye out, as you never know what jewel you might find!

AN APPLE FOR EVERY SEASON

That we know as much as we do about so many old varieties of apple is down to the Victorian writers and nurserymen and women who painstakingly researched and described them. What is more, they recognised the seasonal nature of apples in a way that has been lost to us as the supermarkets have blurred the seasons for all of our fruit and vegetables.

Perhaps the greatest authority was Robert Hogg, the son of an Edinburgh nurseryman, who began his career with the famous Brompton Park Nursery and later co-founded the Pomological Society in 1854. At various times from 1858 he was secretary and chairman of the Horticultural Society's Fruit Committee, and later became secretary of the Royal Horticultural Society. However, he was best known as a writer and editor and his wonderful fruit descriptions, historical research and advice in The Fruit Manual *and* The Herefordshire Pomona *are still relied upon today, and I have quoted him many times in the following pages.*

Later came Edward Bunyard, who succeeded his father, George, in the family's nursery. A food and wine enthusiast and writer, he declared, 'No fruit is more to our English taste than the apple', and in print and on the radio he seduced readers and listeners with vivid and evocative descriptions of his favourite seasonal varieties, such as the 'rich and mellow' Orleans Reinette (see page 150), of which he wrote, 'its brown-red flush and glowing gold do very easily suggest that if Rembrandt had painted a fruit piece he would have chosen this apple', or the Cox's Orange Pippin (see page 84), which in November was, for him, 'the Château Yquem of apples'.

If picked at the right time, or properly stored, his selection of apples would provide fruit from September to the end of the following June. He also understood that within its season each apple had a particular moment when aroma, sweetness and acidity would come together in a perfect storm of flavour. 'The right season to eat an apple is a matter of importance; to catch the volatile ethers at their maximum development, and the acids and sugars at their most grateful balance requires knowledge and experiment,' he wrote. 'Many apples will keep far beyond their period of maximum flavour, and in some this moment is so fleeting that they are hardly worth growing; a week-end away from home might prove disastrous. Times and seasons are therefore but rough guides to the correct moment; experiment alone can decide.'

After Bunyard died, the mantle of protector of British apples was taken up by Philip Morton Shand, a wine connoisseur, who had famously written in his Book of Food *in 1927 that, 'The French have poor taste in apples, liking them merely soft and sweet. After all, no nation can have an impeccable taste in everything, and the inevitable Achille's heel is just as likely to be found in apples as in drawing-room furniture.'*

I wonder if he travelled to the great apple orchards of Normandy, the Loire or Rhône Valley! But I wholeheartedly agree with his conclusion that, 'Who on earth with a spark of individuality in his make-up wants to eat the self same apple every blessed day in the year.'

THE GREAT APPLE TASTING

My approach to the food we grow has always been the same: I want to understand the nuances of every variety in order to discover the best flavours and textures and which cooking technique will suit each best, so with my team we go to extraordinary lengths to do this, whether it is tasting fifty aubergines or forty chillies (an eye-watering experience!).

The orchard is about heritage and beauty, but crucially it is also about flavour; and so we needed to discover which apples to grow for the kitchen. I have never understood my British friends' approach of splitting apples into just two single categories, cooking and eating – or perhaps three, if you add in cider apples. The Victorians identified certain, more acidic, apples as destined for the kitchen, and other 'dessert' apples for enjoying raw; however, they also understood which of the 'cooking' apples, in which season, would make the best sauce, jellies, pies, soufflés or dumplings. But much of that old knowledge has been lost, and it is still far too restrictive for me.

As a chef and a Frenchman, I don't make this simplistic and confusing distinction between cooking and eating apples. It is crucial to me to push the boundaries to understand how to achieve the best flavours and textures from every individual apple, in order to give my guests the best, most sublime apple experience.

So I set my own five specific tests. I wanted to know which apple would give the best juice and how each variety would behave when pureed, baked whole, in a tarte Maman Blanc or a tarte tatin. I do apologise to my English friends for not including pies and crumbles – though I can assure you that I make an excellent crumble (see page 293).

I consulted my expert friends about which apples to taste, especially Britain's most treasured heritage varieties, so Marcus Roberts scoured orchards and walled gardens around the country to assemble the very best sun-kissed examples. Over an exhausting two weeks we tested and tasted over a hundred apples and it was a huge and valuable undertaking, the like of which I don't believe has been done in any other kitchen.

Usually green apples, like Granny Smith (see page 133), make the best juices when you use the whole of the skin – although I must say the best apple juice I have ever tasted is made with the Egremont Russet (see page 105). For puree, or for a pie or crumble, the apple must be very moist and have enough acidity to break down quickly, like Cox's Orange Pippin (see page 84) or Red Windsor (see page 152). I want an appetising colour and characterful flavour that needs no sugar or hardly any at all.

For baking a whole apple (at 170°C/150°C fan/gas 3), I want a fruit like Chivers Delight (see page 71) or D'Arcy Spice (see page 91), which will hold its shape without blistering too much or, worse, imploding or collapsing, while the flesh should remain moist and become meltingly soft. For a tarte tatin, an apple must be tight enough to hold its shape and also have a high acidity. Why? Because we are going to add caramel, and so the apple must combat the sweetness. Our favourites include Cox's Orange Pippin, Devonshire Quarrenden (see page 95), Granny Smith and Braeburn (see page 49). And for a tarte Maman Blanc, I am looking for an apple such as Captain Kidd (see page 59), Lord Lambourne (see page 145), and, of course, the Reinette Grise du Canada (see page 156) of Maman Blanc. These have the perfect balance of acidity and sugar, and enough texture to allow the crescents of apple to keep their shape, but fluff up, and turn a beautiful golden colour.

It was most important to me that our judges were not only our chefs, but our gardeners too – and anyone who happened to be passing by: a guest, a housekeeper . . . we are all-inclusive! For the last thirty-five years my vision for Le Manoir aux Quat'Saisons has been to bond together the garden and the kitchen, where my Executive Head Chef Gary Jones and Chef Pâtissier Benoit Blin ensure that our values are propagated and shared. That is why Le Manoir has such an extraordinary energy. A chef needs to go out into the gardens and understand the provenance and seasonality of a fruit or vegetable, what are the best varieties for specific dishes, and how they are grown; and a gardener needs to come into the kitchen and understand how a fruit or vegetable will be used, and what qualities a chef is looking for. How young or mature a fruit or vegetable is, how its flavour has been affected by the weather, or its level of ripeness . . . all these small variables make a difference in terms of taste. When chefs and gardeners understand and respect each other and the challenges they each face, you have a marvellous creative environment and beautiful food for our guests.

So what did we learn together? Well, as you will discover in the pages that follow, we found that most apples are good at something and some are good at a few. A handful, like Adams' Pearmain (see page 27), Devonshire Quarrenden and Discovery (see page 98), are good at many things; and a few shining stars like the Cox's Orange Pippin, Red Windsor and the rare Cheddar Cross (see page 69) can achieve almost anything. Very occasionally an ancient variety turns out not to be very good at anything, as our rigorous examination exposed the truth that a romantic name and a treasured history may not always be enough to satisfy the demands of our changing gastronomy and our customers' expectations. And so some old heritage apples fell short. But I am not out to ruin reputations, and they still have an important place in our orchard.

Also, I have to acknowledge that, since every variety not only has its season, but its perfect moment when the balance of sugars and acidity combine to produce perfection, we may not have done justice to every one. As Edward Bunyard cautioned in The Anatomy of Dessert (1929), 'Let us dismiss the popular error that a single test is sufficient for a fair judgement of a fruit. Often one hears the phrase, "I tasted so-and-so and did not think much of it." Flavour depends much upon the season, and many varieties require a really hot summer to develop their highest qualities.'

And so, although I have reported our judgement on each apple faithfully, whenever we have tested a variety that is generally looked on with fondness but we have found it to be unpleasant, harsh in its acidity or unwilling to yield its crisp flesh to the softening heat of the hob or oven, we have to ask: did we do this apple a disservice? Did we taste it too early, or too late, to show its full potential? On another day, in a different hour, would it all have been different?

Will Sibley, who has tasted thousands of apples and other fruits in his role as chairman of the trustees at the East Malling Research Centre, is as romantic as this Frenchman when it comes to searching for that moment 'when a particular variety ripens to a certain point on a certain day and the sugar levels are a perfect match for the flavonoids. That is when the magic happens, and you remember it for ever,' he says. 'There are scientific tests you can do to give you a really good idea of the optimum time to eat an apple, of course, but mostly it is about the drama of hitting just the right moment when the acidity and sugars are in perfect balance. A day or even an hour later and it can be gone. I remember doing a tasting involving the Alkmene variety, which *is German-bred, but has the Cox's Orange Pippin as one of its parents and is sold in the UK as Early Windsor. There were about twelve of us on the tasting panel and all of us agreed this was the best apple we had ever eaten. Two days later, it tasted quite different. I even remember my second-best apple experience, sitting on a wall in Edinburgh eating a Laxton Fortune. The flavour was so extraordinary I can still taste it now.'*

In our great taste test I was lucky enough to be presented with yet another glorious example of the Cox's Orange Pippin, and my heart sang. Other apples fared less well, but that is the eternal, mysterious and seductive, yet sometimes frustrating, magnetism of the apple . . . and why you should not take my tasting notes as gospel. Rather, they are the findings of an eternally curious chef, who wanted to understand what each of these apples could contribute to our orchard experience at Le Manoir. I hope they will inspire you to try to seek out some of these old varieties and taste them yourself. Better still, grow them yourself, and demand to know why your favourite variety is not on the shelf in your local shop or supermarket.

ADAMS' PEARMAIN

54 trees in my English orchard
Norfolk/Herefordshire, 1826
SEASON: *early October*
APPEARANCE: *greenish gold, becoming streaked/flushed with red*
BEST FOR: *puree, baking whole and tarts*

For a chef it is such a joy to discover a wonderful new variety of any fruit, and for me it is even more rewarding to find an almost lost apple that is part of the British heritage, even though its true origins are quite obscure. This beautiful old variety was one of the most popular eating apples in Victorian times, thanks to its rich, nutty, aromatic flavour, and quite dry yellow flesh. Now it is almost totally unknown, although it is still beloved by small-scale gardeners. I wish I could introduce more of you to this apple as it is truly majestic, rather gracious, tall and elegantly pear-shaped, and so appetising-looking with its smooth, red-blushed skin of many shades, through gold and orange to deeper red, almost mahogany. The first time I saw it, I knew it had character and I hoped it would offer me some interesting new flavours.

Adams' Pearmain is one of those apples that has fascinated people for centuries because we cannot know for sure where it came from originally: was it Norfolk or was it Herefordshire? All that has been established is that scions (cuttings for grafting) of it were sent to the London Horticultural Society in 1826 by Robert Adams – hence the name. However, Mr Adams originally called the apple the Norfolk Pippin, possibly because he had received the scions from someone in Norfolk, or had found them there himself.

Robert Hogg wrote that he had 'endeavoured unsuccessfully to discover the origin of this valuable apple', before chancing on the possibility that it had also been known by yet another name. 'It was not till I attended the first Pomological Meeting of the Woolhope Club at Hereford,' he says, 'that I obtained a clue as to its history. I there found it exhibited in almost every collection as the Hanging Pearmain, and so widely is it grown in the county, there cannot be any doubt that it is originally a Herefordshire apple.'

TASTING AND COOKING NOTES

I am in awe of this apple, as once we began our immense cooking and tasting tests of well over a hundred varieties it showed its true qualities. It is a wonderful apple for baking and pureeing. Colour is so important to me in cooking, and once peeled, the Adams' Pearmain revealed a lovely yellow flesh which, when diced, broke down quickly with a dash of water into a delectable puree that yielded very easily beneath our forks and needed no sugar.

Next, we baked the apple and it cooked perfectly, keeping its shape and colour, with no explosions, and rewarded us with a melting texture.

Maman Blanc would approve of the way it performed when making her famous tarte. The yellow segments, overlapping in perfect concentric circles, fluffed out but kept their shape, turning gold and lightly caramel-coloured at the edges: just delicious!

Of course, an apple that purees so beautifully will rarely have enough acidity to pass the tarte tatin test. Nevertheless, this apple is a winner in our kitchen, and I long for the trees to bear their fruit!

GROWING NOTES

This is a variety that has been treasured in small gardens, not only for its flavour, but because the upright tree is naturally quite hardy and disease-resistant, especially to scab, and it is relatively vigorous, but can be grown successfully in pots. In our orchard the trees crop well and in most years the apples can be picked from early October and are at their best in late October. If they are stored in a cool, dark, dry cellar they can keep until the end of December, provided the fruits are not too mature when they are picked.

ANNIE ELIZABETH

22 trees in my English orchard
Leicestershire, 1857
SEASON: *late September/October*
APPEARANCE: *green/yellow, flushed with red*
BEST FOR: *baking whole and tarts*

Annie Elizabeth – who was she? The moment I was given this apple to taste my childlike curiosity was aroused. How did she come by this wonderful name? I hoped that Annie Elizabeth would turn out to have been a mysterious beauty, someone's lover perhaps, but the reality is quite different. Although there are several different stories about the christening of the apple, the one that most people believe to be true is a poignant one.

The apple was first grown in 1857 by a magistrate's clerk called Samuel Greatorex, who lived in Avenue Road, Knighton St Mary, in Leicester, and it is said that he later named it as a touching memorial to his illegitimate baby daughter, who died in 1866. Apparently there is a headstone in the graveyard of the church of St Mary Magdalen in Knighton that reads, 'Annie Elizabeth Greatorex aged one'.

The apple received a First Class Certificate from the Royal Horticultural Society in 1868, and was eventually introduced commercially by Harrison's of Leicester in about 1898. It seems that the owner of the nursery, Thomas Harrison, had two daughters who were called Annie and Elizabeth, so you can guess the alternative story! There is even a third idea that Annie Elizabeth was the daughter of a gardener called William Knight, who tended the original tree for Samuel Greatorex!

Whatever the truth, what is also exciting for me is that the first seedling is said to have been grown from a pip of our local favourite, the Blenheim Orange (see page 42), so we can make the connection with our ancient apple of Oxfordshire. I find this quite fascinating as the two apples are very different. The Blenheim Orange has almost white flesh, while the Annie Elizabeth has pale gold flesh and they taste and cook differently. So is it true? Maybe not, but it doesn't matter. I love the idea, because, you know, apples, like people, are made up of a multiplicity of relationships and histories that can reach all over the world, and seedlings rarely grow up to be just like their parents.

Considered by Robert Hogg to be a 'late kitchen or dessert apple', Annie Elizabeth is known to keep well, and it was popular until the 1930s, but then, as orchards around the country began to disappear, so did Annie Elizabeth. Now, however, enthusiasts in orchard groups in many counties around Britain have made it their mission to research and rediscover 'lost' varieties, and one of these groups, Leicestershire Heritage Apples, found that the original old tree still exists. It was identified in 2011 with the help of the current occupant of the house in Leicester, who owned a one-hundred-year-old watercolour painting of the garden that shows the tree looking exactly as it does now.

TASTING AND COOKING NOTES
When you bite into the golden flesh, the apple has a delicious long flavour, with a good balance of sugar and acidity, but when we pureed it, it took too long to break down well, so this is not an apple for a crumble or a compote. A shame, because the colour is so appealing.

Although it makes an excellent tart, there was not quite enough sweetness there, and I knew, of course, that for a tarte tatin it would be a disaster, and it was, because the texture of the apple is more crumbly than tight, which is what you need for a tatin. However, when baked it was beautiful. The apple stayed whole with no blistering, and inside the golden flesh became fluffy, rich, unctuous and perfumed, so I forgave Annie Elizabeth for all her other failings.

GROWING NOTES

This is a heavy cropping variety with a pink, almost mauve blossom, that is relatively easy to grow in the garden – in fact it can grow so quickly that, as William Sibley warned me, 'It can become a tangled mess of branches.' He also advises that you should ensure the trees are on a suitably dwarfing rootstock such as M9 (see page 263). The trees are hardy, vigorous and adaptable, can tolerate mild, wet climates, and are quite resistant to disease, although they are very susceptible to rosy apple aphid, which is not good news! The apples are lovely enjoyed straight from the tree when they ripen in late September but, winds permitting, they can stay on the branches until after the New Year. Provided the fruits are not overripe, they are one of the longest-storing varieties, which can keep until February in dark, cool, dry, frost-free conditions.

ASHMEAD'S KERNEL

6 trees in my English orchard
Gloucestershire, 1700s
SEASON: *early October*
APPEARANCE: *green russet*
BEST FOR: *its history!*

Along my wonderful journey of discovery I could not resist planting a tree – six in fact – with such a venerable, yet mysterious, heritage as Ashmead's Kernel. This intensely sweet-sharp-flavoured variety was first thought by Robert Hogg to have been grown in the garden of one Dr Ashmead, a physician who was supposed to have lived in Gloucester. 'Kernel' is an old word for 'seedling' and the apple's parent is thought to be the Nonpareil, an ancient variety dating back to 1696. However, more recent dedicated research by the Gloucestershire Orchard Trust has found no trace of a Dr Ashmead, and it is now believed that the apple was more likely to have been raised elsewhere in Gloucester by a different Ashmead – William – who was an attorney at law and became a freeman of the city in 1747.

Hogg considered Ashmead's Kernel to be 'A dessert apple of the very first quality, possessing all the richness of the Nonpareil, but with a more sugary juice. It comes into use in November, and is in greatest perfection from Christmas till May.' Morton Shand, who was passionate about championing British heritage apples over French varieties in the early twentieth century, spoke of its 'initial Madeira-like mellowness of flavour', overlying a 'deeper honeyed nuttiness, crisply sweet not sugar sweet. Surely' he asked, 'no apple of greater distinction or more perfect balance can ever have been raised anywhere on earth?'

Such lyrical testimonies, and yet it seems that while the Ashmead's Kernel was celebrated locally, it never really gathered popularity beyond the gardens of Gloucestershire. It is possible that its buff, rustic appearance didn't appeal to the wider commercial market, although it did make its name in America, where it is one of the few named varieties taken over by the early settlers that managed to thrive there.

In recent years, however, thanks to the work of the Gloucestershire Orchard Group, heritage fruit growers and suppliers, this regional treasure is belatedly being celebrated beyond its own county, where, I am told, at the annual tasting of around one hundred Gloucestershire varieties, it has been 'banned' from entering, as it will always win first prize!

TASTING AND COOKING NOTES
Sadly, this is an apple that perfectly proves the truth that age, heritage and an intriguing story do not always translate into a memorable eating and cooking experience, if the season is against it. Marcus Roberts, who tracked down the fruits for our tasting, was hugely apologetic and perplexed because all the examples of this, one of his favourite apples, that he had tried that season were 'off' and unripe, perhaps due to some vagary of the weather. And I must confess that during the tasting process the apple was spat out by both our gardeners and chefs. It did not bake well, and its scores were poor for puree, tarts, tarte tatin and juice. However, I really want to be kind to this grand old apple, about which so many fond words have been written, and acknowledge that it was not tasted in its finest moment, so it will get another chance, another day.

GROWING NOTES

I must tell you that my expert friends have very divided opinions on the worth of this apple for a small garden. Some say it is not an easy variety to grow and would not recommend it at all as, for a start, pollination can be difficult. William Sibley, who has devoted his life to researching varieties that taste wonderful but also crop abundantly, went as far as to tell me that the variety would be 'a complete waste of time', while David Pennell cautioned that 'cropping can be erratic as the flowers are susceptible to weather damage'. Marcus Roberts, however, is quick to jump to the apple's defence, insisting that his own tree, in a semi-exposed-garden situation in the Northamptonshire uplands, is nothing but obliging, fruiting well in most years, as are the same trees he has planted for various other people in the area.

Usually the fruit is picked during October, but David says, 'It is not easy to tell when it is ripe from its nondescript, green, russeted appearance'; and while Marcus agrees, he suggests letting the birds, 'nature's professional sugar detectors', be your guide, as once they start to peck, then you know the apple is fully ripe. Alternatively, very gently press the skin with a fingertip and, if the apple is ripe, the skin will depress a little. The apples can then be stored and tend to be at their peak for the Christmas table, but can keep until around the New Year, although the skin will probably wrinkle and the flesh becomes quite soft.

THE RISE AND FALL
OF THE ENGLISH APPLE

In Victorian times the English apple was revered and cherished as no other fruit. All over the country, skilled nurserymen were researching, experimenting, propagating and grafting, frequently sharing new ideas and varieties with fellow enthusiasts in Europe. In the ornamental gardens of English country houses, apple trees were de rigueur, trained into palmettes and espaliers, in columns and pyramids, with the trees treasured as much for their shape and blossom as their fruit. At the dinner tables of grand houses, apples in myriad sizes, shapes and colours would be arranged in elaborate displays and tasted and discussed like fine wines. Yet already a few cheaper interlopers from America and, later, New Zealand were threatening to dominate the British market.

Despite the valiant efforts of great Victorian fruit experts and writers, like Edward Bunyard and Robert Hogg, to champion English apples, in particular against cheaper foreign imports, the demand for many traditional varieties waned and British orchards began to decline in the early twentieth century. The demise reached its zenith in the 1970s. This time the main culprit, for which I must apologise, was the Golden Delicious, which was imported from France (although it was originally an American apple, see page 122) and aggressively marketed in Britain as 'Le Crunch'. Sadly, its success brought about so many losses for British growers.

The supermarkets that were beginning to push out the small green-grocers wanted a ready supply of uniformly perfect-looking, sweet apples with a long shelf life, so even the national favourites like Blenheim Orange (see page 42), Ribston Pippin (see page 160) and

Worcester Pearmain (see page 167) were sidelined, along with the rarer, more unusual old apples. Only the Cox's Orange Pippin (see page 84) was able to stand its ground. In 2004 orchards began to be 'grubbed up', in order to qualify for EU grants for turning them into open farmland.

Thankfully, two environmental campaigners, Angela King and Sue Clifford, came to the rescue, joining with the writer and film-maker Roger Deakin to launch the Common Ground movement, encouraging the creation of community orchards and designating Apple Days at which local experts could arrange tastings of local heritage apples and run workshops on grafting, or the old skill of artisan cider-making. They celebrated around three thousand varieties in The Apple Source Book, *inviting supportive chefs like me to contribute recipes featuring specific varieties.*

These groups are constantly searching for lost varieties that may still exist, unknown, in a garden or an old abandoned orchard somewhere, and they invite anyone who has an old tree of an unknown variety to send them some apples to identify. Marcus told me the story of one local Oxfordshire apple, the North Aston Nonpareil (or Folk's Apple), one of the rarest and most historical apples of our region, which was almost lost. Its origins are not certain, but it is thought to be a French apple brought from Normandy to Oxfordshire as early as 1594. Marcus and his co-founder of the Mid-Shires Orchard Group found five old trees remaining in the village of North Aston, and from these they grafted new ones, which are now spread around the county, in an attempt to reacquaint people with this historic fruit.

It was in tune with this new mood that I began planning my great orchard project with a huge sense of nostalgia, hope, wonder and excitement.

BEAUTY OF KENT

To be planted in my English orchard
Unknown, 1820
SEASON: *late September/October*
APPEARANCE: *golden yellow with red flush*
BEST FOR: *eating fresh*

How naive I was to imagine that only the French could be so entranced by the beauty of a variety of fruit that they would bestow on her a name like Belle de Pontoise or Belle Fille de Salins. As I began planning my orchard, I discovered that once again I had misjudged the British and that behind the pragmatism of this wonderful nation there is an equally emotional response to the loveliness of an apple. Yes, indeed, my British friends reveal themselves as true romantics, especially when it comes to the fruits of the garden and orchard. And so we can find 'Beauties' all around the country, from the Beauty of Blackmoor, which originates in Bristol, to the Beauty of Moray from Scotland.

Perhaps not as well known as the Beauty of Bath, the Beauty of Kent was a very popular apple in Victorian and Edwardian England, yet no one is sure of its origins, although from its name we have to assume that it was first found or raised somewhere in Kent.

The agriculturalist William Forsyth calls it a 'fine large apple, resembling a Codlin', but says nothing more about its history in his book *A Treatise on the Culture and Management of Fruit Trees,* first published in 1802. All that is known is that it was introduced to the Brompton Park Nursery around 1820. The well-known Ronalds

Nursery in Brentford (see page 164) noted it as: 'A beautiful and much esteemed sauce apple', and in 1884 Robert Hogg wrote in *The Fruit Manual*, 'When well-grown, the Beauty of Kent is perhaps the most magnificent apple in cultivation. Its great size, the beauty of its colouring, the tenderness of the flesh, and a profusion of sub-acid juice, constitute it one of our most popular winter apples for culinary purposes, and one of the most desirable and useful, either for a small garden, or for more extended cultivation.'

TASTING AND COOKING NOTES
Eaten raw, the apple revealed her true beauty, deliciously juicy and perfumed, with a beautiful crunch and clean, crisp layered flavour, but put to the cooking tests she lost a little of her charm. The apple broke down into a pale, grainy-textured puree. When baked it collapsed and the taste floundered. In a tarte tatin it fared better: the apple halves held their shape, but the perfume of the raw apple somehow disappeared, and sadly there was not enough acidity to stand up to the sweetness of the caramel.

GROWING NOTES
The apples grow on an upright tree that is quite vigorous and suitable for all areas, but is something of a reluctant cropper. It is also very prone to apple powdery mildew and woolly aphid and in heavy soils may be prone to canker. In most seasons the fruit is best picked in the second half of September, and while it can be stored, it is best eaten early, as its acidity will fade.

BELLE DE BOSKOOP

8 trees in my English orchard
Boskoop, Netherlands, 1856
SEASON: *late September/October*
APPEARANCE: *quite lumpy, greenish orange/red, often russeted*
BEST FOR: *strudel*

As I was looking at my apple-tasting notes for this book, I found myself wondering how I came to plant eight of these trees in my orchard. Was I seduced by another Belle? Is it because I was influenced by Eveline Noort, the general manager at Le Manoir aux Quat'Saisons, who is Dutch? Or did our head gardener, Anne Marie, decide to sneak the trees into the orchard as she has since confessed that she loves the abundance and beauty of their flowers, which cover the spreading branches in snowballs of small, white and pale, pale pink flowers. And I thought that only Frenchmen could be so romantic!

Then my friend Will Sibley told me, 'Raymond, almost every garden in France that has apple trees will have a Belle de Boskoop, and they are sold in garden centres all around the country. The French seem to love them!' I had no idea, but of course I am almost British now, and in Britain this apple is not well known. I find it so fascinating that a fruit can be perceived so differently in different countries and cultures.

All that seems to be known about the apple's ancestry is that it was discovered in 1856 by K. J. W. Ottolander, whose family had a nursery in the town of Boskoop, near Gouda, which is known for its many centres specialising in ornamental fruit. The variety is thought to be a bud-sport (see page 49) of Reinette de Montfort and it received a Royal Horticultural Society Award of Merit in 1897. It is also known as Schöne van Boskoop or Goudrenet in the Netherlands.

TASTING AND COOKING NOTES
The apple is a huge favourite for cooking in the Netherlands, especially in recipes such as strudel, which, although it is an Austrian dessert, is popular there. However – and I don't want to offend Eveline, the Dutch nation, or all the French families who have a Belle de Boskoop tree in their garden – I have to say that in our rigorous tests the apple achieved one of the worst ratings across all the categories of cooking. Anne Marie defends it as a large apple that slices easily, has a high content of vitamin C, and its flavour develops with age, so it is possible that when we tasted the fruits in October they may not have been at their finest. And so, as I am not out to ruin this Belle's reputation, I am going to be generous and give her another chance to impress me. But then, happy as I am to admire her flowers – as they *are* beautiful – if the fruits do not perform well in my kitchen, I will have to uproot the trees and send them to Anne Marie with love, so that she can plant them in her own garden and admire their magnificent blossom to her heart's content!

GROWING NOTES
One reason for the apple's popularity must be that it crops easily, has good resistance to disease, is suitable for damper regions and is also resistant to the cold, so can be grown as far north as Scotland. The trees are upright, spreading and triploid (see page 263). Harvesting can be from late September and the apples are best held in storage for use from November onwards. As Anne Marie notes, they should store well all the way through to April, and should improve with age.

BLENHEIM ORANGE

49 trees in my English orchard
Oxfordshire, 1740
SEASON: *late September/October*
APPEARANCE: *yellowy orange with light streaks of red,*
creamy yellow flesh
BEST FOR: *eating fresh, juice, puree and tarts*

After forty-six years of living in Oxfordshire, I now consider myself a local boy and so I think I have an intimate knowledge of Blenheim Palace, the seat of the duke of Marlborough, and its glorious history. Of course, the palace takes its name from the Battle of Blenheim, in which the first Duke led the defeat of the 'invincible' French army of Louis XIV! So perhaps it is safer to talk of the famous Blenheim Orange apple instead. The story I was told (and which has been well documented) is that the original tree was discovered growing against the boundary wall of the palace estate by a local man, Mr Kempster, who was a cobbler or tailor. He grew a cutting in his garden in Woodstock, where it was known as Kempster's Pippin, and it became quite famous, attracting tourists who made special journeys by foot, horse and coach just to see the apples. In 1804, however, a Mr Biggs, who was a Worcestershire nurseryman, asked permission of the Duke of Marlborough to market the apple commercially and it was renamed the Blenheim Orange, though many people still preferred to call it after Kempster.

I first tasted this wonderful local apple years ago when I visited Blenheim and admired not only the grandeur of the palace, but also this wondrous fruit: large, perfectly shaped and with a gorgeous orangey-red colour – so appetising. I helped myself to a few apples from the lower branches and, at first bite, the beautiful appearance translated into delicious and unctuous flavours. Such a great balance of sweetness and acidity. I am happy to tell you that I made my peace with the present Duchess of Marlborough at the grand opening of the second phase of Le Manoir aux Quat'Saisons, when I confessed to her that I had stolen some of the family's prized apples, and all is forgiven!

The parentage of the Blenheim Orange isn't known – though it may have been a seedling of the eighteenth-century Golden Reinette – and interestingly the Bénédictin apple, grown by Benedictine monks in Normandy in the nineteenth century, has been found to be identical to it. At the turn of the nineteenth century another nurseryman, the food and wine connoisseur Edward Bunyard, characterised many of the old English varieties, pinpointing the time of year when each achieved the perfect balance of aroma, sweetness and acidity. Blenheim Orange was his December apple, and he praised its 'nutty warm aroma', and went on to say: 'There is in this noble fruit a mellow austerity as of a great port in its prime, a reminder of those placid Oxford meadows, which gave it birth in the shadow of the great house of Blenheim. Like Oxford, too, it adopts a leisurely pace, refusing to be hurried to maturity or to relinquish its hold on life. An apple of the Augustan Age.' Such a wonderful, romantic description.

Like many a great prodigy, Kempster's original tree seems to have been very short-lived. Perhaps it was exhausted by so many visitors eagerly taking cuttings, as the old tree had another special quality: it was one of a small, rare and valuable group of apple trees known as pitchers, as instead of propagating them by grafting, you could take a cutting, 'pitch' it into the ground and it would grow.

Writing about the Blenheim Orange in *The Herefordshire Pomona*, Robert Hogg included a very beautiful and elegiac account of the glorious heyday and sad demise of the original tree, which appeared in the *Gardeners' Chronicle*:

'In a somewhat dilapidated corner of the decaying borough of ancient Woodstock, within ten yards of the wall of Blenheim Park, stands all that remains of the original stump of that beautiful and justly celebrated apple, the Blenheim Orange. It is now entirely dead, and rapidly falling to decay, being a mere shell about ten feet high, loose in the ground, and having a large hole in the centre. Till within the last three years, it occasionally sent up long, thin, wiry twigs; but this last sign of vitality has ceased, and what remains will soon be the portion of the woodlouse and the worm. Old Grimmett, the basket-maker, against the corner of whose garden-wall the venerable relict is supported, has sat looking on it from his workshop window, and while he wove the pliant osier, has meditated, for more than fifty successive summers, on the mutability of sublunary substances, on juice, and core, and vegetable, as well as animal, and flesh and blood. He can remember the time when, fifty years ago, he was a boy, and the tree a fine, full-bearing stem, full of bud, and blossom, and fruit, and thousands thronged from all parts to gaze on its ruddy, ripening, orange burden; then gardeners came in the spring-tide to select the much-coveted scions, and to hear the tale of his horticultural child and sapling, from the lips of the son of the white-haired Kempster. But nearly a century has elapsed since Kempster fell, like a ripened fruit, and was gathered to his fathers. He lived in a narrow cottage-garden in Old Woodstock, a plain, practical, labouring man; and in the midst of his bees and flowers around him, and in his "glorious pride," in the midst of his little garden, he realised Virgil's dream of the old Corycian: "Et regum aequabat opes animis"' [meaning he equalled, in contented mind, the wealth of Kings – such is the powerful romance of the apple!].

Some say that soon after the old tree was reduced to a stump it was burned, and the one sound piece of wood left was made into a commemorative snuff box. However, its offspring, some of which are variants, continue to flourish in gardens and orchards all around the country.

Finally I will share a more personal Blenheim Orange secret with you. My wonderful long-suffering assistant of eighteen years, Leanda, lives in a cottage just beyond the walls of Blenheim Palace, almost beside the site of the original tree, and I am lucky to receive, every year, a basket of beautiful Blenheim apples from the estate. I must be a good boss!

TASTING AND COOKING NOTES

The Blenheim Orange apples that Marcus Roberts found for the Raymond Blanc Richter Scale taste test were picked from a tree on a Victorian fruit wall, and they showed so many strengths. As an eating apple this variety has a beautiful taste and its texture is crisp, though more crumbly and less tight than a Cox, and it makes a good single-variety juice. It pureed beautifully: the diced pale flesh broke down quickly with a tiny amount of water and it was delicious, needing no added sugar.

When baked, it held its shape very nicely, although there were a few blisters in the skin, and the Maman Blanc tarte experience was quite lovely and memorable, as the perfumed slices of apple fluffed beautifully and took on a gorgeous golden colour, again with hardly any sugar needed. This apple is not made for tarte tatin, however, as its flesh is not acidic or firm enough. You need a lower-sugar apple, such as a Chivers Delight (see page 71) or Granny Smith (see page 133), to counterbalance the sweetness of the caramel in this dessert. Nevertheless, I truly love this apple. It is a wonderful eating variety, and it has so many qualities in the kitchen, so why can I not find it in every grocer's shop in Oxfordshire? To me it is incomprehensible.

GROWING NOTES

The Blenheim Orange tree is vigorous and strong and will grow very big. Along with the Bramley's Seedling (see page 51), it is often the last to survive in old derelict orchards. Being a triploid (see page 263) and a partial tip-bearer (see page 170), you might have to consider pollination and not prune too heavily. Also, notes David Pennell, the variety 'can be slow to establish the cropping habit'. However, the Blenheim Orange also grows well on dwarf rootstock, which is more suited to a smaller garden, and in this format seems to be much less reticent in bearing fruit.

Although the apples are very special eaten straight from the tree, usually in late September, they can be stored until around mid-December to early January if they are in good condition and not too mature when they are picked. Marcus Roberts remembers that, traditionally, Blenheim Orange apples were sold in trays and at Christmastime these would be adorned with more fancy packaging as people bought them especially for the festive table.

A GOLDEN CHILDHOOD

I grew up playing in orchards, helping to tend them, and frequently, with my friends, launching raids on our neighbours' cherry orchards, where the temptation of the big black, juicy fruits was too much to resist.

Our house was in a very rural part of France, just in between the beautiful elegant region of Burgundy and the rugged Jura Mountains. Behind the house that my papa built, breeze block by breeze block with his own hands, we had our own apple tree, an old ornamental pear tree and a cherry tree, which provided us with beautiful fruit almost throughout the year. However, the greatest fruit gardens of my childhood were tended by my grand-père, who had been a successful farmer but became a very poor man when his large herd of cows suffered a viral epidemic, and so he lost his farm; everything. But then he had the good fortune to become the groundskeeper of a chateau in the village at Serre-les-Sapins, close to Pouilley-les-Vignes, about ten miles from our home, which had a huge vegetable garden, cascading terraces where herbs grew, an orangerie, and a magnificent orchard.

The house that my grandparents lived in by the chateau was very simple, with no heating, just a fire, and water drawn from the well, but the extensive orchard gave them so many riches, and it was heaven for a small boy to venture through. Franche-Comté is normally quite a cool region in winter, and yet this corner was a perfect microclimate for peaches, including the small, crimson Pêche de Vigne (see page 239), tiny golden Mirabelles de Metz (see page 251), cherries and plums. There were hundreds of trees, many trained in espaliers, palmettes and cordons against the walls. Everything grew in abundance and my grandfather was master of it all. In my school holidays I served my apprenticeship with him, helping him with his tasks. He knew so much about the varieties and he taught me about seasonality, the soil, how to add the manure, and how to prune the trees, although I wasn't very good at that! It was hard work, but of course we had fun too.

While my grandfather grew the most heavenly produce, my mother and grandmother would use some of the fruit in simple but beautiful desserts. By God, both women knew how to cook! My grand-mère was one of the most renowned cooks in the county, so when a dignitary would visit Besançon, or there was a big wedding or celebration, she would be called on to prepare a dinner. She was so ahead of her time, creating dishes like blanquette de veau *with lemon and yoghurt, the most extraordinary milk and tarragon liqueur, or macerating fruit with herbs. She was a genius in the kitchen, as was my mother. They both made their delicious desserts effortlessly; it was like magic.*

One of the first lessons I learned from Maman was, 'You shall waste not.' What fruit was not used immediately would be bottled, preserved or my grandfather and the local men would turn it into alcohol: Poire William, plum brandy, apple brandy, mirabelle eau de vie. The cellar below our house was the magical place where all these treasures were stored.

BRAEBURN

26 trees in my English orchard
Nelson, New Zealand, 1952
SEASON: *late October*
APPEARANCE: *green gold, flushed with red*
BEST FOR: *eating fresh, tarte tatin, juice and puree*

It is strange how little is known about the genesis of this apple, since it is a relatively recent variety and one of the most famous, grown all over the world. All we can say is that it was a chance discovery by a farmer, O. Moran of Waiwhero, in the Moutere Hills, near Motueka, Nelson. It is thought that the Lady Hamilton variety was one parent and possibly Granny Smith (see page 133) the other, as both apples were growing nearby at the time. The new apple was taken up and marketed by the Williams Brothers of the Braeburn nursery nearby, hence the name.

What marked this apple out from some of the other imports that began to dominate the British supermarket shelves was that at its best it had much of the depth of flavour and sweet-sharp intensity of the best traditional English apples. Of course, British farms were keen to plant it themselves, but they struggled to grow it on a commercial scale. Will Sibley remembers that this variety would never ripen, 'even if the fruit was left on the tree until December; it would just become starchy'. However, this is a very clever apple, which easily produces bud-sports or singular branches, which behave differently from the rest of the tree. As Will explains it: 'What happens is that the sun's radiation hits a flower bud on one small branch of a tree, causing a genetic twist that makes the branch behave in a completely different way to the rest of the tree. Some of these sports are remarkable and when they are grafted they produce different clones, each with their own slightly different characteristics, usually cosmetic – for example some might have a slightly higher colour, or they might keep a little better – but in terms of flavour they are all recognisable as Braeburn.'

In 1981 an earlier-ripening 'Hillwell' clone was developed from a sport by Mr and Mrs John Hill in Hastings, which meant that many countries that don't have the sunshine hours or intense light levels of New Zealand could now grow Braeburns. France was one of the countries to grow these Braeburns successfully and in the early 1990s Will introduced this clone to Britain, grafting the first trees for trials at Rainham in Kent. Thanks to this success, English growers are now able to produce smaller crops of quite beautiful Braeburn apples, and since this is a variety that we value in our pâtisserie and kitchen at Le Manoir, we have planted twenty-six trees in our orchard.

TASTING AND COOKING NOTES
Fresh and juicy, with great aromatics, this is a lovely apple to eat straight from the tree. It makes a very pleasant juice and although its quite tight flesh takes a while to break down, it makes a very good puree, compote and sauce, with no sugar needed.

Because of its compact flesh, it also takes a long time to bake whole, although its flavour and textures are enjoyable. Its sugar levels are high enough to make a very good tarte Maman Blanc, but again its tightness stops it from being magical. Of course its texture is a bonus, and so it makes a divine tarte tatin.

GROWING NOTES
This is a long-season apple and so it needs a good summer in order to ripen well in this country. Also it is not easy to grow organically, as it is not disease-resistant. The trees are moderately vigorous and spreading. The fruit can be picked from mid-October and stored for use from November through to March.

BRAMLEY'S SEEDLING

21 trees in my English orchard
Nottinghamshire, 1809
SEASON: *early October*
APPEARANCE: *green yellow, sometimes with a red blush*
BEST FOR: *puree (but only with lots of sugar)*

When I became the new custodian of Le Manoir aux Quat'Saisons back in February 1983, I was so happy to discover, amongst the magical grounds of this beautiful house, a mini orchard of ten trees. I had no idea which varieties they were as it was winter, but I knew enough to recognise that they were probably fifty to seventy years old, and they were apple trees, and I imagined making jam or gelées and creating magnificent desserts with the apples they would bear.

Next came the beautiful spring snowballs of white and pink blossom and, as summer followed, the small fruits became bigger and bigger until every branch was laden with huge green apples, so green it was as if they had been painted and so big that I thought they must have come from America! And of course I had to taste one. I took an enormous bite ... what a mistake! I spat it straight out, as the level of acidity almost blew my head off and my taste buds were assaulted by the aggressive, astringent sourness. On that day – and please, my dear British friends, forgive me – I became the sworn enemy of the Bramley apple. I know it is revered in Britain, and there are many of you who might be tempted to hang me from a branch of a Bramley apple tree, but before you do, let me tell you why I am not fond of this apple. For me, it doesn't fit with the way we think about modern gastronomy – yes, it will puree in a few minutes, but it is so sour that you have to add almost an equal amount of sugar to create an acceptable flavour, and, as we all now know, too much sugar is a pretty effective weapon against good health and taste.

Although I may not love this sour apple, one thing I must say is that the story behind its discovery is very sweet. In Church Street in the village of Southwell, Nottinghamshire, somewhere between 1809 and 1815, a young girl, Mary Anne Brailsford, planted some pips from the apples her mother was preparing to cook. One seedling grew into a tree, which produced 'very fine apples in 1837'. Later, the cottage and garden were bought by Mr Matthew Bramley, a local innkeeper and butcher. It wasn't until 1856 that Henry Merryweather junior, the teenage son of a local nurseryman, impressed by a basket of the apples he saw being carried, asked where they came from and gained permission to take cuttings from the tree to grow in his family's nursery, on the condition that they were registered as Bramley's Seedling. The first recorded sale of the apples is in Henry Merryweather's book of accounts for October 31, 1862, which states that three apple trees were sold for two shillings.

By the early 1900s, Bramley trees were widely planted all over Britain, and by the time of the Fruit Census of 1944, held in the National Archives at Kew, there were more than two million Bramley trees in existence.

Nottinghamshire is not the only place that has become famous for its Bramleys. In 1884 sixty seedlings from Henry Merryweather's nursery were planted in Armagh, in Northern Ireland, which is known as the Orchard County, and in 2012 the Armagh Bramley was awarded Protected Geographical Indication (PGI) status by the European Commission in recognition that: 'The unique growing conditions in Armagh result in a firmer, more dense fruit than would be grown elsewhere.' I am intrigued. This is clearly a Bramley that I must try!

The original tree in Southwell, which was recognised as one of the fifty 'Great British Trees' by the Tree Council in 2002, is still visited by people from all over the world and is now two hundred and ten years old, which is at the extremity of what is possible for an apple tree. It came down in a storm in the 1990s, but it showed how incredibly resilient an apple tree can be when it grew a new branch from the trunk and carried on producing apples. Next it contracted the lethal honey fungus infection and was thought to be dying, but so treasured is this tree that the University of Nottingham have stepped in and bought the cottage and garden so that their horticultural experts and students can nurse it and try to extend its life. I am told that clones taken from it have produced fruit that is much smaller, redder and not so sour, so they can be pressed into apple juice or used for compotes without added sugar, and even eaten raw. One grower in the Midlands has devoted a whole orchard to original-clone Bramleys and is hoping to make a success out of his sugar-free Bramley sauce! Supermarket Bramleys also seem to be smaller, with flushes of colour and less acidity. I have now tasted half a dozen from various stores and they are all so different.

And then there are Crimson Bramleys, which were also discovered in Southwell, but much later, in 1913, so we are going to plant some in the orchard. Perhaps, along with the Armagh Bramleys, I might like these apples better!

TASTING AND COOKING NOTES
To me the classic Bramley is a ball of acidity and water, so as soon as you expose it to heat, the flesh implodes and, of course, it makes quick and excellent-looking puree very quickly. However, as I have said, it needs too much sugar, and the overuse of sugar is something I have always battled against in my kitchen and pâtisserie. But, knowing how much my English friends disagree with me about this apple, as I began writing this book, I decided to conduct an

experiment. I diced a large 200g apple from my own tree into 2cm cubes and cooked it with 50ml of water. In exactly two minutes the chunks had entirely imploded and completely pureed. Upon tasting, I screamed; the acidity was that powerful. I needed 100g of sugar to make the apple edible, but after adding such a quantity, it resulted in both the sugar level and acidity level being too high. Next, I pureed the equivalent quantity of supermarket Bramleys, and was amazed that they only needed 50g of sugar. The flavour was still quite acidic, but enjoyable – so perfect for a crumble.

Talking of which, I confess that I had the best apple crumble experience when I was invited by Clare Scheckter to Laverstoke Park, the organic/biodynamic farm started by her husband, Jody, a former Formula One World Champion. Clare very kindly gave me the recipe, which was her mother's (see page 293). Imagine my reaction when I found out that the apple Clare had used for the dessert was a Bramley! Of course I was sure that it must be a cross-breed and not a pure sour Bramley. It was after this lovely experience that I decided I must not give up on this apple, which I had been so insulting towards, because my British friends cherish it so much. So I persevered to try to find some way to use Bramleys in the kitchen at Le Manoir. And I succeeded. Eventually I found that, yes, it can make a lovely chutney, and also an excellent filling for Christmas mince pies (see page 295), because the added vine fruits sweeten it enough without the need for so much sugar. I even use it sometimes in my famous Brown sauce (see page 271). Also, since Bramleys produce large volumes of juice, a little can be useful mixed into the juices of other apples, particularly sweet ones, to introduce some acidity and create an overall more balanced flavour.

GROWING NOTES
Bramley's Seedling trees are quite disease-resistant, and although they prefer sunshine, they can tolerate cool temperatures and so are

grown all around the UK, though they can be sensitive to frost even in the green-bud stage. They are famous for their longevity and can grow very big unless they are controlled. David Pennell feels that they can be 'too large for many modern gardens and a struggle to grow even as a trained tree', while William Sibley adds that if they are pruned strongly on a regular basis, this reduces the size of the crop. However, some growers have cultivated Bramleys on dwarf rootstock, which produce large amounts of fruit.

The apples can be picked for cooking or storage from early September, but it is best to delay until later in the month or into October to allow the fruit to mellow slightly. William advises that: 'As the tree gets older, say beyond twenty years, then the fruits will store into the New Year and up until February, otherwise until early December', and his tip is: 'For some unknown reason the apples store better in hay than on racks.'

CALVILLE BLANC D'HIVER

To be planted in my French orchard
France, 1598
SEASON: *mid-October*
APPEARANCE: *ribbed and yellow with red blush*
BEST FOR: *eating fresh*

Writing this book has been such a joyful journey of discovery because each fruit has its own story and connection to history, geography, sometimes politics, often love, and even art. How could I resist the romantic idea of an ancient heirloom apple from France, immortalised in Monet's still life *Apples and Grapes*, which he painted in 1880? I must say this is not a handsome apple. Calville is the prefix given to hundreds of apple cultivars that have a particular lumpy appearance, and this one is quite ribbed, sometimes knobbly and oddly shaped, indicating its antique origins. But perhaps its distinctive form engaged Monet more than its sleeker cousins, as the six Calville Blanc d'Hiver fruits sit proudly and sturdily on the table, drawing the eye away from the smaller, perfectly round apples that also feature in the painting, which may have been the Api variety that was popular at the time.

The personality of the Calville Blanc d'Hiver clearly outshone its looks in French kitchens too, as in its day this apple was one of France's most beloved varieties. It is thought to have come originally from Normandy, and was first mentioned in 1598 by the Swiss botanist Johann Bauhin under the synonym Blanche de Zurich (this is an apple that has over two hundred and fifty synonyms on the National Apple Register!). It is recommended in many of the influential French fruit books of the seventeenth century, which were republished in

English, so it is likely that it was known in England in the early part of the seventeenth century. It was said that its Champagne-like flavour and texture made it a favourite apple for 'wet sweetmeats' and especially *tarte aux pommes*, according to Joan Morgan in *The New Book of Apples* (2002), and at the beginning of the nineteenth century it was fetching high prices in the London markets.

In 1884 it was mentioned by Robert Hogg in *The Fruit Manual*, along with Calvilles for other seasons: Calville Blanche d'Été (summer) and Calville Rouge d'Automne (autumn). Hogg called it 'a valuable winter apple, admirably adapted for all culinary purposes, and excellent also for the dessert.' I must say I find it strange that he gave it the feminine name Calville Blanche, as if an apple can be characterised as masculine or feminine, and to me this is a masculine-looking apple!

It is also one of the varieties that was grown by the third US President, Thomas Jefferson, at Monticello, just outside Charlottesville, Virginia, where the Renaissance-style house, vegetable garden and 'fruitery' in which he eventually grew one hundred and seventy varieties, from Virginian cider apples to European peaches, almonds and cherries, were built and tended largely by slaves.

TASTING AND COOKING NOTES
I was grateful to be given some of these old and rare apples and eager to put them to the taste test. You might think that because this is an intriguing old French variety I would have been tempted to be more generous with my ratings and less impartial in my views. Not so! My French Republican values insist on one man or woman, one vote, and that means all my chefs, gardeners and invited guests place their vote before me, though sometimes inexperienced young chefs may be only just forming their palates, and my lovely gardeners can be looking for different characteristics, so I have to step in and make the final judgement. And in this case I have to say that the romance

of the Calville Blanc d'Hiver ends with its beautiful story – for the time being, at least, as this is a variety that can keep until March, changing its character as it matures, and so if re-tested at various times later in the year, it might surprise us.

In October it was a good, crisp apple for eating, though rather leathery-skinned, slightly bitter and quite challenging; however, by January it is said to be soft, juicy, medium-sweet and aromatic. It made a dense, sharp puree, but the pieces resisted the heat and remained quite chunky and firm, so before cooking they would have to be diced very small. Although this was said to be a classic apple for a tart, the slices lacked the intense flavour and attractive colour and texture that I look for. In a tarte tatin, the apple halves held well, but were a little grainy and lacked the acidity to counterbalance the sweetness of the dark caramel base.

The apple performed better when baked whole, as it kept its shape, but once more it revealed its sturdiness as it took 45 minutes for the flesh to soften properly. Overall it was quite 'nice', but such an average experience is not enough to make it into my kitchen, so sadly the October apple didn't live up to my hope that I might have rediscovered a long-lost French treasure.

GROWING NOTES

The trees are hardy in cool temperatures but are weak growers, best suited to warmer areas. They are fairly resistant to disease, although the codling moth can attack the fruit and aphids may damage the foliage. The fruit can be harvested around the middle of October and kept until March; however, while on the tree it can struggle to ripen properly. As David Pennell warned me, 'This is one of those varieties that seems to need very good summer growing conditions, especially heat and sunshine'; so the traditional advice is to grow the trees against a wall for warmth.

CAPTAIN KIDD

21 trees in my English orchard
Hawkes Bay, New Zealand, 1962
SEASON: *mid-October*
APPEARANCE: *deep red*
BEST FOR: *eating fresh, juice and tarts*

Maybe because apples so often have romantic names, or because the French word *pomme* is feminine, I tend to think of them as female (and thus I hope you forgive me for sometimes referring to them as 'she'). However, with this apple it is impossible, as Captain Kidd sounds so much like a swashbuckling pirate on the high seas, which makes me wonder how this apple got its name. The answer is the frustrating one that we arrive at so often when we play fruit-detective: no one really knows.

Captain Kidd is a handsome, deep red sport of Kidd's Orange Red. Dedicated growers are always looking to improve on an already brilliant apple and sometimes a branch of a tree will give rise to a bud-sport (see page 49), which might produce fruit that is more highly coloured and attractive, ripens earlier or later, or has a slightly more distinctive flavour. In which case cuttings from these sports are used to develop a new cultivar of the original.

Both apples are called after the man who raised them: James Hutton Kidd, a tailor's son who was born in 1877 in Hexham in Northumberland, which may explain why the apples have a very English character to them, even though the family emigrated to Christchurch in New Zealand when he was a child. James trained in agriculture and then, with his brother Wilfred, began growing apples. His true passion was the science of growing: experimenting with new techniques, researching disease prevention and especially breeding new varieties. In particular, he wanted to try to combine the appearance of some of the best newer varieties with the more complex flavour of the famous old English apples.

Kidd's Orange Red was a great achievement: a cross of the Delicious (not the French Golden Delicious, but a different, American apple) with the renowned Cox's Orange Pippin (see page 84). Initially he called it by the rather dull name of Delco, but when he sold the propagation rights in the early 1930s to the nursery firm of Duncan and Davies, they renamed it Kidd's Orange Red.

Kidd continued his breeding programme until the Second World War, when he transferred his seedlings to the New Zealand government's Appleby Research Orchard close to the major fruit-growing region of Nelson, and sadly he died in 1945 before he could witness the emergence of the Captain Kidd variant in 1962, which was raised in the orchard of Robin Osborne in Twyford, Hawkes Bay. (Incidentally, he also never saw the later development of his most famous apple, originally known as D8, but later renamed Gala (see page 112).)

Sometimes a sport can result in a better-looking or longer-keeping apple at the expense of flavour, but in the case of Captain Kidd nothing of the eating and cooking quality of Kidd's Orange Red is lost; the apple just has a richer red colour.

I was expecting that the Captain Kidd would triumph in our tests since it has the Cox's Orange Pippin in its heritage, which is the best apple I have ever tasted. And I wasn't disappointed. We loved the apple so much that we planted twenty-one trees in our orchard, and also decided to put in four Kidd's Orange Red, too, though we have yet to reap their first fruit.

TASTING AND COOKING NOTES

Raw, this is an exciting apple: juicy, crunchy, with a tight flesh and fabulous flavours, and it made a delicious single-variety juice with a gentle and well-balanced sweetness and a big apple flavour. I wouldn't recommend it for a puree, though, as it didn't break down. Baked whole it had an excellent texture and flavour, and in a tarte tatin the aromatics were seductive and layered, but the texture did not hold so well and there was not enough acidity to combat the caramel. The Captain was clearly saving his greatest qualities for the Maman Blanc tarte test. Not a single apple rated as highly in our tastings for this. The tart looked glorious, fluffy and golden, and the acidity of the apple carried the sweetness and flavours with wonderful aromatics including a faint scent of rose petal.

GROWING NOTES

Captain Kidd has beautiful crimson blossom, is resistant to mildew and scab but can be prone to apple canker. It is a triploid variety (see page 263), but is a little easier to grow than Kidd's Orange Red. Harvested in mid-October, the apples can keep well through to January.

CATSHEAD

5 trees in my English orchard
England, around 1600
SEASON: *late September/October*
APPEARANCE: *green with red flashes,*
boxy-shaped, sometimes ribbed
BEST FOR: *heritage value!*

I am thankful to Marcus Roberts for bringing me this strange, quite misshapen and ancient apple variety, amongst many others. This is an apple with several different names, which is mentioned often in seventeenth- and eighteenth-century literature, where it was hailed for its size and its slightly conical, chunky shape and ribbing. Many of these more ancient varieties are 'coined', or angled and irregular in shape, and someone somewhere must have thought that this one resembled a cat's head.

It is such a venerable apple that it is featured in the Elizabethan Orchard that has been restored by the National Trust at Lyveden in Northamptonshire. This is the historic estate that was in the Tresham family from at least the fifteenth century, then in 1600 Sir Thomas Tresham began an ambitious and unfinished lodge and gardens, known as the New Bield, which was dreamed up as a tranquil and contemplative hidden retreat in which he could practise his Catholic faith in the face of persecution in Protestant England. Sadly his project was never completed and the lodge and elaborate gardens remained much as they were in 1605, the year he died, and in which his son, Francis, was implicated in the Gunpowder Plot and died in prison at the Tower of London.

Robert Cecil, Secretary of State to King James I, who received a number of trees grown at Lyveden New Bield from Lady Tresham in 1609, called it 'one of the fairest orchards that is in England', and since 2000 the National Trust have been replanting the ancient orchard, filling it with varieties mentioned in Tresham's letters, garden plans, and records of local sixteenth- and seventeenth-century apples.

Strangely, as it was so well known in its day, virtually nothing seems to be known about the Catshead's origins. In 1678 John Worlidge, in his book *Vinetum Britannicum, Or a Treatise of Cider*, mentions that 'Cats head ... by some called the Go-no-further, is a very large Apple, and by its red sides promises well for Cider.' Later, in 1709, John Arthur Phillips, in his poem *Cyder, A Poem in Two Books*, wrote of 'the Cat's-Head's weighty orb, Enormous in its Growth'.

And in the following century, William Ellis, who styled himself 'A Farmer, of Little Gaddesden, near Hemel Hempstead in Hertfordshire', wrote in *The Modern Husbandman, Or, The Practice of Farming* (1750) that 'The Dumpling or Cats head' is 'a very useful one to the farmer, because one of them, pared and wrapped up in dough, serves with little trouble for making an apple-dumpling, so much in request with the Kentish farmer for being part of a ready meal, that in the cheapest manner satiates the keen appetite of the hungry ploughman, both at home and in the field; and therefore has now got into such reputation in Hertfordshire, and some other Counties, that it is become the most common food with a piece of bacon or pickle-pork, for families.'

I love this idea, which is similar to the pasties that Cornish workers would take into the mines, some of which would be filled with beef and swede (confusingly called turnip in Cornwall) in one end and apples or other fruits 'for afters' at the other end. In the South Midlands and Bedfordshire, there was a similar savoury and sweet version called the 'Clanger'. It is also possible that the Catshead is actually the same apple as the Anglesey Pig's Snout, considered a rare old Welsh apple, which shares the same shape and is also said to have been wrapped in pastry and baked for farm labourers to take out into the fields for their lunch.

TASTING AND COOKING NOTES

I was intrigued by the apple's odd name and wondered if I might discover some feline grace and character within, but disappointingly, having tasted the Catshead and put it through the cooking tests, I can say that I would not want to have it in my kitchen as it failed catastrophically in every test. Unfortunately, it is another prime example that not all heritage varieties are 'best', as they don't necessarily have the gustative qualities we look for today. However, we have kept five Catshead trees in the orchard out of deference for its history and heritage and its appearance of grand antiquity.

GROWING NOTES

The tree crops heavily and is very resistant to scab. The apples are usually picked in late September and if kept cool will keep until January.

CHARLES ROSS

6 trees in my English orchard
Berkshire, around 1890
SEASON: *September*
APPEARANCE: *yellowy green with red/orange streaks*
BEST FOR: *its history*

What I have loved about delving into the history of the apple varieties we chose for our orchards is that in my mind I now have pictures of the huge diversity of people who first grew them. When I walk amongst the trees I imagine their excitement at finding a wonderful seedling growing in a hedgerow, or triumphantly cross-breeding two great apples to create an intriguing new variety.

Surprisingly few English apples bear the name of the person who first raised or found them, but this apple is one of them. Charles Ross was the head gardener at Welford Park near Newbury, in Berkshire, from 1860 to 1908. The estate dates back to Saxon times, but the present house was built in the seventeenth century and was home to many generations of the Eyre-Archer-Houblon family. Charles Ross became head gardener in the time of Charles Eyre and the estate was famous for the new apples that he bred – around thirty named varieties.

The irony is that the apple nearly didn't bear Ross's name at all, as he generously called most of his apples after other people. Charles Eyre, Houblon and Welford Park Nonsuch were varieties named for his employers. Others were christened after friends, and he originally called the Charles Ross, which was to become his most famous apple, after the famous eighteenth-century fruit breeder, horticulturalist and writer on apples and pears Thomas Andrew Knight, who was a founder member, and later president, of the London Horticultural Society (now the RHS).

The new variety was exhibited as the Thomas Andrew Knight apple in 1890 and received an Award of Merit from the RHS in 1899, which is a highly prestigious acknowledgement, often of years of work dedicated to the creation of a new fruit. The same year, it was renamed the Charles Ross, at the insistence of either Captain Carstairs, who rented Welford Park around this time, or Charles Ross's friend, the nurseryman William Pope.

Many of Ross's varieties were crosses involving the great, quintessential English apple, the Cox's Orange Pippin (see page 84), and that is true of the Charles Ross. The other parent is Peasgood Nonsuch, a Lincolnshire apple first grown from a pip by Mrs Peasgood in Grantham, when she was a child in the 1850s.

As always with these old English apple stories, one small thread of history leads to another, so forgive me if I take a little detour here. Mrs Peasgood moved to the historic Lincolnshire town of Stamford, taking her apple with her, which was later promoted by the famous local nurseryman Thomas Laxton in 1872, before he moved his nurseries to Bedford. Stamford now has its own community orchard group and they have discovered that this one town alone has a huge apple heritage. Forty-four varieties are now known to have been raised in the Stamford area in the nineteenth century by three people: Thomas Laxton, another nurseryman, Robert Brown, and Richard Gilbert, the head gardener at the famous Burghley House. I imagine all of these men experimenting and grafting away, seeing who could produce the best varieties. I wonder if they were in competition with each other, or maybe they worked together? Only a few of their apples, like Barnack Beauty, which I have in my orchard, and Lord Burghley and Allington Pippin, which we included in our great apple tasting, are still in existence; but the search is on for 'lost' varieties with wonderful local names, such as St Mary's Street, The Butcher and The Parcel Post, which may still be growing in someone's garden, somewhere.

But to return to Charles Ross. I can fully understand why, in search of a little miracle, he chose the Peasgood Nonsuch to cross with the Cox's Orange Pippin, as it was known as an apple that was good for eating and cooking. The word 'nonsuch' or 'nonpareil' in an apple's name means 'without equal', and the RHS called it 'one of the most handsome apples in cultivation'.

TASTING AND COOKING NOTES

We were very excited to taste this apple, since so many good things were written about it. However, in our kitchen tests I was not convinced of its qualities. Yes, it is a big and truly handsome apple, and it was pleasant, juicy, light and refreshing to eat fresh, but beyond that there was no drama, no delightful surprises, and none of the hoped-for bursts of flavour.

Whether it was pureeing, juicing, baking or making a tarte tatin, I am sorry to report that the apple was sub-average in all the cooking challenges. Yet I am told, interestingly, that this variety is very heavily planted for a leading brand of apple puree for babies, as it is thought to have the perfect acidic balance, so it is curious that it didn't puree well. I suspect that the apples we tasted were not at their best. As always there is the question of tasting at the right or wrong moment. By that I mean that if an apple is picked too early it will not have had time to develop its full taste, texture and sugar levels. And if picked too late, it can lose a great deal of its moisture and texture. Perhaps, after all, 'l'erreur est humaine' – it is the human beings that are to blame and not the apple! I have six trees and this year I will personally pick the fruit with Anne Marie at the perfect point of ripeness to ensure a fair trial.

GROWING NOTES
The Charles Ross grows well on smaller rootstocks, so it is a good tree for smaller gardens, and generally crops well with quite big, showy, colourful fruit. Picked in mid-September the apples can keep until December, but the fruits tend to soften and become mealy.

CHEDDAR CROSS

21 trees in my English orchard
Bristol, 1916
SEASON: *August*
APPEARANCE: *greenish yellow, with a red flush*
BEST FOR: *everything, especially tarts*

This apple reminded me that you should never pre-judge anything. I must admit the name Cheddar Cross did not conjure up any expectations of gastronomical glory, and yet this apple truly surprised me. It was introduced to me by Marcus Roberts, and it is a lovely apple to look at: blushing red with golden stripes. Then, when we began to test it in the kitchen, I was taken aback by its fantastic qualities.

This is a relatively new apple compared to most of the heritage varieties we have planted in the orchard. It was raised in 1916 by G. T. Spinks, who was a fruit breeder at the Long Ashton Research Station in Bristol. He christened his apples after English towns and counties, adding 'cross' as the suffix, so there is also a Gloucester, Exeter, Plymouth, Taunton, Hereford and Newport Cross.

Nurserymen often experiment with bringing together two apples with opposite qualities in the hope of finding a happy and harmonious medium, but they are rarely successful. As a chef who also likes to mix tastes and textures, I think that if I were an apple breeder I would be tempted to work with apples with different, but not opposite, qualities, as this is what Spinks did with the Cheddar Cross with great success.

Its parents are the crisp little red apple Star of Devon, and the older Allington Pippin, raised by Thomas Laxton some time before 1884.

The latter is a variety that is not often seen today, but it was one of the great Victorian favourites, and no wonder, as it is itself a cross between two great apples, the King of the Pippins (see page 154) and the Cox's Orange Pippin (see page 84). All this illustrious ancestry shows itself in the Cheddar Cross and yet, ever since it was introduced to the market in 1949, it has only been grown commercially on a small scale, which is a great shame.

TASTING AND COOKING NOTES

It is rare to find an apple that performs well in all of our kitchen tests, but the Cheddar Cross almost equalled the Cox's Orange Pippin in showing itself to be good at everything. What a happy discovery! When tasted from the tree, it was bursting with juices, flavours and aromatics. It made an almost perfect creamy and delicious-tasting puree, with no sugar needed. Baked whole it cooked beautifully and the flesh was plump and fluffy, but also melting, with a lengthy layering of flavours.

Maman Blanc would have smiled when it came to the tarte Maman Blanc test, as the concentric layers of apple crescents turned a beautiful gold and the aroma was divine – so good I was transported back to my childhood, when I would smell the tart baking the moment I opened the door of our house. When we made a tarte tatin with the Cheddar Cross it was a little lacking in the density, fleshiness and acidity that makes for perfection, yet it was still delicious.

GROWING NOTES

This is a variety that is generally resistant to scab, but can be susceptible to mildew. If the apples are picked in late August they can be enjoyed into September, but their skins can become greasy if they are stored for longer. A good variety to grow against a wall, as an espalier or palmette.

CHIVERS DELIGHT

52 trees in my English orchard
Cambridge, around 1920
SEASON: *mid-late October*
APPEARANCE: *slightly flattened, golden with orange-red flush*
BEST FOR: *eating fresh, juice, baking whole and tarte tatin*

Being an Oxford boy – albeit with a funny French accent – and having a competitive edge, I doubted that a Cambridge apple could really beat an Oxford apple, but I had to eat some humble apple pie as I discovered that Cambridgeshire has a long tradition of fruit growing and, amongst the many orchards and growers the county has witnessed, the Chivers family stand out. They are believed to have been descended from the Huguenots, who settled in Cottenham at the end of the seventeenth century, and in around 1817 they moved to the nearby village of Histon. In 1825 Britain's first railway opened and the rapid expansion of the network began changing the distribution of foods and opening up new markets. When a station was built in Histon, Stephen Chivers, who was a market gardener, started an orchard in 1850 close to the tracks and sent his sons to open a distribution centre in Bradford. After a while it became clear that the majority of their fruit was being bought by manufacturers of jam, and the sons convinced Stephen that they should begin making their own.

Despite the success of their jams, marmalades and jellies, and their pioneering canning operation, the family considered themselves farmers first and foremost, and as well as growing fruit, they raised livestock and cereals on nearly eight thousand acres locally. Between 1920 and 1936 the family began developing their own apple varieties and Chivers Delight was the best known and the most successful. In the first half of the twentieth century it was hugely popular, but has since fallen out of favour. And I wonder why, because I love this apple.

Could it be that this orphan fruit suffers from not having a known illustrious parentage (although there is a suggestion that the Cox's Orange Pippin (see page 84) may be involved somewhere in its heritage)? Well, now it has a new champion. I loved this apple so much that I have planted fifty-two of their trees in my orchard, which always delight with their abundance of blossom. Then, in October, every branch bends under the heavy weight of these good-looking, plump and colourful fruits – Anne Marie often catches me munching one straight from the tree when I think she is not looking – and I will fight for their reappearance in shops and supermarkets.

TASTING AND COOKING NOTES

Mostly the Chivers Delight is classified as a 'good eating apple' – and it is true that this beautiful apple often graces the fruit bowls at Le Manoir aux Quat'Saisons – but this pigeonholing is a crying shame because I found it to have so many more exceptional and surprising qualities. Straight from the tree it is a joy. My heart sang as it has all the characteristics of a great apple: honeyed, yet refreshingly juicy, crisp, aromatic and delicately sweet; and it makes a delicious juice.

Admittedly it is not an apple to puree, as, despite it having a delightful perfume, sweetness and acidity, it didn't achieve the desired smooth consistency. Baked whole, however, the Chivers Delight was a star: no collapsing here, the apple stood proud without a blister, firm but melting. Its distinct honey flavour, although sweet, was counterbalanced by a refreshing acidity and the layered aromatics were long-lasting.

After this I was looking forward to a very special tarte Maman Blanc experience, but sadly I was disappointed. It wasn't the flavour that was lacking, but the balance was thrown as the acidity disappeared. This was a twist in the plot that defied logic, and it became even more curious when, to my surprise, the apple made a divine tarte tatin. This I cannot explain, as normally the dessert needs tart, acidic, compact flesh from apples like Cox's Orange Pippin and Granny Smith (see page 133), but these apples have the opposite characteristics to Chivers Delight. Nevertheless, the halves of apple kept their tight shape, yet were fully cooked, moist, and somehow their wonderful honey flavours and perfume did not make the tart too sweet. I believe the Tatin sisters who invented this famous recipe a century earlier would have loved to have been offered a basket of Chivers Delight.

GROWING NOTES
Easy to grow in the garden and resistant to many pests, although prone to canker, the Chivers Delight will do best in a sunny spot and autumn sunshine will produce the best fruit, as the apples ripen quite late in the season (mid-to-late October). In our orchard the trees are great croppers and if the apples are kept cool they can be stored until around January time.

CLAYGATE PEARMAIN

7 trees in my English orchard
Surrey, 1821
SEASON: *October*
APPEARANCE: *green overlaid with orange/red and often russeted*
BEST FOR: *puree and baking whole*

The nature of apples is that a seedling can spring up anywhere from a pip thrown down by a passer-by, and some of the very best varieties have been found by chance in the most unlikely of places. This is the case with the Claygate Pearmain, which the horticulturalist John Braddick discovered growing in a hedge close to his home in Claygate in Surrey, and went on to become a favourite in Victorian gardens and the orchards of country houses.

Braddick was quite the explorer, travelling the world in search of new varieties, as well as busily raising thousands of fruits, from apples and pears to cherries, peaches, apricots, plums and grapes, back home. All of these, as he wrote in a letter to *The Gardener Magazine* in March 1827, he hoped would 'gladden the hearts of horticulturalists for many years to come. As they are produced,' he promised, 'I will make them known to the public, with as much facility as is in my power.' So it is amusing that he found his most successful fruit almost on his doorstep.

He exhibited the Claygate Pearmain to the Royal Horticultural Society in 1821, where it received a First Class Certificate. Robert Hogg called his find, 'A valuable and highly esteemed dessert apple of the first quality,' while Bunyard considered it was 'fully deserving of a place in the best dozen dessert apples'.

TASTING AND COOKING NOTES
This venerable heritage apple did well in our tastings, despite its age, and even exceeded most of the modern varieties. Eaten raw, its flavour was pleasant, rich and nutty, although it is a shame that it has a slightly leathery skin; and when juiced it was tasty but lacking in a vital sharpness.

It made a good puree, with a big apple flavour, very well balanced between acidity and sweetness, and requiring little sugar; however, it could be considered a little on the dry side. The rich, nutty flavour carried over into the baked apple, which kept its shape and texture and was simply delicious. But when baked in a tart, the dryness was more noticeable, so that the dessert was good, but not remarkable. And when it came to the tarte tatin, the apple really showed its limitations as it crumbled a little and lacked the crucial acidity to combat the sweetness of the caramel. However, as this is a late-keeping variety, it may be that the apple will perform differently if we test it again when it is at its optimum ripeness.

GROWING NOTES
The trees are non-vigorous and keep a good compact shape, which is good news for smaller gardens, though as they are partial tip-bearers (see page 170), they need careful pruning to avoid losing fruit. The RHS recommends this variety as an excellent source of nectar for attracting bees, and it can cope with northerly, colder areas with higher rainfall as the trees have good resistance to disease, especially scab. The apples should keep well through to February, with the colour softening to yellow as the fruit is stored.

THE APPLE STORE

The cellar beneath our house in Franche-Comté was the huge family garde-manger (larder), which was the exact footprint of the house that my father built with his own hands, filled with treasures: hundreds of bottles and jars of preserved fruits and vegetables in neat rows, the beetroots, parsnips and chicory lifted from the earth floor on wooden slats and covered in jute, and the inevitable barrel of local wine dripping slowly from its tap into the earth. It stays in my memory like a rich, still-life oil painting.

Underneath the bottles and jars would be the apples that had not been used straight away, which my father would keep in the dark until January or beyond.

But that was yesterday. Today we have almost lost the understanding of the seasonality of all foods and so storing apples has also become a forgotten skill. On our supermarket shelves there are fruits available every day of the year, imported from across the world, from countries like New Zealand, Chile and South Africa, but don't forget that these apples too have been stored. They cannot be eaten straight from the tree, so instead they are picked before they are fully mature, and kept in what the industry calls controlled atmosphere storage, in which temperature, oxygen, carbon dioxide – and importantly, the natural ripening gas, ethylene – are controlled. The apples effectively 'go to sleep' for up to six months or even a year before being brought out into the ambient temperature, so they 'wake up' abruptly and haven't had the chance to develop all their characteristic sugars and flavours slowly throughout the autumn. Of course, taste, juiciness and nutrients are all affected, especially taste. That sums up modern fruit today.

In days gone by, families knew which varieties were in season when, and how long each would keep. Storing apples was a crucial element of ancient food security because they could be made into pies and puddings and would provide a valuable source of nutrition through the cold winter months. The great Victorian pomologists also understood this, detailing every nuance of each fruit and its keeping properties with characteristic lyricism. As Edward Bunyard wrote in The Anatomy of Dessert, *'What fruit can compare with the apple for its extended season, lasting from August to June, keeping alive for us in winter, in its sun-stained flush and rustic russet, the memory of golden autumnal days?'*

The importance of variety is something I have always known, as in our family an apple was not just an apple, a pear not just a pear, a potato was not just a potato. Each had a season and a purpose. One thing we proved in our tastings of so many varieties together was that not every apple should be picked from the tree and eaten in September/October, however ripe it may look. Many mid-to-late October apples, more often the harder acidic varieties, like Court Pendu Plat (see page 81), want to be kept, often well into November or December, when they can be brought out for Christmas.

Straight from the tree, many early apples can be challenging, but as they store, these 'keepers' continue to ripen slowly, and as more of their starches turn to sugars they develop more complex flavours. Even some varieties that have traditionally been classed as 'cookers', and are too fiercely sour to eat straight from the tree, become mellow and sweet enough to grace the fruit bowl or eat with cheese. There are some apples, such as the ancient Gloucester variety Green Two Year Old, which were said to keep from one season to the next!

It may seem old fashioned, but there is a certain beauty and romance about nurturing and maturing your own apples, and it is a very easy thing to store them in a cool, dark place. You can buy special apple racks, but a slatted box will do. Keep each variety separate as they will ripen at different times (if necessary, wrap each one in newspaper), and make sure the apples don't touch, as we all know the saying: 'one bad apple spoils the barrel'.

COURT OF WICK

4 trees in my English orchard
Somerset, around 1790
SEASON: *late September*
APPEARANCE: *yellow gold with red flecks*
BEST FOR: *eating fresh*

The most fascinating aspect of some of these ancient varieties of apple is the mystery that surrounds them. This, of course, can be frustrating too, because between legend and true history there are often so many different stories and theories.

There is only one real source of information about this old Somerset apple, sometimes called the Court of Wick Pippin, and that is Robert Hogg. In his *Fruit Manual*, he tells us that the variety 'originated at Court of Wick, near Yatton in Somersetshire'. It is said to have been raised from the seed of the Golden Pippin – so at least we have a clue as to one of its parents. It was first propagated by a Mr Wood, who was a nurseryman in Huntingdon. He called it Wood's Huntingdon and distributed it under that name in around 1790, but how and when Wood's Huntingdon became Court of Wick we may never know.

In fact, this apple's likely birthplace is a Jacobean manor house and chapel in the village of Claverham, Yatton, called the Court de Wyck. The original house was built before 1338; between 1660 and 1670 it was enlarged and, at the beginning of the eighteenth century, it was considered one of the finest properties in the area. At the time of the discovery of the apple, it would have been the absentee seat of the Rt Hon. John, Earl Poulett, who became the fourth earl and seventh baron in 1788, and whose family owned the manor over a span of two hundred years, but rarely lived there. Sadly, by 1814, the manor had become almost uninhabitable and it was pulled down, leaving behind only the fourteenth-century chapel and tythe barn. The orchard in which the Court of Wick apple was most likely raised had long since disappeared.

In its day this was clearly a very popular apple. In *The Fruit Manual*, Robert Hogg quotes the agriculturalist John Billingsley, who published a survey on the *General View of the Agriculture of the County of Somerset* in 1798, in which he noted: 'The favourite apple, both as a table and cider fruit, is the Court of Wick Pippin, taking its name from the spot where it was first produced. It originated from the pip or seed of the Golden Pippin, and may be considered as a beautiful variety of that fruit. In shape, colour, and flavour it has not its superior.' And, writing almost eighty years later in *The Herefordshire Pomona*, Hogg was still praising the variety in quite poetic terms, as 'one of the best and most valuable dessert apples. The rich and delicious flavour of the fruit is not inferior to that of the Golden Pippin ... In some places, as on the Hastings Sand, the colour of the fruit becomes a fine clear orange with a somewhat carmine cheek on the side next the sun; the same rich tint is observed in some localities in Herefordshire.'

TASTING AND COOKING NOTES
Although quite small and unremarkable-looking, when you bite into the Court of Wick, there is a big apple flavour and a slight hint of acidity and my expert friends tell me that, thanks to its aromatics, it makes a wonderful cider. But now, I have to confess, the notes from our cooking tests for this apple have mysteriously disappeared, so until I can taste the next crop from the orchard, I cannot tell you more!

GROWING NOTES

Although the Court of Wick was first grown in Somerset, it is a variety that is known to cope with cold and windy conditions and it has good resistance to canker. According to Joan Morgan in *The New Book of Apples*, it was said to withstand even 'most severe blasts from Welsh mountains'.

COURT PENDU PLAT

8 trees in my English orchard
Franche-Comté, France, 1613 or earlier
SEASON: *mid-late October*
APPEARANCE: *flattened; greenish yellow with*
pinky-red flush, often russeted
BEST FOR: *eating fresh and puree*

The name *court pendu* is often confused with *corps pendu* which translates to 'hung body', and projects terrible imagery of corpses of apples hanging on barren branches of trees ... but I will stop being dramatic, as the name actually means 'hanged short' and only refers to the anatomy of this specific variety, whose stalk is so short that the apples appear to almost rest on their branches.

In France there are many apples that bear this name, including Court Pendu Gris, which is supposed to date back to the 1400s in Normandy, where it was on sale in the market at Rouen in 1420, and may have featured in the potager of King Louis XI. There is also a Court Pendu Rose, Rouge, Doré and Violet, as well as Court Pendu apples appendaged with the names of different regions, such as Dordogne, Limousin, and a Court Pendu Royal.

I was so excited to learn that this very rare and ancient variety was found in my region of Franche-Comté. It was first documented by the Swiss botanist Johann Bauhin, who cited the apples in his posthumously published work, *Historia Plantarum Universalis* (1650), completed with his son-in-law, Jean-Henri Cherler, after the apples were discovered in 1613 growing in the middle of some Gallo-Roman ruins at Mandeure, close to my home in Le Doubs.

In Britain the apples were widely grown in the time of Elizabeth I, but are thought to have been introduced much earlier by the Romans, making this variety one of the oldest still in cultivation, and so I have planted eight trees in our orchard to try to ensure its survival.

A big Victorian favourite, both for its flavour and the attractiveness of the tree, it could often be found in formal gardens. Robert Hogg considered it 'a valuable dessert apple of the first quality; in use from December to May. The tree is of small growth, very hardy, and an abundant bearer. Grafted on the paradise stock it makes excellent bushes and espaliers. The blossom of this variety expands later than that of any other variety, and on that account is less liable to be injured by spring frosts; and hence it has been called the Wise Apple.' I very much like the idea of having wise apples in my orchard.

Unlike most apples, which can be eaten off the tree when ripe, this one only ripens as it is stored, and then not until Christmas – this of course was a quality that was much valued in its heyday when there was no such notion as year-round apples in supermarkets.

TASTING AND COOKING NOTES
First I have to say that our taste test in October was too early in the season for this variety, and as Marcus Roberts, who brought me the apple, was keen to impress upon me, we would not experience it at its full potential.

Despite its tough exterior and youthfulness, this old French apple did actually deliver well. It had a well-balanced and rich flavour and was refreshing, due to its low level of sugar (though of course it was not fully ripened and this would most likely change as the starches turned to sugar and complexities of flavour built up during storage). Interestingly, the apple also had a faint aroma of pineapple, giving it a very distinctive character.

It offered a good-quality puree, but didn't measure up to its competitors such as the Blenheim Orange (see page 42), Red Windsor (see page 152) or the Cox's Orange Pippin (see page 84) in the other tests; and it simply did not want to bake whole, remaining dense and slightly grainy under heat, although the flavour stayed interesting and it retained its notes of pineapple. The promise was there, however, and so we must give this ancient and intriguing apple the full re-tasting that it deserves, to discover whether disappointments might turn to triumphs.

GROWING NOTES
Due to late flowering, this variety has good resistance to frost as well as disease, particularly scab and mildew, so if you can find a tree, it is also perfect for a garden as it is not vigorous and is small and upright with a characteristic spreading form. Being a late-flowering variety, however, you may need to consider providing a pollination partner (see page 263) if it shows a tendency not to set the fruit. If picked in mid-to-late October and stored, the apples will become more mellow, sweet and scented as they keep through to February.

COX'S ORANGE PIPPIN

54 trees in my English orchard
Buckinghamshire, 1825
SEASON: *late September*
APPEARANCE: *greenish gold with orange/red flush*
BEST FOR: *everything*

I will never forget the summer's day, about thirty years ago, when I joined William Sibley at a tasting of heritage apples laid on by the Royal Horticultural Society at Le Manoir. That tasting stays with me for two reasons: first, it inspired me to dream about my beautiful orchard project, and second, one of the apples stood head and shoulders above the rest. Her beauty was not immediately obvious from the outside, as she does not have the showy prettiness of a Chivers Delight (see page 71), Adams' Pearmain (see page 27) or Devonshire Quarrenden (see page 95), but once I took a bite I knew I was tasting the best apple of my life. I was overwhelmed with a sensory explosion of aromatics, clean, long, complex flavours, which balanced sweetness with acidity, and a crisp texture.

For years I mistook this apple for a Queen Cox until Will pointed out that it was actually a Cox's Orange Pippin that I had been so blown away by (I am so bad with names I still get the names of my sons Olivier and Sebastien mixed up, so now they call me 'Henri'!). This is one of the most glorious of all British apples, which was famous in its day, and is still one of the most popular, widely grown and available varieties of all time, so familiar to us in Britain that, like an old friend, we rarely even feel the need to use its full name. And it is almost as if there is a sense of mutual admiration, as these apples like to stay at home in the British climate where they feel comfortable, and really don't travel well. So, unlike many varieties, they are rarely grown in other countries.

Richard Cox, the lucky man – or genius – who first raised this extraordinary apple, was a brewer from Bermondsey in East London, who must have been quite wealthy because he was able to retire to his Georgian country house, The Lawns, in Colnbrook, Buckinghamshire, where he devoted himself to his garden. Some time around 1825 he made the historic decision to cross-pollinate two of his trees: thought to be the Blenheim Orange (see page 42) and the Ribston Pippin (see page 160), though this has never been confirmed. As a result he chanced upon an apple that connoisseurs still think is one of the finest of English fruits, thanks to its gloriously complex and aromatic balance of sweetness and acidity.

Commercially, however, it had a slow start and wasn't actually marketed until around twenty years later. It was first taken up by a local nursery, E. Small & Son, who propagated the original tree and began selling the variety in the 1840s with limited success. It won a major award in 1857 and a decade later the apple was faring well in the hands of another local firm, Royal Nurseries, in Slough, who began marketing the apple on a large scale from 1862. Up until 2012 it was the all-time favourite apple in Britain, until along came the New Zealand Gala (see page 112).

Marcus Roberts told me an amusing anecdote about one of the most renowned and innovative of the great Victorian fruit growers, Thomas Rivers. His nursery in Sawbridgeworth, Hertfordshire, was founded by his grandfather in 1725, and the old orchard, which still contains some six hundred trees, is currently being restored by volunteers in the Rivers Heritage Site and Orchard Group. Rivers was apparently asked at a fruit show to recommend his top twelve apples. He said that for his first three he would plant Cox. When asked for the next three, he answered 'Cox'. As to the next three, he chose Cox again, and when asked for his final three, he hesitated and then replied, 'Why, I should plant another three Coxes!'

Roald Dahl even mentioned the Cox's Orange Pippin in his book *Danny, the Champion of the World*, in which Danny quotes his father as saying that one of 'the nice things' about the apple is that 'the pips rattle when it's ripe'. Such is the extraordinary magnetism of this apple that it is no wonder that it has been called into action so many times to cross-breed with other varieties.

So, you might ask, if this is such a heroic apple, why is it that a Cox bought from the supermarket can often be disappointing? Well, the answer is complicated, but it is important, so I hope you will bear with me . . .

The great irony is that the British love for the Cox, which reached its peak in Victorian times, also contributed to the story of the great decline of the English orchards, which had begun early in the nineteenth century, if not before, with the import of cheap apples from America, Canada and, later, New Zealand. This was so concerning to the Victorian champions of the English apple that, in 1883, connoisseurs, nurserymen and gardeners alike came together to stage the National Apple Congress in the Chiswick Gardens of the Royal Horticultural Society. An unprecedented 1,545 varieties were identified and paraded according to their county in a bid to choose and promote the best traditional varieties in the face of their New World rivals. As always the English way was to divide the variety into 'dessert' and 'cookers' and a list of sixty of the best of each was drawn up. The most popular dessert variety turned out to be the King of the Pippins (see page 154), followed by Cox's Orange Pippin, with its parent, Ribston Pippin, in third place.

As a direct result of the Congress, fruit growers were encouraged to give up local and even regional varieties and concentrate instead on the 'national' favourites, but as far as the Cox was concerned, this was a difficult choice, because as esteemed as the apple was, and is, it is regrettably very susceptible to disease, particularly scab, and is one of the most difficult apples to grow. Many clones were produced and favoured by different nurseries, but these often resulted in differences in the apples, though many are interesting in their own right. (I have decided to plant some Crimson Cox, which is a clone discovered in about 1913 by John Harris of Haynes Farm, Carey, Herefordshire, and introduced to the market in 1928, along with Queen Cox, which I now know to be another highly coloured clone!)

Growers struggled to produce enough fruit to satisfy the market until, in the 1920s, sulphur sprays were developed and deployed against the scab (the heavy use of sulphur is something that I hate, by the way, and have vowed to avoid it in my orchard even though it is at the cost of a smaller harvest and the scourge of disease).

By the late 1960s and through the 1970s, commercial growers were faced with a new and overwhelming competition, which I am sorry to say came from the Golden Delicious (see page 122), an American apple that was extensively grown in France and which was aggressively marketed in Britain as 'Le Crunch'. This coincided with the rise of the supermarkets, who demanded perfect, beautiful-looking fruit in reliably huge quantities.

Not only was the Cox's Orange Pippin tough to grow, but it was still being raised on old-fashioned 'paradise' rootstock (see page 120) known as 'type 2', which produced bush trees in which the apples in the centre were often hidden in the dense foliage, away from the sun, so they appeared too green for the supermarkets' liking. So the search was on to find a clone that could deliver not only a bigger crop, but an apple with a higher colour, and sadly flavour was lower down the list of priorities.

To cut a long story short, a huge amount of money was thrown into the project, which was begun at Long Ashton Research Station, part of Bristol University. Around five thousand cuttings were whittled down to about one thousand and, in 1982 to 1983, these were sent to William Sibley at East Malling, so he could assess and work with growers to choose the highest-yielding clones that produced the best-looking fruit. Without these attributes, as Will says, the supermarkets would simply not have been interested in this holy grail of English apples.

The research roughly coincided with the introduction of new root-stocks. The traditional paradise stock, says Will, 'without a shadow of doubt imparted some flavour', but now there was a move towards the new M9 rootstock (see page 263), which produced more manage-able, better-cropping trees, whose fruit could be picked easily from ground level, but again flavour was not the main consideration. 'The combination of clones chosen for looks, and the loss of the type 2 rootstock,' Will believes, 'changed the face of the commercial Cox's Orange Pippin for ever.'

This collision of two important factors is partly what accounts for the fact that a supermarket Cox, even when it is good, is rarely extraordinary. Often the apples are grown with irrigation (some-times in New Zealand) in climates and soils not best suited to them, sprayed with chemicals and then picked not fully ripe and subjected to gas-storage, refrigeration and long-distance transport, so that the apple you eventually buy can be a pale travesty of its former glorious self.

So much has happened to this apple in its long and complicated history that it is possible that we will never today taste a Cox's Orange Pippin that is bursting with all of the superlative flavour sensations that the Victorians loved so much. Yet, to go back to that tasting thirty years ago, a Cox that is grown in sunshine and allowed to ripen to its full potential on the tree, then picked at the perfect moment, can still completely blow you away!

Just such an apple was the goal for Marcus Roberts as he searched for samples for our great tasting, and the ones he found, he told me, were the best that *he* had ever tasted, picked from a thirty-year-old tree, which was planted against a Victorian fruiting wall of hand-made brick at a manor house in Northamptonshire. The apples had been allowed to ripen naturally with a full measure of sunshine, helped by the warmth of the old wall, and sure enough, the moment I tasted one I was in love again.

TASTING AND COOKING NOTES

What this apple may have lacked in looks it absolutely made up for in that extraordinary explosion of flavours and textures, and it made a fantastic, low-sugar fresh juice. Although it has a tight flesh, the Cox breaks down very well into a golden puree, in which the per-fume and layers of flavour are still extraordinary. The apple baked beautifully, without splitting or blistering, and, once cut, the flesh was juicy, aromatic and appetising. It made an excellent tarte tatin, and, although it has less acidity than a Granny Smith, it compen-sated with its freshness and intensity of perfume. In a tarte Maman Blanc, however, it performed to its absolute best, which was quite remarkable considering it scored so well in all the other tests. For this tart its bouquet and complexity were just perfect: it was a true and exquisite apple experience.

GROWING NOTES

Although suited to the cool British climate, the trees are still not the easiest to grow, as they don't like the coldest and wettest sites and, as we know, they are prone to diseases such as scab and canker as well as damage from aphids. They can produce small fruit if allowed to over-crop, and may not bear fruit at all some years. So they are probably not the best choice of tree if you are only going to plant one (particularly if you eschew non-organic methods and even some of the permitted 'organic' sprays) as there are other Cox-like apples that will reward you with most of the joys, without the woes. However, if you have a clay soil or you live in Essex or in the East of England – these are the regions where the Cox grows best – it might be well worth a try. Alternatively, you could plant a tree, grown on dwarf rootstock, in a medium-to-large pot in a favourable spot. Harvested from late September into October, the apples can be stored until early January.

D'ARCY SPICE

To be planted in my English orchard
Essex, 1785
SEASON: *early November*
APPEARANCE: *greenish, with red flush*
BEST FOR: *baking whole and tarts*

On a late-summer's day, right behind the magnificent ancient abbey in Oxfordshire that is the home of my best friends, Michael and Martine Stewart, I met the apple expert Dr Barrie Juniper – an extraordinary man who loves to share his knowledge of the history of the apple and all its varieties (see page 12). Behind the wall of the abbey there stood his orchard, the oldest that I had ever encountered. I felt privileged to enter such a secret and sacred place. Amongst all the rare, ancient varieties, including Grenadier, Court Pendu Plat (page 81) and Catshead (page 62), Barrie proudly introduced me to this wonderful apple, the D'Arcy Spice.

You might think, from its name, that this late-season heritage apple has a French background, but it is not so. Nor, sadly, does it have anything to do with the hero of Jane Austen's *Pride and Prejudice* – what a romantic story that would be.

However, this apple is not without its aristocratic connections. Its name reflects not only the rich, warm and spicy flavours it develops as it matures, but also the fact that it was found, in 1785, in the garden of the grand fifteenth-century timber-framed and moated D'Arcy Hall in the village of Tolleshunt D'Arcy, near Maldon in Essex, where there is still a row of the apple trees at the approach to the house.

It is an apple that seems to have fallen victim to the often muddled, multiple-naming of ancient apples that the great Victorian pomologists tried to resolve, as at one time it was also known as the Baddow Pippin, since, in 1848, Mr John Harris, a nurseryman at Broomfield, near Chelmsford, propagated it from grafts taken from one of the original old trees, and sold it under that name. Then, a few years later, the Rivers Nursery of Sawbridgeworth (see page 85) put it in *their* catalogue, but they called it Spring Ribston.

The village of Tolleshunt D'Arcy, which gave this apple its true identity, has a curious history too. The first part of the name is said to come from Toll's 'funt' (fountain) and it has twelve entries in the Domesday Book, but in its early days the second part of the name would change according to the name of the local landowner. Unusually the succession was passed down through the female line and, as the women married, the village would add the name of the latest husband. So at one point it was known as Tolleshunt Tregoz, then Tolleshunt Valoines and Tolleshunt de Boys.

In the early fifteenth century a de Boys daughter married John D'Arcy and he began the building of D'Arcy Hall (for all her importance in the story, the daughter's name is unknown). The D'Arcys were quite a formidable family in the area. John's father, Robert, Lord of Maldon, married a wealthy heiress, Alice Fitz Langley, and began building the historic Moot Hall in the town as a private residence, and his grandfather, Henry D'Arcy, was Sheriff of London.

Perhaps because of the family's prestige, when the village became Tolleshunt D'Arcy this was the last name-change. The hall, which was finished by John's son, Anthony (who became Sheriff of Essex and Hertfordshire), remained in the family until 1593 and there are houses and streets in the village that bear their name, and memorials to them in the local church.

But back to the apple! The tradition in Essex was that the fruits would be left on the tree to develop their flavour until Guy Fawkes' Day. Then they were harvested and put inside cloth sacks, which were hung from the branches until December, as going into Christmas and New Year the fruits become softer, sweeter, and develop the nutmeg spice flavours for which they are famous.

Barrie Juniper encouraged me to try planting some trees in our orchard at Le Manoir as, although they seem to love their native Essex, if they find the right spot elsewhere and can enjoy a hot summer, they produce delicious fruit; and Marcus Roberts promised me that the D'Arcy Spice was 'a real keeper; a classy beauty', which in her best years would yield a small but glorious harvest. Having met the D'Arcy Spice in her youth, I can tell that when she reaches her full maturity, she will be truly lovely, so we are planting ten trees to see how well they do in my corner of Oxfordshire.

TASTING AND COOKING NOTES
Our mammoth apple tasting took place in October, but this was not the optimum timing for the D'Arcy Spice, which needs to further ripen in order to develop its fruit sugar and show its full potential and beauty. When eaten raw the skin of the apple was quite thick, but the flesh was crunchy and juicy with an interesting layering of flavours, and when juiced it held both the flavour and colour well. Its youthfulness was evident when we pureed it, as the flesh didn't break down well enough and the colour was a greyish-white with a green hue; however, when baked this plump apple stood proud with no blistering whatsoever and, even though it lacked the maturity to show all of its flavours, it had a wonderful complexity.

Baked in a tart the segments fluffed out beautifully and the great moisture of the apple combined with its sugar to create an appetising golden colour. Once again the early harvest meant that the flavour was slightly too tart, but it was still magnificent. We even had a good result with a tarte tatin, although, to be critical (and I am a very stern judge!), it fell short of the true experience, as although it had the perfect acidity it showed signs of collapse. But it had a lovely warm, spicy flavour, and throughout the tasting it tantalised us with the promise of more to come as the fruit developed.

GROWING NOTES
This is a tree that is available from more specialist suppliers, but it is not common and is not a steady cropper or strong-growing. It has good resistance to disease, likes sandy soil and dry conditions and loves a cool summer followed by a warm autumn, which will allow its spicy flavour to develop. When picked from mid-October onwards the apple can be kept in store until April in some seasons.

DEVONSHIRE QUARRENDEN

48 trees in my English orchard
Devon, 1678
SEASON: *August/September*
APPEARANCE: *deep crimson with occasional red flecks in the flesh*
BEST FOR: *eating fresh, puree, tarts and tarte tatin*

I never stop being amazed by the way a fruit can evolve and travel from one country to another. Imagine, this variety of apple is at least three hundred years old! And, despite having Devonshire in its name, it is originally from France. It is thought that Quarrenden comes from its probable birthplace of Carentan in Normandy, famous for a fierce battle that took place there during the D-Day landings.

Somehow the apple found its way to Devon, where the local accent and pronunciation seems to have turned it into Quarantine or Quarrenden (often written as Quarendoun or Quaryndon). I realise my English friends must have had the same struggles with the French language as I myself had with English when I first arrived in Great Britain. In fact, it took me three days to reach Oxford from Devon as nobody could understand what I was saying when I explained I wanted to go to 'OxFORDT'. I felt quite alien, so I have a great deal of empathy for those locals who translated this lovely Carentan apple into Quarrenden.

The apple is mentioned by the Hampshire agriculturalist John Worlidge in his book *Vinetum Britannicum, Or a Treatise of Cider,* published in 1678, where, in yet another variation of the spelling, he calls it the Devonshire Quarrington and pronounces it to be 'a very fine early Apple'.

It is likely that it became the parent of a Kent apple called Ben's Red, which, confusingly, is also sometimes sold as Quarrenden. However, little else is known about its history after it crossed the Channel, except that by Victorian times this very attractive fruit, dressed in its deep crimson, was widely grown all over the country, where it was said to fetch a good price. Robert Hogg, who also struggled to find out much about its history, called it a 'very valuable and first-rate dessert apple', and praised its 'fine, cooling and refreshing vinous juice'. It is also listed in *Scott's Orchardist*, the extensive catalogue produced by the nursery of J. Scott of Merriott in Somerset in 1872, as 'one of our most highly esteemed fruits either for eating or for cider making'. However, it is now rarely seen, and so its praises need to be sung. Because this apple was so loved by all our tasters, I have planted forty-eight of the beautiful trees in our orchard, and I hope to introduce our guests at Le Manoir aux Quat'Saisons to a fine Devonshire Quarrenden experience.

TASTING AND COOKING NOTES
Juicy, with a great crunch and a surprising hint of strawberry, this is simply a delicious apple when eaten raw. It also made excellent juice and a very lovely puree, but was clearly not an appropriate apple for baking whole. Although the flavour was excellent and it kept its red-berry perfume, the flesh remained too firm.

Most remarkably, this old apple could have been made for the tarte Maman Blanc. The fluffy slices kept their distinctive character with a lovely balance of acidity and sweetness. And, what is even more exceptional, this apple also performed brilliantly in a tarte tatin – a feat that very few apples that make a good puree can achieve. The apple halves stayed firm, but the flesh was moist and the apple's special flavour counterbalanced the sweetness of the caramel – it was just divine.

GROWING NOTES

The trees are a triploid variety (see page 263), but crop well and are known to tolerate quite windy, wet locations (though some old-time gardeners recommend a sheltered location with light soils to get the best from them). David Pennell warns 'not to allow the tree to over-crop or it will get into the frustratingly biennial cycle of bumper crops one year, followed by next to nothing the next'. The apples are early ripeners, so are best enjoyed straight from the tree in late August, and they will only keep until September.

DISCOVERY

28 trees in my English orchard
Essex, 1949
SEASON: *mid-August*
APPEARANCE: *deep red flush over pale yellow green, the flesh*
is often flushed pink
BEST FOR: *baking whole, tarts*

I love this apple because it is the first to be picked from the branches in our orchard, and the first to grace the fruit bowls for our guests at Le Manoir aux Quat'Saisons. The apples are quite beautiful, with their rich red skins and creamy white, occasionally pink-flushed, flesh; and straight from the trees they make wonderful eating apples, delivering a great sensation of freshness.

Discovery is one of the earliest cropping of the English varieties, which was first raised in 1949 in the midst of calamity. A workman on an Essex fruit farm, George Dummer, grew a number of seedlings from the pips of Worcester Pearmain apples (see page 167) and decided to plant the best one in his front garden in Langham – but as the poor man only had one arm, his wife had to help him and then, unfortunately, there was another disaster as she managed to slip and break her ankle. So the seedling waited for several weeks covered by a sack before it could be planted, showing remarkable resilience. Despite the frosts it not only survived (and is still there today), but produced great crops of red apples, which, unlike many early varieties, had the virtue of staying on the tree long enough to ripen properly. What a wonderful little love story, that also gives a tiny window on life in the

British countryside after the Second World War, when people still hoped to discover a new jewel of an apple.

Originally known as Dummer's Seedling, it was later taken up by a nurseryman, Jack Matthews, from Thurston in Suffolk, who had been a pilot during the war and initially called the apple Thurston August. Matthews specialised in buying grafts and launching a new variety of apple each year. The year 1962 was the turn of Thurston August, which was presented to the market under yet another new and more dramatic name: Discovery. Its known parent, the celebrated Worcester Pearmain, clearly gave the apple its colour and hint of strawberries, and though its other parent isn't known, it is thought to have been the equally famous Beauty of Bath.

As the Discovery is one of the first apples of the season to be harvested, there was a tradition of sending some to the Queen Mother on her birthday each August. Being the trailblazer for the season is the key to its continued commercial success. However, you could question whether it is actually a great flag-bearer as, although it is cheerful-looking and fresh-tasting (and being small and red, it is appealing to children), like many of the early apples it is a little one-dimensional, being without the length of keeping of the later apples. However, having put it through its paces in our taste test, my answer to that is yes, the Discovery has a place in the kitchen.

TASTING AND COOKING NOTES
The attraction of this apple is that it is an English variety available in August, but like most early apples, although it is deliciously juicy with a refreshing flavour (and it makes a pleasant, sweet juice), it lacks the complexity, depth of flavour and richness of later-season apples. The appeal of early apples has sometimes been compared to that of Beaujolais Nouveau, the first wine to be made from the new

harvest, which is light and delicate and summery, but has none of the character of later wines.

Yet when Discovery was exposed to heat, we had a different story. The flesh crumbled into a pleasant puree with a light pink hue. It was a little watery, but it required hardly any sugar. And the apple was sumptuous baked whole. The skin blistered lightly, but inside was a very fluffy flesh with light, but good aromatics.

There was a small triumph in the Maman Blanc tarte test. The fruit turned pale gold and fluffed out in an appetising way, but with a less perfumed flavour than a Devonshire Quarrenden (see page 95) or a Cox's Orange Pippin (see page 84). I thought the apple would implode when it came to the tarte tatin, but it held its shape very well, and produced a fresh and delicate experience. What it lacked in richness it made up for in delicate scents: though more eau du cologne than heavy perfume!

So, overall in the cooking tests, if you will excuse the pun, this apple was a true and unexpected Discovery.

GROWING NOTES
We have twenty-eight Discovery trees in our orchards and they look wonderful when the apples are fully ripened and red. They also have the advantage of being relatively easy to grow, and so this is a variety that is good for a small garden, especially in colder areas as it is quite hardy and the blossom is tolerant to frost. It is not too vigorous, if a little slow to come into fruit, and you can judge when to pick the apples at their best around mid-August – however, they will only keep into September.

EDWARD VII

To be planted in my English orchard
Worcester, 1902
SEASON: *October*
APPEARANCE: *waxy-skinned, yellowish green,*
sometimes with pale reddish flush
BEST FOR: *puree and baking*

An apple fit for a king? As I have explained in the introduction to this book, as a chef and a Frenchman I have never understood the English idea of classifying apples into two single categories: eating or cooking. It is something that is quite alien to me, but it is a distinction that has been enshrined in British history since it was taken to new heights at the dinner tables of grand Victorian houses. Certain 'cookers' would be selected for particular puddings, which would be followed by elaborate displays of fresh apples for the 'dessert', and new varieties were often bred specifically for either purpose.

However, most of those designated as cooking apples began to be edged out by the Bramley's Seedling (see page 51), which saturated the market once it began being grown commercially in the early 1900s. So this 'cooker', the Edward VII, may have arrived a little too late to the party in the year of King Edward's coronation in 1902.

Classed as a very late cooking apple, and thought to be a cross between our local Blenheim Orange (see page 42) and the Golden Noble (see page 128), it was first recorded by William Rowe, a well-known nurseryman, 'seedsman and florist', in Worcestershire, which was a huge centre of apple (and pear) growing, with orchards specialising in grafting and breeding new varieties. I can almost picture the busy William as, according to an Orchard Survey of the City of Worcester done in 1999, he had a shop selling produce at 65 Broad Street in Worcester, along with outlets in nearby Claines and Droitwich, as well as his nursery in the hamlet of Barbourne. It was from here that he is thought to have introduced the Edward VII apple to the market in 1908. However, although it became popular in gardens, it was never really grown commercially on a large scale, despite winning first prize from the Royal Horticultural Society for best new culinary variety the following year.

The apple belongs to a small group that has one or more vertical 'suture' lines, or hairlines, in the skin, which, although faint, are often useful clues for experts on Apple Days at which people bring along fruits from their gardens hoping to learn their identity.

In our orchards the Edward VII is only now about to be added, as one day I went out to look at the trees, and they were nowhere to be seen. It turned out that somehow they had been forgotten in the original planting, for which we must beg a royal pardon!

TASTING AND COOKING NOTES
As a French Republican, I was rather in awe of an apple named after a king, and I must say it created a great deal of expectation. Even more so as the Edward VII apple is a cross between the Golden Noble, which is acidic and tart, and Blenheim Orange, which is a large, well-balanced apple with a spectrum of great qualities. Such a parentage should make it a good apple for sauces and purees, and while it didn't reach any great heights in our tests, it certainly didn't disappoint. It created a very good and flavourful juice and pureed very well, resulting in an appetising pale yellow colour with a tinge of green – it reminded me a little of the Bramley's Seedling, but it was far less astringent. It also baked well, retaining a firm and tasty

flesh. However, I am afraid to say that this kingly apple would not have made the cut for Maman Blanc's tarte, and when it came to the tarte tatin it simply collapsed – but if I was an English chef, I would say it would make a fantastic pie.

GROWING NOTES
The tree doesn't need too much space as it is hardy and upright. It is also quite problem-free, and has natural resistance to most of the usual apple diseases. It flowers quite late in the spring, so falls into the 'wise apple' group that can avoid damage from late frosts. Although it is regarded as slow to come into fruit and is not a heavy cropper, it is a useful apple for the garden as the fruit can be picked in mid-October and, properly stored, will keep through to April.

AN APPLE A DAY?

Well, you cannot take it completely literally that an apple a day will keep the doctor away, as the old saying goes, but there is some long-standing and new evidence to back up the relationship between health and apples. They are a fantastic and rich source of both insoluble and soluble fibre, as well as vitamin C and various phytochemicals, which help protect a cell's DNA from oxidative damage. And a new study (2019), published in the journal Frontiers in Microbiology, *has found that 'Freshly harvested, organically managed apples harbour a significantly more diverse, more even and distinct bacterial community, compared to conventional ones', according to Professor Gabriele Berg from Graz University of Technology in Austria, one of the authors of the research. As a result, organic apples could be healthier for the gut, and tastier than conventional ones.*

One medium apple provides 50–80kcal, 0g of fat and 12–19g of carbohydrates, while the sugar content varies greatly depending on variety, with Gala (see page 112), followed by Pink Lady, Jazz and Fuji towards the top end of the scale, satisfying the trend towards sweeter apples. However, these apples lack the more complex flavours of older varieties like Cox's Orange Pippin (see page 84).

Thanks to their fibre content, apples have a low glycaemic index, as the fibre helps to slow down the conversion of carbohydrates into glucose. Of course, this requires you not to strip away the fibre. An apple will always be at its most nutritious when organic, fresh, raw and whole, with its skin on. For juice too, fresh is always best. The cloudier or less processed the better, as clear apple juice requires a filtration and pasteurisation process that destroys a great number of the apple's health benefits. So I like to think that, yes, maybe one fresh, organic apple a day might keep the doctor away!

EGREMONT RUSSET

110 trees in my English orchard
Somerset, 1872
SEASON: *late September/October*
APPEARANCE: *yellowy-gold to orangey-brown russet*
BEST FOR: *juice*

Many years ago, one of my guests at Le Manoir aux Quat'Saisons gave me a gift of a bottle of Egremont apple juice from a grower in Norfolk. He told me that this apple juice had been lightly sterilised for safe keeping. I remember it well because instead of offering him a glass of Champagne to show my gratitude, I opened his bottle of apple juice there and then as I was so curious to taste it, and so we shared it. To this day, it was the best apple juice that I have ever tasted: pure nectar, rich and multilayered with a great depth of flavours, complex aromatics and a surprising delicate, lingering nutty flavour at the finish. From that day the Egremont Russet has been in my heart, so much so that we planted one hundred and ten trees in my orchard.

This classic apple is the most famous of a whole family of russet apples that were in vogue during the Victorian era. The name refers not to the flavour but to the rough, sandpapery nature of the skin. Most have fallen out of fashion, but to its huge credit, the Egremont Russet is a true survivor. It is one of the few Victorian apples to retain its place in British hearts – and find its way into the supermarkets, where, unusually, you can find good, flavoursome examples – although my friends Barrie Juniper and Marcus Roberts would argue that the more obscure Brownlees' Russet, which was raised in Hemel Hempstead in about 1848, is *actually* the best of the russets.

Yet the Egremont variety is an apple that keeps its heritage a closely guarded secret. Even its birthplace is not known for certain. It is thought that it was originally grown by Lord Egremont and a Mr Slater in the famous fruit gardens of the Egremont Estate in Petworth, Sussex. No mention of it has been found amongst the varieties known to have grown there, but Fred Streeter, the famous horticulturalist, journalist and BBC broadcaster on gardening, was convinced that this was the apple's birthplace. Streeter was a remarkable man who left school at the age of twelve to pursue his ambition to become a gardener, was wounded in France in the First World War, and in 1926 was invited by the third Baron Leconfield to be head gardener at Petworth House, one of the famous estates designed by Capability Brown, where he developed the fruit growing.

Despite Streeter's convictions, the first record of the Egremont Russet was from the nursery of J. Scott of Merriott in Somerset in 1872. John Scott started this famous nursery in the mid-nineteenth century, and it stayed open, championing old varieties, until 2009. From the beginning the nursery was famous for its catalogues, or *Orchardists*, which not only listed the varieties, but also looked at the history of apples and discussed aspects such as grafting and training the trees.

Scott, like many of his fellow Victorians, expressed 'great annoyance' at the confusing multiplicity of names by which apples were known around Britain. In his *Orchardist*, second edition, dated 1872, he wrote: 'no one but he who embarks in forming a large collection of apples can tell the difficulties that have to be encountered ... I now never trust the correctness of a name, until I have proved it.' His way of doing this was to acquire duplicates, 'in some cases a dozen trees, all under one name – I plant them side by side to see how many of them are alike, and when I find a fair proportion having the same character, then I conclude I may with some degree of safety select those that are alike as the true sort . . . I have now examined about 1,100 sorts of Apple, and consider that I have got them pretty correct . . . In conclusion,' he wrote, 'I have no hesitation in saying that my stock of fruit trees is one of the finest in the kingdom, covering thirty acres.'

Surely, then, in the extensive listing of his nursery's varieties, we might find out something more about this apple, and how it came to arrive in Somerset? We found a copy of the *Orchardist* and there it was, amid the descriptions of twenty-eight russet apples with long-forgotten names, the listing: *Russet, Egremont* – but followed by nothing, only white space! What a disappointment. Why no more information? Was this absence of detail because the apple was so newly arrived that there had not been time yet to get to know it? There is so much more I would still love to discover about its history and others like it, but for now all we can say for sure is that at the turn of the twentieth century the Egremont Russet became hugely popular after Bunyard, in *The Anatomy of Dessert*, hailed it as one of the 'richest late autumn fruits'.

TASTING AND COOKING NOTES

When an apple makes an extraordinary juice it can often mean that it doesn't like to be pureed – and sadly this was the case with the Egremont Russet. It baked whole quite well, but the flesh was rather meaty and dry. However, in a tarte Maman Blanc it had some good layered perfume and richness, although that meatiness remained, so the apple slices were lacking in moisture. This was also a factor in the tarte tatin, in which the halved apples held well, but the overall experience, although good, was unexciting. Nevertheless, I very much love this apple and it has found its true place at Le Manoir aux Quat'Saisons as the base of our own apple juice.

GROWING NOTES

The Egremont Russet is a good, small tree for a garden. It crops well, especially against a wall, where it can also be trained as an espalier, as it will do best in a sunny spot. However, the trees can also cope with cooler, wetter areas. The variety is late-flowering, which is an advantage as it can avoid the frost. The fruit is resistant to scab, though the foliage can be affected, and it is vulnerable to woolly aphid. The apples, when picked in late September, will store through to December.

ELLISON'S ORANGE

3 trees in my English orchard
Lincolnshire, 1904
SEASON: *mid-September*
APPEARANCE: *green gold, flushed and striped with red*
BEST FOR: *tarts*

This apple brings together the stories of two prominent families in Lincolnshire at the turn of the twentieth century: the Ellisons and the Pennells.

Ellison's Orange, like many an old English apple, was raised by a clergyman. It is interesting how often these men of the Church were also renowned as keen and knowledgeable horticulturalists.

The Reverend in this case was Charles Christopher Ellison. Generations of the Ellison family had been prominent members of the local community in Lincolnshire since 1740 and Charles Christopher became vicar of Bracebridge and Rector of Boultham in 1874. Clearly a man of many talents, he was an expert in decorative metal-turning and even had his own lathe room, but he was most famous for growing and breeding roses and fruit. Four acres of his garden were filled with roses, and he is said to have had around one thousand five hundred fruit trees, so the annual opening of his gardens to the local community was a highlight of the social calendar.

Ellison's brother-in-law was Joseph Shuttleworth of Hartsholme Hall, whose heavy-iron-manufacturing company was one of the largest employers in Lincolnshire, and his head gardener was one Albert Wipf, about whom little is known, except that he was born in Basle, Switzerland, arrived in Britain as a teenager in 1850, and by 1871 was settled in as gardener with his first wife. It was he who teamed up with Ellison in 1904 to cross a Cox's Orange Pippin (see page 84) with an old French apple of the Calville Blanc family – most likely the Calville Blanc d'Été or Blanc d'Hiver (see page 56). The result was this apple, which they named Ellison's Orange after the Reverend.

The roses that Ellison bred were listed in the catalogue of his friend Charles Pennell, whose family founded their nursery in Bracebridge in 1780 and opened seed shops in Lincoln and Grimsby. It is one of the few famous nurseries from this era that is still in existence today, now in the hands of the seventh and eighth generation of the Pennell family. Naturally, the Reverend Ellison launched his new apple with the Pennells (in 1911) and in true Christian spirit the money raised by sales of the fruit was used to fund the retirement of Mr Wipf the gardener.

TASTING AND COOKING NOTES
This is considered one of the most important of the Cox-style apples, and it is often said that the depth and intensity of flavour is comparable, although it is especially noted for its intense aniseed flavour, something it definitely does not inherit from the Cox. In our tastings we found it to be a good apple, but not a great one. It juices well, but needs to be combined with another more acidic juice, otherwise it can be intensely sweet. Its performance was average in all of the kitchen tests, except when baked for a tarte Maman Blanc, when it showed a little more of the complex aromatics you would expect from an apple with such an interesting lineage.

But, as we know, the timing is so crucial and we may have tested it too early for it to show its full potential.

GROWING NOTES
Apple experts of the past recommended this variety for gardens, and the trees are quite hardy, though not too tolerant of high rainfall as they are susceptible to canker. They can crop well, but tend to be biennial. When picked in mid-September the apples will store through most of October, but they can soften quite quickly in storage, so three weeks is about the maximum.

GALA

10 trees in my English orchard
Wairarapa, New Zealand, 1934
SEASON: *mid-October*
APPEARANCE: *gold, with scarlet flush*
BEST FOR: *nothing so far!*

Gala is the apple that always seemed to me to encapsulate the unfortunate shift in recent decades towards fruit that is bred primarily for sweetness at the expense of complexity of flavour. Of course it is an apple that is extremely successful due to its attractive appearance and colour, and as it is grown all over the world in both hemispheres it can be in the supermarkets all year round. So it has become the dominant variety.

Over 80 per cent of the apples we buy these days are from supermarkets. And according to the latest statistics from British Apples and Pears for 2018/2019, Gala accounted for 59,379 tonnes, compared to 27,209 for Braeburn (see page 49) and 11,817 for Cox (see page 84). This put Gala at its highest levels since 2008/9 and – how depressing – Cox, which is a wonderful apple, at its lowest.

But for me Gala is not a great apple. A great apple, like the Cox at its best, has a beautiful balance of acidity and sugar. Although it is true that the percentage of sugar in Gala is no greater than some other commercial apples, it tastes sweeter due to its lack of acidity and as a result it is mono-flavoured, and not very exciting.

Gala was the outcome of the most famous experiment carried out by James Hutton Kidd of Hexham in Northumberland, who moved to New Zealand with his family as a child (see page 59) – though he didn't live long enough to see its world dominance. It is a cross between Golden Delicious (see page 122) and Kidd's Orange Red, which Kidd had earlier bred from a cross between Cox's Orange Pippin and an American apple, also called Delicious, so it was inevitably going to be an easy crowd-pleaser. Originally known as D8, the apple did outstandingly well in trials alongside nine hundred other apple varieties from around the world, and it was named Gala and released in New Zealand in the 1960s. In the 1980s it was exported to Europe and the US, where it recently overtook Golden Delicious as the nation's favourite apple. And a redder sport, Royal Gala, has now become accepted as the standard for red apples.

Having said all of this, I must tell you that I decided to plant ten Gala trees in our orchard. You might wonder why I would do this when I don't have a great affection for this apple, but I wanted to see whether there was a difference between a Gala apple that has been allowed to develop its sugars fully on the tree and has been grown completely without chemicals, with a lot of love, and a supermarket apple that may have been grown the other side of the world, picked when not fully mature and kept in controlled atmosphere storage.

TASTING AND COOKING NOTES
In order to revisit my opinion of the Gala apples found in most supermarkets, as I was writing this book I bought two packs at different times, one imported from South Africa and one from Chile, to taste and cook. I can report back that the testing of this variety did nothing to change my mind.

Eaten raw, this apple never gave me joy and, as expected, these examples were mealy, sweet, lacking in acidity and hopelessly mono-flavoured, while their juice had an equally disappointing flavour.

While cutting each batch of apples I was surprised to see the difference in the colours of their flesh: some were white, some yellow. Pureeing took 26 minutes and even then the Gala would not break down. Interestingly the white-fleshed apples took much longer than their yellower counterparts.

The apple held its shape well when baked and, to be fair, the flavour did improve, though not dramatically. In a tarte tatin, the apple segments became mushy and the result was oversweet.

But as I have said, I know that this apple, like so many modern commercial apples grown and exported in high volumes, is a victim of long storage in a controlled atmosphere, which I believe dulls down the flavour. So I am very much looking forward to tasting my own Gala apples this year to see if there is an appreciable difference.

GROWING NOTES

Although Gala originates from New Zealand, it is grown extensively in South America and South Africa, as well as France, so is known to tolerate a surprising spectrum of climates and can do well in Britain. However, it prefers a dry climate. In wet conditions it can be susceptible to fungal infections like apple canker and scab. Gala can flower profusely and over-crop if the 'fruitlets' are not thinned in July. Picked from mid-October the apples can be stored into early January.

GEORGE CAVE

17 trees in my English orchard
Essex, 1923
SEASON: *early/mid-August*
APPEARANCE: *quite small, green/yellow with red flush*
BEST FOR: *tarts*

This is one of those secretive and rather mysterious English apples that you won't easily find, and little is known about its heritage, even though it is one of the relatively 'newer' English varieties we have planted in the orchard. However, it does have quite a following amongst enthusiasts who know their apples.

It was almost certainly raised from a chance seedling in 1923 by George Cave – and some say that its parents were the Beauty of Bath and Worcester Pearmain (see page 167), which, according to Marcus Roberts, would certainly account for the fact that it ripens early (like both of these apples) and softens when it is kept, like the Beauty of Bath. But we may never uncover the full story.

And who was George Cave? Perhaps the First Viscount George Cave, lawyer and politician, who was Home Secretary under David Lloyd George and later Lord Chancellor? It seems not. Or perhaps the George Cave who worked at Kew Gardens, before taking over the botanical gardens of Calcutta and Darjeeling? Again, it seems not. No, it looks like this George Cave was a chemist from Dovercourt, near Harwich in Essex, about whom virtually nothing is known, although thanks to a former entomologist from East Malling, Jack Briggs, writing in the *Independent* newspaper in

1994, we have this small shred of information: Cave, according to Jack Briggs, 'was "shoved out" (his words) of his chemist's business in Dovercourt', and 'his apple was rescued from a dustbin at Dovercourt by his daughter and grown on, before being tested at the National Fruit Trials where it compared favourably with the then standard "Beauty of Bath". Cave wanted "no pecuniary advantage" from his apple and sent it to Pye of Morley Fruit Farms, Ferndown, Dorset, to distribute.'

Strangely, this last piece of information is at odds with the accepted detail that the apple was not marketed until 1945, when it was acquired by Seabrook & Sons of Boreham in Essex, who gave the apple its name. I can testify that it *was* Seabrook who promoted the variety, so much so that it was known locally just as Seabrook's Apple. The reason I know this is that my good friend William Sibley's first job was with Seabrook – long before he became involved with the East Malling Research Station – and he remembers the thousands of George Cave trees that were grown there. 'The apple could be delicious straight from the tree, like Beauty of Bath,' he says, 'but the problem was that it just didn't keep well. After about a week it would be almost inedible. However, before the Discovery variety arrived in the 1960s, this was the first English apple of the season, and so it would always fetch a good price.'

TASTING AND COOKING NOTES
The George Cave is crisp and juicy when eaten straight from the tree, and it did make delicious juice, but like many early apples it lacks the complexity of flavour and aroma of the later fruits. When it came to the kitchen tests it didn't fare well as a puree, as the flesh remained tight and did not break down easily; neither did it perform well baked whole, as the flesh, instead of becoming fluffy, dried out quite heavily.

However, when it came to the tarte Maman Blanc it was a different story. There was no drying of the apple slices, which turned an appetising colour with plenty of juice, and there was a wonderful texture and tartness to balance the great apple flavour.

Sadly, the same could not be said for the tarte tatin, where it was not a success. Just as when it was baked whole, it remained too resilient and did not deliver its full flavour.

GROWING NOTES
The trees crop well, but you may need to be ready to pick the apples as soon as they are ripe as they can have a tendency to drop from the tree in mid-August – this is another reason to suspect that one of the apple's parents may be the Beauty of Bath, which gives growers a similar problem. Like most early varieties, George Cave apples don't keep, and will soften and turn mealy in a few days.

ANCIENT AND MODERN

Thanks to a huge work of research by my friend Barrie Juniper (together with David Mabberley, one of his students), which was published in 2006 as The Story of the Apple, *we now understand that apples were growing millions of years ago in the high peaks of the Tian Shan Mountains in East Asia, between Kazakhstan and Western China. Here, perhaps interacting with seeds of a cherry-sized wild apple dispersed by birds from the Asian region that is now China, a vast diversity of apples flourished. The nineteenth-century traveller Victor Vitkovich proclaimed these naturally occurring groves to be 'a marvellous garden where apples and pears look down on you from the trees and beg to be eaten'.*

It was a Russian scientist, Nicolai Vavilov, who in the 1930s first put forward the theory that all modern-day apples are direct descendents of the Tian Shan apples, and in the 1990s DNA testing proved him right. Such is the remarkable genetic complexity of the apple – and it happened to be the notorious Golden Delicious (see page 122) that was tested – that fifty-seven thousand genes were identified, more than any other plant studied. What is more, the genome sequence was indistinguishable from the Tian Shan apples.

About 1.75 million years ago, the mountain range remained above the glaciers of the ice age that covered much of Western and Central Europe and, according to Barrie's theory, the pips, which of course are the seeds, of the apples were spread by bears, deer and wild pigs, and later horses, donkeys and traders, along the 'Silk Road' to Europe and onwards to England.

I love the idea that apples, like people, are made up of a multiplicity of connections. What makes the apple world so vast, complex and intriguing is that wherever an apple core is dropped, or the pips distributed by a bird or an animal, these seeds can grow into a tree, but the fruit it bears will not be an exact reproduction of the parent tree. Like children, each seedling or 'pippin' will be different, even if only in a small way, and most will grow up to be quite unremarkable, but every so often a sibling or cousin will turn out to be so extraordinary, and become so famous, that everyone will, literally, want a piece of it.

Human beings, ever experimental, learned from ancient times that the way to reproduce an apple variety most faithfully was to create a clone by taking a cutting (known as a scion) and graft it onto rootstock (another plant with a well-developed root system) – the practice is even mentioned in the Bible – and Barrie Juniper believes that many grafted varieties would have passed from Babylon to Greece and Rome, and then the Romans most likely brought them to Britain, establishing the first orchards.

What is very exciting is that scientists at Cornell University in New York have gone back to the ancient Tian Shan varieties in a bid to unlock their secrets and develop new varieties. They have linked up with botanists at the Kazakhstan Academy of Sciences to collect seeds and scion wood from the ancient apple forests, which are now being grown and screened around the world in order to increase the genetic diversity of apples in the West, and hopefully also to discover valuable traits of resistance to disease and drought.

Here in Britain we have our own superlative research centre at East Malling (NIAB EMR), which has been able to capitalise on the work done on the apple genome in relation to its own breeding

programmes. In a quiet corner of Kent, twenty-five miles down the road from the National Fruit Collection at Brogdale, this centre of excellence has been at the forefront of nearly all the big scientific and technical advances that have shaped the way we grow the fruit that we eat today, and which varieties we will eat tomorrow.

This best-kept secret began over a century ago in 1913, with nine hectares and a small laboratory. The early pioneering work focused on the old 'paradise' rootstocks that had been used for hundreds, if not thousands, of years to propagate trees. The idea was to develop newer grades of rootstock, which would help control tree sizes, allowing young trees to fruit earlier, and more prolifically, with better, larger fruit in less dense, bushy foliage. They could also be harvested more easily. As a result of this key advancement, it is now possible to grow forty to seventy tonnes of apples per hectare, where once it could only be four to seven tonnes – so a tenfold increase in a hundred years. At the height of their research, Malling rootstocks were used in 80–85 per cent of global apple production – so nearly every apple we eat today has a connection to this corner of Kent. What a remarkable story.

Today their scientists are tirelessly developing new fruits in the time-honoured manner of selecting varieties with the most desirable genetic traits and crossing them in the hope of producing a brilliant-tasting, wonderful-looking fruit that will grow prolifically with good resistance to pests and diseases. This, of course, was the holy grail for Victorian scientists and nurserymen, who were the great trailblazers. The ultimate prize is the same, only the science has moved on.

The first time I visited East Malling was a complete revelation to me. I was totally blown away by this world of science and the scale of detail and research that goes into the development of a new fruit variety – imagine, from the time of pollination, it can take twenty-five years of trialling before a new variety of apple is released commercially.

On one occasion I was looking for new varieties of strawberry and I was invited to wander into a field of some six thousand plants bearing berries of every shape and size that were being trialled. I was overwhelmed by the heady spectrum of perfumes and flavours, from sharp to sweet, with notes of sage, pineapple, lemon, peach ... and the palette of colours, from white through to deep red, almost purple. With the Beatles' 'Strawberry Fields Forever' playing in my head, I must have tasted sixty to seventy different selections, until I felt as though I was turning into a big strawberry myself. I learned so much, and what made me so happy was that although the trials were looking into shape, colour, resistance to disease, generosity of cropping, above all they were looking for fruits that were full of the wonderful complexities of flavour that, as a chef, I long for – my favourite incidentally was the Marshmello variety, which we now grow at Le Manoir.

The work of East Malling is needed more than ever today. Increasing populations and increasing affluence mean that, as a society, we are going to have to produce as much food in the fifty years between 2000 and 2050 as we did in the five hundred years between 1500 and 2000. So the goal for apples is now one hundred and ten to one hundred and twenty tonnes per hectare, with more resistance to the pests and diseases that are the bane of a grower's life – believe me, I am beginning to know!

GOLDEN DELICIOUS

To be planted in my English orchard
West Virginia, USA, 1890
SEASON: *late October/November*
APPEARANCE: *large, yellow gold*
BEST FOR: *eating fresh, baking whole, tarts*

I must tell you that at first I did not want to have any Golden
Delicious in my orchard. Why? Because this is an apple that is as
much hated as it is loved. There is no doubt that it was one of the
main culprits responsible for the disappearance of so many beautiful
heritage varieties from the shelves and for the consequent decima-
tion of British orchards, after it flooded the British market from
France in the 1970s. Also, I had always found this greeny-yellowy
supermarket apple – not really golden at all – to be quite pleasant,
but bland. It seemed to be lacking the character, complexity and
balance of sweetness and acidity of a Cox's Orange Pippin (see
page 84) or Blenheim Orange (see page 42). So, I decided, I cannot
plant this apple.

Then, in a conversation with my good friend Marcus Roberts, he
told me that he had experienced a moment of revelation on a frosty,
late-December afternoon, when he had come across a tree in the
gardens of Yarnton Manor in Oxfordshire, on which the fruits were
still hanging, and were truly golden and glowing on the barren
branches – such a dramatic spectacle. When he tasted one it had
a yielding texture and a sweet, sublime flavour that truly lived up
to the apple's name. He realised that there is a world of difference
between a Golden Delicious that is allowed to fully ripen on the tree,

and the supermarket apple, which is grown on the other side of the world, picked when pale and unripe, and stored for up to twelve months before it appears on the supermarket shelves in Britain.

So I decided to think again about the Golden Delicious. And when I looked into its parentage, I was astonished to discover that this is not a French apple, as I had thought. However, it has quite a story to tell, and it is the story of two American families: the Mullins and the Starks.

Although the apple's parentage isn't known for sure, it is thought to be a natural cross between the very popular Virginian apple Grimes Golden and possibly the Golden Reinette. The Grimes Golden apple already had its own romantic story, as it is said to have been raised from a pip planted by the legendary pioneering missionary and nurseryman John Chapman, who was known as Johnny Appleseed, because wherever he travelled throughout the Northeastern states of America he planted apples.

The original Golden Delicious seedling was found on a farm owned by L. L. Mullins in the hills of Clay County, West Virginia, in 1890. In 1962, the *Charleston Daily Mail* published an interview with one J. M. Mullins, 'now a man in his 87th year', who told the story of how, as a fifteen-year-old, he was sent out by his father with a scythe to mow the fields, where he came across a little apple tree no more than twenty inches tall ... 'I thought to myself, "Now young feller, I'll just leave you there," and that's what I did. I mowed around it and on other occasions I mowed around it again and again, and it grew into a nice lookin' little apple tree and eventually it was a big tree and bore apples.'

The piece of land on which the tree was growing later passed to his uncle, Anderson Mullins, who decided to send some samples of the apples to the well-known Stark Brothers Nursery in Louisiana, now run by Paul Clarence Stark, the sixth generation of the family. Almost a century earlier in 1816, James Hart Stark had been one of a small band of pioneers from Bourbon County, Kentucky, who made the journey to the fertile banks of the Mississippi in covered wagons. He took with him scions from Kentucky apple trees and from these he built up his nursery, growing and developing new varieties through the generations.

One of the family's own varieties was a yellow apple known as Stark's Delicious and for many years they had been searching for a late-keeping apple with a similar appearance and flavour. Now, out of the blue, a package arrived from West Virginia containing three yellow apples. When they tasted them there was huge excitement, because these apples looked like the popular Grimes Golden, but they tasted like Stark's Delicious. Experts were called in, and one of the apples was sent to Colonel Brackett, a pomologist at the Department of Agriculture in Washington. Paul Stark recalled, 'Friends present at the time told us how the Colonel came hurrying into the office, a little slab of this wonderful yellow apple perched on his knife blade, exclaiming, "Taste *this!* Here's an apple with an even *better flavour* than Grimes Golden."'

So Stark set out on a one-thousand-mile railroad trip, finishing with a twenty-mile horseback ride through the wilds of the West Virginia mountains to the Mullins' farm.

'Back of the house I saw an orchard,' he wrote later. 'But – here came the dismal disappointment! Every tree I could see was nothing but wild seedlings – miserable runts. Dejected and sick at heart, I turned around to leave – when – I SAW IT! There, looming forth in the midst of the small, leafless, barren trees, was a tree with rich green foliage that looked as if it had been transported from the Garden of Eden. That tree's boughs were bending to the ground beneath a *tremendous crop of great, glorious, glowing golden apples!* I started for it on the run. A fear bothered me, "Suppose it's just a Grimes Golden tree after all!" I came closer and I saw the apples were 50 per cent larger than Grimes Golden. I plucked one and bit into its crisp, tender, juicy-laden flesh. Eureka! I had found it. The long sought for *perfect* yellow apple had been discovered. The "Trail of the Golden Apple" had reached a successful end. And, just as I had eaten my apple, core and all, I turned to see Mr Mullins, with a "I-told-you-so" smile on his face, climbing the hill to welcome me.'

The story continues that Mullins sold the tree (some say for fifty dollars, other say five thousand dollars), together with the patch of ground around it, and Stark took a bundle of cuttings home with him, arranging for a burglar-proof cage to be put around the original tree. Two years later, in 1916, his grafted trees bore fruits, which were named Golden Delicious. The new variety was instantly popular, especially at railroad stations, where the apples were sold to passengers for their journey.

What is not so well known is that the Golden Delicious was also introduced to England in 1926 by Edward Bunyard's nursery, and it was a popular variety in Kent orchards in the 1930s. However, it was not at its best in the English climate, whereas in France it flourished. In the 1960s French farmers in Algeria were forced out of the country, and when they returned to France, President Charles de Gaulle suggested that, with the help of grants, they might take up fruit growing in the valleys of the Loire and Rhône.

The variety they were encouraged to grow was Golden Delicious, which in this climate was the perfect commercial grower's variety. Big and high-yielding, it was easy to grow, resistant to many diseases, and it was good at everything: eaten fresh it was sweet and juicy, it pureed well and it baked well. It was such a winning apple that when, in the 1970s, the supermarkets in Britain began to dictate the standards, the French seized the moment and marketed the apple to them as 'Le Crunch'. Unfortunately for many British growers of traditional varieties, the campaign was so successful that they could not compete against these shiny, uniform-looking apples, which didn't even bruise, and for each lorryload reaching our shores, many traditional English apple trees were grubbed up. In our local shires, many fine collections of trees ended up on the bonfire and in the space of just seven years Britain's share of the apple market declined from 60 to 38 per cent.

Of course, this was a huge disaster, for which I and my fellow orchard enthusiasts around Britain are still trying to make amends. Yet I find I cannot blame the Golden Delicious, as its only crime was that it was too good, and it was supported by a huge campaign. Thanks to Marcus Roberts I now have a beautiful image in my mind of the mythical golden apples hanging on their barren branches at Christmastime. I really want to know what such a completely ripe fruit, grown properly and picked straight from my own tree, might taste like. And so, finally, we are planting a few of these trees.

TASTING AND COOKING NOTES
Before we committed to Golden Delicious in the orchard, I decided that I needed to taste the very best samples of these apples that I could find, handpicked for me in France. When they arrived at our kitchens and I opened the box, just as Paul Stark did over a century ago, I could understand how he must have felt to discover these deep, rich yellow-coloured apples, heavy and gorgeous, inside.

Eaten raw, all the elements of a good apple were present: a wonderful crunch, great juiciness, fabulous acidity, a good equilibrium and a surprising and complex layering of flavours. And the apples made an enjoyable juice.

I could tell that they would cook well, and they did. Baked in every form, they filled the kitchen with lovely aromas and kept their shape while fluffing out incredibly. The tarte Maman Blanc looked like a glorious painting, with tastes and textures to match, and although lacking a little in acidity, the apples also made a good tarte tatin, if a little too sweet, with delightful perfumes. I learned a huge amount from this tasting, especially that imported apples, picked green and held in suspended animation, can never compare to fruit that is allowed to linger on the tree and tasted at the optimum moment.

The decision was made. We would plant some trees, leave the apples on their branches as late as possible, and see what flavours we can achieve in our corner of Oxfordshire.

GROWING NOTES
Although the Golden Delicious has found its favourite home in France, it can still grow well in the UK but will need a sheltered, warm spot, preferably against a wall. A warm autumn helps, as the apples should be left on the tree as late as possible, preferably into mid-November. The apples can then be stored for another three months or so. As with Gala, it is easy to allow this variety to overproduce large numbers of small fruit – so if too many of these 'fruitlets' set, thin them down to two on each fruiting spur. This will help to ensure a consistent crop of good-sized fruit year on year.

GOLDEN NOBLE

To be planted in my English orchard
Norfolk, 1769 or 1820
SEASON: *October/November*
APPEARANCE: *pale green turning to gold*
BEST FOR: *juice and puree*

I had high hopes that the Golden Noble would turn out to be an ancient treasure as it was introduced to me by Barrie Juniper, amongst many old varieties almost lost to the world. I tasted it on a late-summer's day in the still of his ancient orchard, as the sunlight cut through the laden tree, and I was struck by the fact that the apple was not gold at all, but a pale green. Barrie explained that as the apples were left to mature on the tree they would turn a beautiful gold and the fruit sugars would also develop their flavour and texture. Although the apple was traditionally considered an alternative to Bramley's Seedling (see page 51) for cooking, Barrie had recommended it to me as a 'delightful, delicate-fleshed, sharp dessert apple to eat with strong cheese', and in this wonderful, wild, historic place I could not help but be completely charmed by the promise and the imagery.

Edward Bunyard hailed the Golden Noble as the best apple of all for a pie. 'And what should an apple do in a pie?' he asked. 'Well, I think it should preserve its individuality and form, not go to a pale, mealy squash, but become soft and golden. In flavour it must be sharp or what's the use of your Barbados sugar? It should have some distinct flavour of its own, not merely a general apple flavour. Fulfilling all the conditions comes Golden Noble, golden before and after cooking, transparent in the pie, and in every way delectable.'

According to Robert Hogg, the apple was said to have been discovered by Patrick Flanagan, who was head gardener to Sir Thomas Harr – though this is most likely Thomas *Hare*, who was the second baronet of Stow Hall near Downham, Norfolk, the estate that had been in his family since 1553. There were three incarnations of Stow Hall, all of which have been demolished, and the Golden Noble seems to have been found in the time of the second building, whose gardens were designed by the leading nursery of the day, Lee and Kennedy of Hammersmith. Flanagan, who was also an expert on the growing of melons, supposedly took a cutting from a tree he found in an old orchard nearby and presented it to the Horticultural Society of London in 1820.

That Flanagan was the first to recognise the Golden Noble, however, is thrown into some doubt, as an apple going by the same name was also listed much earlier, in 1769, in the catalogue of William Perfect in Pontefract, Yorkshire. William and John Perfect were well-known nurserymen and seedsmen whose business had been in their family since the early 1700s and continued until a century later.

It seems the Golden Noble was also a well-travelled apple, as it appears under the name of Gelber Edelapfel in *Deutsche Pomologie*, the beautifully illustrated book of German apples published by Wilhelm Lauche, nurseryman, apple expert and chairman of the German Pomological Society, just before his death in 1883.

TASTING AND COOKING NOTES
This is another apple that we put through the taste test straight from the tree in October, and probably did it an injustice as this is an apple that needs either to be left longer on the tree or stored for a while for it to express all of its qualities. Nevertheless, when we juiced it, it was delicious, full of wonderful flavours, though quite astringent and sharp. It was no surprise that it broke down very

easily into a beautiful puree with a delightful yellow hue, and this, for me, is where this apple's strengths lie: in purees and pies. And of course it will come as no surprise that I prefer it to the Bramley as it requires so much less sugar to give it a pleasing taste. When baked, the apple's unripeness and acidity made it quite sharp and so it didn't perform well in a tart or tarte tatin. The apple was clearly begging for another month on the tree in order to develop all of its flavours, and so it must and will be given another chance to show us why it was so valued historically.

GROWING NOTES

The trees are good for gardens as they are moderately vigorous, fairly upright and, as they are relatively late-flowering, this can help protect them against frosts, though they can still be caught out. Although not heavy croppers, they come into fruit quickly and if picked in October can be stored and used into December, when they will sweeten enough to become a quite sharp eating apple. This is one of the varieties whose skins become greasy during storage, though of course this doesn't matter if they are peeled.

CRAB APPLES

Wrapped around the archways that frame the pathways through my orchard, our crab apple trees create their own spectacle. First, it is their blossom that captivates me. From gentle pinks to vibrant reds they are a celebration of spring. And the apples that follow are just as eye-catching in their shades of yellow, gold, orange, crimson and almost purple. I have even created a new garden for them, interplanted with large purple imperial clematis, across from the wildflower garden, where the abundance of their foliage creates a privacy reminiscent of the romantic, secluded orchards of Shakespeare's day. Their blossom offers the bees from my bee village a rich source of pollen, and this happy chef has a wonderful source of fruit for crab apple petit fours (see page 297).

At Le Manoir we have planted six very different but beautiful varieties of crab apple: Golden Hornet, Robusta, Red Sentinel, Gorgeous and John Downie.

These wonderful, tiny, tangy ancient fruits are so much a part of our orchard heritage, woven into ancient folklore, magic and myth. It was said that if you threw the pips of a crab apple into the fire while saying the name of your love and the pips exploded, then your love would be true.

Medieval orchards consisted mainly of crab apples, along with some cultivated apples, and wild and cultivated pears. Grown from pips or cuttings, they were good pollinators and produced hardy apples for cider or for fermenting to make verjuice, which was taken as a tonic, or used as a souring agent in cooking. They were most popular roasted and served in bowls of hot ale, sugar and spice, at Christmastime, or for the Wassail Bowl, which would be passed around in the ancient tradition of blessing the apple trees in order to ensure a successful year.

'When roasted crabs hiss in the bowl,
Then nightly sings the staring owl . . .'

So goes the Winter Song, which closes Shakespeare's Love's Labour's Lost. *And in* A Midsummer Night's Dream, *the mischievous Puck teases that:*

'. . . sometime lurk I in a gossip's bowl,
In very likeness of a roasted crab,
And when she drinks, against her lips I bob . . .'

GRANNY SMITH

16 trees in my English orchard
New South Wales, Australia, 1868
SEASON: *mid-October*
APPEARANCE: *bright green with crisp white flesh*
BEST FOR: *eating fresh, juice, tarte tatin*

Will we ever find a British apple, I wonder, that has the same characteristics as a Granny Smith? Because, of course, it is not a native apple, though it is so familiar that many people think it is – and, as with Kidd's Orange Red and Captain Kidd (see page 59), we can claim a big connection, since all three apples were raised by English emigrants to Australasia. And after all it was a Granny Smith that featured on the Beatles' Apple record label – what could be more English than that?

So who was Granny Smith? Well, the story is a lovely one of an unexpected reward for hardship and courage. Maria Ann Sherwood was a farmer's daughter from Peasmarsh in Sussex who married Thomas Smith, a farm labourer, in 1918 when she was eighteen years old. They lived in the village of Beckley, surrounded by orchards, and it is likely that Maria worked on local fruit farms (records suggest her father-in-law may have been the tenant of a farm growing pears and hops). However, the depression of the 1920s and 1930s meant times were tough for farm workers, especially as more machinery began to be introduced. Beckley was hit hard. For many families there was no work, the poorhouses were full, and it appears that the parish supported around two hundred families to emigrate to Australia in search of a new life. So in 1938 the Smiths, with their five surviving children, set sail aboard the *Lady Nugent* and settled in the farming community of Eastwood, just north of Sydney.

This much we know, but the rest of the story is an intriguing mix of truth and legend, involving an apple tree that mysteriously appeared on the banks of a nearby creek. According to one version, Maria threw the core of a crab apple out of her kitchen window and the seedling that grew from one of the pips produced so much green fruit that some said the branches had to be propped up to save them from breaking.

In 2018, when the Granny Smith apple celebrated its one hundred and fiftieth birthday, it was revealed that a letter had been found, written decades later by Maria's grandson, Benjamin Spurway, which appeared to confirm the essentials of this story. And it tells of the hard work, 'determination and courage' of the family as 'they cleared, ploughed and cultivated' the land they had acquired until 'the day came when their ambitions were realised and a beautiful orchard took the place of wilderness'.

According to Spurway, his grandfather, Thomas, took a market stall in Sydney where the family sold their fruit, but when he came home penniless, after stopping off at a pub on the way, Maria, by now a granny, took over the stall, making the trip by horse-drawn cart. One day at the market another grower gave her some French crab apples from Tasmania so that she could test their cooking qualities. She made two pies with them, and then, writes Spurway, 'granny just leaned out of the window and dropped the peel and skins, going out afterward and poking in the seeds with her fingers'. Some time later, the seedling appeared, and when it began to bear fruit, she realised the potential, carefully nurtured it and began propagating it and marketing it in Sydney. A relative, Edward Gallard, is credited with first growing the new variety commercially in 1868 – sadly, however, this was only two years before 'Granny' Maria died.

There is another small variation on the story, told by Tom Small, the son of another fruit grower, who claimed that he and his father visited the Smiths when Tom was twelve years old, and Maria showed them a tree that had sprung up and that was bearing a few green apples. They tasted them, and Tom's father recommended grafting some cuttings. When asked where the tree had come from, Maria apparently told them she had brought a case of rotting Tasmanian French crab apples back from the markets and tipped them out at the site where the tree now grew.

Whatever the exact details of the story, by the 1930s Granny Smiths were being exported to Britain and grown all over the southern hemisphere. In 1950, to honour Maria, the Granny Smith Memorial Park was established near her home in Eastwood, now a suburb of Sydney, where a Granny Smith festival is held every year.

The problem with growing green apples like the Granny Smith on a commercial scale in Britain is that they don't like the vagaries of the British climate, which is rarely predictably extreme enough for them. They prefer very cold winters in which they can lay dormant, followed by warm summers. But, despite the supermarket dominance of sweet apples like Gala (see page 112), 'we English' do still love to munch a crisp, sharp, juicy Granny Smith, so for many years the search has been on to find an English equivalent. In 2005 the Greenstar was launched, which was an interesting cross, developed in Belgium from a Granny Smith and a sweeter French apple called Delcorf, which was raised in 1956 by George Delbard in Malicorne (see page 9) and is also known as Delbarestivale®. This apple looks like a Granny Smith and is noted in the same way for its creamy white flesh, crispness and juiciness, but it is sweeter, with little acidity, and it has made little headway as the British public are quite stubbornly loyal to Granny Smiths.

I wanted to try growing some Granny Smiths in our orchard, and so we planted sixteen to see how well they would do, as for me this is a valuable apple for tarte tatin.

TASTING AND COOKING NOTES
This is the variety for anyone who enjoys a sharp, tangy apple with just enough sugars to make it a lovely eating experience. Skin on, it makes the best juice. Pale green, it doesn't require any sugar and is packed with flavour. I know, as I drink a glass most mornings.

In the kitchen, due to the dense nature of their flesh, the apples take far too long to break down, so they don't puree well, nor do they bake well. In a tarte Maman Blanc the slices become quite dry, but when it comes to the tarte tartin, this apple is triumphant: its tight flesh allows it to hold its shape well, and its acidity counterbalances the rich sweetness of the caramel perfectly. The only other apples that can compete are the Cox's Orange Pippin (see page 84), Chivers Delight (see page 71), Red Windsor (see page 152), and Devonshire Quarrenden (see page 95).

GROWING NOTES
Granny Smiths make for small trees that crop well, but in our climate we usually have to use them more for cooking than eating fresh, as much more warmth tends to be needed to develop their full sugars and flavour. But I have to report that my trees are in great shape, with plenty of good-looking fruit, and if we pick them around mid-October they should keep for use in the kitchen until April.

HANWELL SOURING

To be planted in my English orchard
Oxfordshire or Warwickshire, 1813
SEASON: *mid-October*
APPEARANCE: *greeny yellow, flushed with red*
BEST FOR: *its history*

This local medium-large apple was recommended to me by my friend
Marcus Roberts as similar to the Bramley, 'but with a better flavour',
and one that he urges people to plant instead, as it is far more interesting and historic. So, of course I was excited to try it, especially as I
was also told by my other friend Barrie Juniper that it was traditionally used to make the apple sauce for goose at Christmas.

'Souring' in the name relates to the apple's high level of acidity and
takes us back to Shakespeare's time in the Mid-Shires, when apples
were often classed as 'sourings' or 'sweetings' – a very early example
of the puzzling and unshakeable English desire to classify apples as
either 'dessert' or 'cookers'.

Sadly there is little certain history about the precise origins of this
apple, so I cannot entertain you with a romantic story of a seedling
found by chance in a hedgerow, cottage garden or the manicured
and ornamental orchards of the landed gentry ... there is only the
general assumption that the apple was either discovered, or raised,
in Hanwell, near Banbury, in the very north of Oxfordshire (or what
the locals like to call 'Banburyshire').

Most sources until now have suggested that the variety was first
referenced in 1820, when, in a volume of the *Transactions of the*

Horticultural Society of London, it is noted that the Reverend William Thomas Bree, of Allesley, near Coventry, 'exhibited at the last meeting in May, 1820, specimens of an apple, called the Hanwell Souring, a remarkably good keeper', which he believed to take its name from Hanwell village. However, Detective Marcus Roberts has found new evidence of an earlier link, which leads him to believe that perhaps the apple was already known just over the border in Warwickshire. He delved into the county archives where he discovered a reference to Hanwell Souring in a hand-drawn 'experimental' orchard plan dated 1813. This links perfectly to Reverend Bree (or W. T. Bree, as he signed himself), as his home village of Allesley is in Warwickshire.

Bree was a well-known botanist and authority on natural history who contributed to many publications, and in a volume of *The Gardener's Magazine* of 1829 he recommended that the Hanwell Souring, 'a baking or kitchen apple' and a 'good bearer and excellent keeper', should have a place in any orchard. 'I have found [the apples] very good in the end of July, and have no doubt they would have kept longer had I not had occasion to use them,' he wrote. However, he concludes, 'the apple is not, I believe, generally known in the nurseries, nor, perhaps, much cultivated out of the midland counties'.

Writing much later, in 1884, in *The Fruit Manual*, Robert Hogg also considered the Hanwell Souring 'an excellent culinary apple of first-rate quality; in use in December, and keeps till March.' And in *The Herefordshire Pomona* he added that, thanks to its strong acidity, 'it retains its flavour better than any other late keeping variety'.

Marcus also formed another theory after he was given some wood of a rare, old, rustic Warwickshire or South Midlands apple, which he had not heard of before, called 'Annual Sweeting'. When grown, the fruit that it produced was small and sweet, and it occurred to him that 'sweetings' and 'sourings' may historically be paired in the region. So if there was an Annual Sweeting, it was perfectly possible that there was also an Annual Souring, and the name 'Hanwell Souring' could simply be a derivation of this.

As a final thought on this perplexing apple, since it has so little romance in its history, let us create some of our own! Imagine if Barrie Juniper's assertion that this was the apple to make sauce for the goose was echoed by Shakespeare himself, in this scene from *Romeo and Juliet*:

MERCUTIO: I will bite thee by the ear for that jest.
ROMEO: Nay, good goose, bite not.
MERCUTIO: Thy wit is a very bitter-sweeting; it is a most sharp sauce.
ROMEO: And is it not well served in to a sweet goose?

How wonderful it would be if this acidic 'bitter-sweeting' immortalised by the Bard was actually a 'souring' and, not only that, but the Hanwell Souring!

TASTING AND COOKING NOTES
In Shakespeare's time this quite acidic apple would probably have been considered a treat, as in those days there was so much less sugar in the national diet. Acidity is a wonderful quality because it is actually a catalyst for flavour, but in excess it can also murder it. Sadly this was the case in most of the tests that we put the Hanwell Souring through, although it is less acidic than the Bramley's Seedling (see page 51). It did make a beautiful puree, if quite white in appearance, but it required quite an amount of sugar to balance the explosions of acidity, and in my kitchen that is not a good thing. Yet this apple was not mono-flavoured and it had a wonderful, layered richness, so I have no doubt it would make some beautiful pies, crumbles and sauces; but it will not bake well, as that is against its nature.

GROWING NOTES

The trees are moderately vigorous, hardy, and don't appear to be unduly afflicted by pests or diseases. They grow well on dwarf (M27) rootstocks (see page 263), which produce nice-looking small trees that display the ripening fruit attractively, so they lend themselves to a smaller garden. The apples are picked in mid-October and when stored correctly can keep as late as April.

KESWICK CODLIN

4 trees in my English orchard
Lancashire, 1793
SEASON: *mid-August*
APPEARANCE: *pale green yellow*
BEST FOR: *puree, juice and its heritage*

Thinking about this apple took me back to my first encounter with the word 'coddle', which is where 'codlin' or 'codling' comes from. I immediately fell in love with this word and wanted to know more about it. This was at the start of my extraordinary adventure in Great Britain, when I arrived here in 1972, not as a chef, but as a waiter, working at The Rose Revived, an inn in Newbridge in the Oxfordshire countryside. My English was atrocious and incomprehensible, and so one of the very first things I did was look for a classic British cookery book, which might help me make myself understood in the restaurant, and also I wanted to immerse myself in British food, cooking and culture. I was lucky to find the perfect one, *The Constance Spry Cookery Book*, written by both Constance Spry and Rosemary Hume – it was the best thing to happen to me! One day when the chef left, the boss asked if anyone could cook. I put myself forward, and on that day I bought the tallest hat, so high that I could barely enter the kitchen, took hold of the frying pan, and my life changed for ever. In no time, the restaurant became renowned and so by day I was in the kitchen and in the night-time I would return to my beloved book, which I still treasure to this day.

This book had everything: not only wonderful recipes, but information about varieties, science, nutrition, British food history, culture and so much more. And through this book I learned some lovely English terms that don't exist in French. One of the instructions given was for 'coddled eggs' and I was mesmerised by this beautiful name, which seemed to me to describe an act of love, as the eggs were to be put into boiling water and then the pan taken from the heat and kept 'in a warm place on the stove for 8–10 minutes', so that the eggs cooked very, very gently. And so it made perfect sense to me when later I discovered that an old English apple that was called a codling would quickly become soft and tender when baked in its skin.

Shakespeare, as Marcus Roberts likes to tell me, knew his apples, and there is a scene in *Twelfth Night* in which Olivia asks Malvolio, 'of what personage, and years' is the emissary sent by Duke Orsino. To which he replies, 'Not yet old enough for a man, nor young enough for a boy; as a Squash is before 'tis a Peascod, or a Codling when 'tis almost an Apple.'

Baked codlins were a favourite London street food in the late eighteenth century, so much so that the famous pantomime clown Joseph Grimaldi included a song in his act on the London stage, called 'Hot Codlins', which was a big hit with his audiences:

> 'A little old woman,
> her living she got
> by selling hot codlins,
> hot, hot, hot.
> And this little old woman,
> who codlins sold,
> tho' her codlins were hot,
> she felt herself cold.
> So to keep herself warm,
> she thought it no sin
> to fetch for herself
> a quartern of . . .'

... at which point the audience would all shout 'gin!' and Grimaldi would reply in mock horror: 'Oh! For Shame!'

Marcus recommended the Keswick Codlin as one of the best examples of the codlin apples, a Victorian favourite for jellies to compliment meat dishes. He inspired me with his talk of a beautiful crop of lemon-yellow apples hanging from an ancient tree in the National Trust orchard at Canons Ashby House, one of the oldest country houses in Northamptonshire, which had been in the Dryden family from the sixteenth century.

However, the Keswick Codlin's start in life was anything but glamorous. According to Robert Hogg in *The Herefordshire Pomona*, 'This excellent apple was first discovered growing amongst a quantity of rubbish behind a wall at Gleaston Castle, near Ulverstone, and was first brought into notice by one John Sander, a nurseryman at Keswick, who, having propagated it, sent it out under the name of Keswick Codlin.'

Hogg considered it to be 'one of the most valuable of our early culinary apples. It may be used for tarts so early as the end of June, but it is in perfection during August and September'. And he goes on to say that, in the *Memoirs of the Caledonian Horticultural Society*, the agriculturalist Sir John Sinclair noted: 'The Keswick Codlin tree has never failed to bear a crop since it was planted in the episcopal garden at Rose Castle, Carlisle, twenty years ago [1813]. It is an apple of fine tartness and flavour, and may be used early in autumn.' However, in 1862, as Joan Morgan points out in *The New Book of Apples*, it was somewhat upstaged by the arrival of the new Grenadier variety, which was promoted as 'an improvement' as it produced larger fruit.

TASTING AND COOKING NOTES

Although the Victorians considered this apple to be an early cooker, once ripe it can be zingy, lemony and refreshing, edging towards overly aggressive, eaten straight from the tree. It made an appetising, attractive pale green juice, which required no sugar and didn't discolour quickly.

Unfortunately, though – and I hope my Lancashire friends will forgive me – it didn't fare too well in most of the kitchen tests we put it through. I knew this apple would fail when baked because of its acidity and water content. However, as expected, it did well in the puree test. It is very easy to understand why. This apple is packed with juices and has a high acidity level, so it transformed very swiftly to a pleasant puree, yet because there is also some good sugar presence it only required a small amount of additional sugar. So clearly this is an apple that is destined for purees, and even pies, rather than a tarte tatin or tarte Maman Blanc. And since my rule is that if an apple of ancient heritage can do even one thing well it is enough to earn its place in our orchard, we now have four Keswick Codlin trees growing.

GROWING NOTES

In Victorian times the trees, which are upright and spreading, were valued for the beauty and the fragrance of their blossom as well as their fruit, and were often trained over arches to form arbours or tunnels. They are resistant to scab and relatively easy to grow, albeit sometimes biennial. Having been discovered in Lancashire, they are used to more northerly situations and, once established, they usually crop heavily, but the apples don't store or travel well, so you really need to appreciate this variety over about a four-week period, i.e. if you pick them in early to mid-August they will not keep beyond September.

LORD LAMBOURNE

26 trees in my English orchard
Bedfordshire, 1907
SEASON: mid-September
APPEARANCE: bright red flush and streaks over gold
BEST FOR: tarts, eating fresh and juice

Tracing a family tree is always fascinating and illuminating because the people who have gone before us help make us who we are today – and it is the same for apples and their ancestors. Whenever I bite into a wonderful, aromatic apple with a complexity of flavour, I feel it is a safe bet that it will have the heavenly Cox's Orange Pippin (see page 84) somewhere in its heritage. In this case, one of the parents of the Lord Lambourne is James Grieve and, although it is not proven, one of *its* parents is thought to be the Cox.

This is a gorgeous and perfectly shaped apple, flushed and streaked with iridescent red over gold. It was raised by the Laxton Brothers, Edward and William, prolific breeders of apples and the sons of the horticulturalist Thomas Laxton, who began his plant-breeding in Stamford, Lincolnshire, before moving his nursery to Bedford, where he was known especially for his peas and strawberries. He was one of the earliest nurserymen to use scientific methods in his plant-breeding, and he carried out experiments and trials for Charles Darwin.

The brothers decided to concentrate on apples and launched twenty-seven new Laxton varieties, along with new pears, plums and strawberries. Many of their new varieties, from the Allington

Pippin and the early Laxton's Advance to the Christmas variety, Laxton Superb, certainly involved the Cox's Orange Pippin; however, the Lord Lambourne is a cross between James Grieve and the Worcester Pearmain (see page 167). It is said to be called after Amelius Lockwood, who, following a career in the army, was Conservative MP for Epping from 1892 to 1917, when he was raised to the peerage as Baron Lambourne; and between 1919 and 1928 was president of the Royal Horticultural Society, hence the tribute.

Unfortunately, the Laxton Brothers' history is tinged with tragedy. When William died, Edward continued the nursery with his son, also called Edward, but known as Ted, until in 1942 Ted was killed during an air raid, when his home was bombed in a direct hit. Edward was awarded the MBE in 1951, but he died the same year. Such a sad story; but what a huge legacy the brothers left behind, especially this magnificent apple, which is still treasured and can be found in many nurseries today.

TASTING AND COOKING NOTES
Eaten from the tree, the Lord Lambourne is top tier. Crisp to the bite and with thin skin and juicy flesh, the genius of this apple is that it has combined the acidity of the James Grieve with the aromatics of the Worcester Pearmain and its frequent hint of strawberry, to give a big, layered, well-balanced flavour, with a little sugar present. Its juice was fabulous, and although it didn't excel as a puree, baked whole or in a tarte tatin, it delighted us with one of the two best tarte Maman Blanc experiences of all the one hundred and twelve apples tested. It was surpassed only by the tiniest of margins by the ultimate champion of the tarts, Captain Kidd (see page 59). The concentric apple segments fluffed out and turned from pale creamy white to an appetising gold, their flavour and texture were outstanding, and their perfume filled the entire kitchen, lingering on and on.

As with people, it is quite rare to find an apple that is good at absolutely everything – though, of course, some are – but I believe that to excel at only one thing is to be blessed. And truly the Lord Lambourne delivered a moment of pure gastronomic ecstasy.

GROWING NOTES

This is a good variety to grow in a garden, as the trees are quite compact, of medium vigour, and should give a good, regular, crop of apples. Also the variety is now largely disease-free. The trees are partial tip-bearers (see page 170), so it is best not to prune them heavily. When picked in mid-to-late September, the apples can be stored until November.

THE BEAUTIFUL ORCHARD

Our orchard is all about flavour, heritage and purity – meaning no chemicals – but it also had to be about beauty and structure, because I cannot separate these. I have never forgotten the first time I saw the magnificent fruit and vegetable gardens at Le Jardin du Roi at Versailles, and I wanted to further merge our two cultures by introducing the English and French varieties alike to the kinds of romantic arches, espaliers, cordons and palmettes that I admired there. Even in the depth of winter, when trained in this way, the sculptured, naked branches are a majestic sight to behold.

And the espalier system, especially, is not just for adornment. It is a brilliant system, designed by Jean-Baptiste de La Quintinie, the genius director of Versailles under Louis XIV, to produce abundant healthy fruit.

In a traditional bushy fruit tree, the dense inner branches and foliage keep out the light and harbour humidity, the best conditions for pests, and so often the fruit does not form or ripen well. But with an espalier tree, palmette, cordon or step-over, in which the branches are trained and flattened against a wire, fence or a warm, protective wall, the fruit can see the sun as it goes through its revolution from morning through to evening. And the breeze circulates through the leaves and branches, drying the fruit, helping to fend off disease. Importantly, too, the trees are at a height that makes it easy to pick the fruit.

With the help of David Pennell, William Sibley and Xavier Guillaume, who planted our six hundred French heritage varieties, we created an orchard in which the trees are planted and trained on a post and wire system, which is based on the classic Versailles system, but also evokes the structural and ornamental walled gardens of the great country houses of the Victorian era. On either side of the central arched walkway, rows of different varieties of trees are trained in low-level step-overs – literally low enough to step over – fans, columns, espaliers and cordons grown in single and double 'U' shapes, partly to give a constantly changing pattern of colours and shapes of blossom and fruit, and partly to limit any disease from spreading within a single variety. The rows of lavender will blaze purple in summer and soften to silver grey in winter to accentuate the structure, and soon the bee village, gypsy chicken houses (see page 246) and thousands of cane fruits will embellish the orchard even further.

I had a powerful image in my mind of a wonderful event that I would call Le Manoir Blossoms. It would celebrate all of our fruit trees in springtime, adorned with fluffy clouds of pink, white and purple flowers. It would be a sight to behold. I would invite our London guests to come to the countryside and they would wander through the orchard against a cinematic sunset, and experience the beauty of the blossoms. Of course the reality is very different. In my enthusiasm and inexperience I had forgotten that every tree is different and so blossom never happens all at once. I was so disappointed. More humble pie for me.

ORLEANS REINETTE

41 trees in my French and English orchards
France, 1776
SEASON: mid-October
APPEARANCE: green/gold to orange and russeted
BEST FOR: tarts and tarte tatin

This was a great favourite of the Victorian nurseryman, writer and connoisseur Edward Bunyard, who is thought to have first tasted it in 1914, when some of the apples were found amongst a box of Blenheim Orange (see page 42) that had been sent to his family's nursery to be identified. 'Its brown-red flush and glowing gold do very easily suggest that if Rembrandt had painted a fruit piece he would have chosen this apple,' said Bunyard. In his view the apples combined the flavours of Ribston (see page 160) and Blenheim with 'an admirable balance of sweetness and acidity ... and for those who incline to the "dry" in food or drink Orleans Reinette is an apple meet for their purpose, rich and mellow, and as a background for an old port it stands solitary and unapproachable'.

We know little else of this apple's heritage except that it was recognised by the Dutch horticulturalist Johann Knoop in 1776, but is thought to have been growing in France much earlier than this. When it first arrived at the Bunyard nursery the firm originally introduced it under the name of the Winter Ribston, but corrected this when it was realised that the apple was already known as Orleans Reinette.

Academics have never quite agreed about what kind of apple the word 'reinette' describes. Certainly it is not French for 'little queen', as once suggested. The sweetest story, even if it is not true, is that the name derives from the rainette faux-grillon, the rare little grey/green/brown Western chorus (or Western striped) frog from Quebec. After all, as Robert Hogg wrote, 'Reinettes are always, or ought to be, spotted with russet freckles . . .' like the belly of the frog. However, Hogg, like many others since, leaned towards the explanation that the word may be derived from the Latin *renatus*, meaning 'rebirth', as an old English word for a pippin (or seedling) grafted onto another seedling was a 'renate'. Therefore a 'reinette' was simply a grafted apple.

TASTING AND COOKING NOTES
When properly ripe this is a good, crunchy, rich and complex-flavoured apple, which leans towards astringency. It is the kind of tangy apple I hope more people will discover in the future when we win the battle against so much sugar in our diets!

Thanks to its slight lack of moisture and its tight flesh, however, I did not expect it to puree well, and I was right. It did bake well whole, although some tightness remained, preventing it from fluffing out as the best varieties do. When it came to the tarte Maman Blanc, the apple crescents did fluff out a little and were transformed into an appetising gold colour. Some delightful flavours emerged, though the characteristic tanginess remained, which not everyone may enjoy. In a tarte tatin, however, this tanginess was an attribute, combating the caramel very well to produce a delicious dessert.

GROWING NOTES
The trees are vigorous and should crop well from a young age; however, they can be erratic and are also known for a tendency to drop their apples without warning around harvest time. If picked in mid-October the fruit can be stored until January.

RED WINDSOR

17 trees in my English orchard
Worcestershire, 1985
SEASON: *late September*
APPEARANCE: *deep scarlet*
BEST FOR: *everything*

The Red Windsor is one of those rare apples that excels at every-thing, and to understand why it is so special we need to delve into its family history. The apple is a red sport of the Early Windsor, the name under which the German Alkmene variety was marketed when it began to be grown in Britain. I had heard about the Alkmene from the great craftsman William Sibley, who told me he was lucky enough to taste an example of this variety at just the perfect moment when its acidity, sweetness and layers of flavour were in total harmony.

Of course it came as no surprise to learn that one of the Alkmene's parents is the Cox's Orange Pippin (see page 84), which was crossed with a nineteenth-century German apple, Geheimrat Doktor Oldenburg, in the 1930s by Professor M. Schmidt and H. Murawski at the Kaiser-Wilhelm Institute for Breeding Research in Münchenberg. The new variety became popular in Holland as well as Germany, and in 1978 a Dutch fruit farmer in Suckley, Worcestershire, decided to bring over some Alkmene trees to act as pollinators for his Cox's Orange Pippins. By the time the Alkmene trees began fruiting in the early 1980s the farm had been sold to a company called Fox Fruit. The new owners found the unusual name of Alkmene difficult to market, so they changed it first to

Fox's Delight, and later to the more crowd-pleasing and patriotic Early Windsor.

And so finally, in 1985, we arrive at the Red Windsor (at first called the Red Alkmene), which was a bud-sport found on the branch of one of the trees growing on the farm, and which produces apples that are a richer red colour, but very similar in flavour to the Early Windsor/Alkmene. It is such a wonderful apple, so I have to ask, why can we not find it in shops and supermarkets?

TASTING AND COOKING NOTES
As soon as we tasted the Red Windsor I could discern the heritage that so impressed Will. At its peak of ripeness this apple had all the qualities of a great apple: crisp and juicy with a big injection of rich, layered flavours, acidity and a delicate perfume. It made a lovely juice and it pureed well and quickly. Whole, it baked wonderfully well, although as it is a small – but perfectly formed – apple, you might need two per person.

When it came to the tarte Maman Blanc, the apple was simply exquisite, and incredibly it made one of the best tarte tatins of all the varieties we tested.

GROWING NOTES
The Red Windsor has the advantage of being self-fertile, disease-free, and the blossoms have some resistance to frost. The variety is also a compact grower which crops well. The apples stay on the tree when ripe and so don't have to be picked at once, but when harvested in mid-to-late September the fruit can be stored until December.

REINE DES REINETTES
(KING OF THE PIPPINS)

24 trees in my French and English orchards
France, 1770s, and England, 1880s
SEASON: early October
APPEARANCE: orange red, with some russeting
BEST FOR: tarts and tarte tatin

The Reine des Reinettes is close to my heart as it is one of the best-known apples in France. So, of course, I had to have some trees in my French orchard. But you can imagine my surprise when I discovered that the King of the Pippins trees that we had also planted in the English orchard are believed to be the same variety! So we have a French Queen and an English King gracing our orchards. And they are one and the same.

The English King was so popular in Victorian times that he was voted the nation's favourite in the great Apple Congress of 1883. The variety is said to have been brought up in England in the 1800s by Mr Kirke, a nurseryman from Brompton in London. In the West Midlands the apple is known as the Prince's Pippin, which is just one of a hundred or so different names. Some say the variety was first known in Britain as the Golden Winter Pearmain; however, Robert Hogg, while acknowledging that in Herefordshire the two names were interchangeable, believed these to be two different apples. In *The Fruit Manual*, he called the King of the Pippins 'one of the richest flavoured early dessert apples, and unequalled by any other variety of the same season; it is ripe in the end of August and beginning of September', but described the Golden Winter Pearmain separately as 'a beautiful and very handsome apple of first-rate quality . . . in use from the end of October to January'.

The French Queen, by contrast, is a much older lady, who can be traced back to around 1770 or even much earlier, probably in Normandy. I will always know this apple as Reine des Reinettes, but I am delighted to have an English King and a French Queen happily co-existing at Le Manoir aux Quat'Saisons. In fact, that perfectly sums up the story of my great orchard adventure.

TASTING AND COOKING NOTES

In our big tasting the Reine des Reinettes underperformed. Clearly our samples were underripe as the flesh was tight and sharp and the sugars had yet to develop fully. This was both disappointing and surprising since I know this apple well, and when fully ripe it is wonderfully fresh, crisp and juicy and makes excellent juice and cider. In a tarte Maman Blanc it will usually fluff out nicely, but in its underripe state it was lacking in sugar and remained too compact, but of course this was a bonus when it came to the tarte tatin, as it performed very well.

GROWING NOTES

The trees are fairly hardy and will tolerate a wetter climate. This is also a variety that will grow well in large pots. If the fruit is picked in the first half of October it can be stored into December.

REINETTE GRISE DU CANADA

48 trees in my French orchard
Normandy, France, 1800s
SEASON: *mid-October*
APPEARANCE: *yellow green, flushed with red and russeted*
BEST FOR: *tarts, baking whole and puree*

In our house on almost every Sunday throughout autumn and winter, my mother would make wonderful desserts, such as baked apples in a semolina soufflé, compotes, and, of course, her iconic *tarte aux pommes*. Lunch was a ritual, beginning with crudités, followed by smoked ham or a roast chicken and a salad made with local cheese – and then, at last, the glorious dessert would arrive. My mum swore by one variety of apple for her tarte, which we grew in our garden and she always called simply 'the Reinette'. I must have peeled hundreds of these apples as my mother's minion in the kitchen, and I always assumed the variety to be either the very local Reinette Grise Comtoise or the Reine des Reinettes, which is known all over France. It was only after I visited my aunt – my mother's younger sister – that I discovered the variety my mother swears by is actually the Reinette Grise du Canada, which is equally well known in France. And it is not from Canada!

Despite its name, this is a very old French apple, which is thought to have originated from at least the turn of the nineteenth century.

At first I planted four trees in our orchard, but since learning that this was the true Reinette for tarte Maman Blanc I put in forty-four more, so there will be plenty for our kitchens.

TASTING AND COOKING NOTES

The apple does not make the best juice, but baked whole it is magnificent, with the russeting of the skin breaking beautifully. It also makes a rich and complex-flavoured puree with a creamy texture, and no sugar is required.

Though it is not the best apple for tarte tatin, it makes a fantastic tarte Maman Blanc – actually the very best – with every crescent fluffing out gorgeously and transforming to a rich gold. Very little juice escapes and towards the end of the cooking the apples take on a darker gold on the edge of the crescents. The kitchen fills with their perfume, just as I remember in my mother's kitchen. And, as it was for the whole of our family on most Sundays, it is so difficult to wait patiently until the tart comes out of the oven and then cools down, as it is a delight that must be eaten when just warm so the pastry has a lovely biscuity quality.

GROWING NOTES

This is a variety that will tolerate most well-drained soils. The trees are strong-growing and should crop well. When harvested in mid-October the fruits are capable of being stored until February.

PURE – BUT NOT SIMPLE

From the very beginning of our journey at Le Manoir, I have demanded purity in our gardens and in all the food we serve to our guests. It is about who I am, a child of the forests and hillsides where no chemicals touched the food that my father or my grandfather grew, and this is what I pass on to my young chefs. It is deep rooted in our culture. I know where every fish that comes into our kitchens is from, how it is caught, and everything about the welfare of the animals that provide the beautiful food for our guests. We must have full provenance of all our ingredients. I have even cut down our wine list by half to concentrate on purity, and with my team of sommeliers we looked for the best organic and biodynamic artisans who care about their vines, nurture their soil, and minimise the use of sulphur and copper. The world of wine, with its charming and seductive labels, has been one of the most secretive, but I believe more and more people are wanting to know what exactly has gone into the production of their food and drink and this movement is now irreversible.

Therefore it was crucial to me that our orchard must be grown in a totally holistic way. In conventional growing almost three hundred pesticides may be routinely used and these often remain in non-organic food, despite washing and cooking. Statistics from The Soil Association tell us that government testing in 2017 found pesticide residues in 47 per cent of British food, and many of these contain more than one pesticide. Between 2011 and 2015, 100 per cent of oranges and 86 per cent of pears tested contained multiple pesticide residue.

By contrast The Soil Association only permits twenty different pesticides (and no herbicides), most of which are innocuous food substances. However, some spraying with sulphur and copper is still allowed, albeit in restricted doses.

For over thirty years at Le Manoir we have worked with The Soil Association and Garden Organic and grown our twelve gardens without a single chemical, and I was not prepared to compromise now. I researched every system of organic growing and every assurance scheme and could not find any alternatives, so I decided we would use nothing at all.

At first we had good yields, but the trees suffered from many diseases, and I soon began to understand why these sprays are permitted by The Soil Association. Organic fruit growing is not easy. It takes hard work and constant vigilance to keep the orchard healthy and combat many diseases, such as scab and peach leaf curl, and I have to accept that we need help. Yet I am still convinced we can find an alternative to copper, sulphur and other chemicals. So we plan to talk to the growers in organic and biodynamic orchards and vineyards, especially in the wetter parts of the UK and in other countries that have similar climates, in the hope of pooling knowledge, and I will go on to work with The Soil Association on trialling alternative ideas, perhaps even the kind of artisan tissanes that might have been used in ancient times. They are now working with scientists and growers to look into growing without copper, especially, and there are trials taking place to monitor the value of possible solutions, such as mulching with fresh willow woodchip. Purity is not simple, and so we have also decided to bring in a full-time orchard specialist to advise us at Le Manoir.

I accept that we will rarely have the high yields of fruit that a conventional orchard can achieve, but I would rather have a smaller harvest of the most delicious fruit than give my guests produce that has not been raised according to the pure ethos that is in my heart and soul and that of Le Manoir. They will have the best. This is who I am.

RIBSTON PIPPIN

24 trees in my English orchard
Yorkshire, 1707
SEASON: *October*
APPEARANCE: *green overlaid with orange and red streaks*
BEST FOR: *eating fresh, juice, tarts and tarte tatin*

This apple's story is very endearing to me as it links an old English apple, which was highly esteemed by the Victorians, to its true heritage in Rouen in Northern France.

One version of the apple's history (it is also sometimes called the Glory of York), is that Sir Henry Goodricke, whose seat was at Ribston Hall near Knaresborough in Yorkshire, travelled to Rouen, perhaps on the Grand Tour that the gentry used to take around Europe. While he was there he tasted a local Normandy apple and kept three pips, which he planted when he returned home. Another version is that the three pips were sent over to him from Normandy by a friend. Whichever is correct, it is agreed that he planted all three pips, two of which came to nothing, but the third grew up to become one of the Victorians' favourite table apples, and the probable parent of my all-time favourite, the Cox's Orange Pippin (see page 84). Some say that the gardener who grew the successful tree was called Robert Clemesha, while others believe that it was the father of Robert Lowe, who was the nurseryman at Hampton Wick. Whoever it was, they had raised a new treasure.

Robert Hogg suggests in his *Herefordshire Pomona* that the Ribston Pippin enjoyed a steady rise to fame rather than becoming a sudden sensation, but by the end of the eighteenth century it was a celebrated fruit. It also had a compatriot bidding for English hearts in the Margil, a variety that may have been introduced by one of the most fashionable English garden designers and nurserymen of the day, George London, after a visit to the gardens at Versailles. London co-founded the Brompton Park Nursery in 1689 and his prestigious clients included Queen Anne and the gentry of many of England's grand houses, such as Longleat, Chatsworth, Burghley House and Castle Howard.

The two French apples began to rival old English favourites such as the Golden Pippin as they were sweeter (though nothing like as sweet as today's modern varieties) and more complex and aromatic. Over the dinner tables of the gentry, the qualities of the Ribston Pippin or Margil versus the likes of the Blenheim Orange (see page 42) or the newer Cox's Orange Pippin would often be hotly debated and argued over in the same way as the relative merits of fine wines. And in one of many literary references to the apple, Charles Dickens, in *The Pickwick Papers*, describes a character at a card party as 'a little hard-headed Ribston-pippin-faced man . . .'

By the time Hogg came to publish the *Pomona* between 1878 and 1884, he was able to declare of the Ribston that 'this delicious Apple needs no encomium. It is as highly appreciated as it is generally-known.' By way of illustration, he noted that in one single nursery, that of Richard Smith and Co. in Worcester (see page 167), three thousand Ribston Pippin trees were being propagated every year to satisfy the demand for them in ornamental gardens.

Hogg also wrote that the original tree stood until 1810, when it was blown down 'by a violent gale of wind. It was afterwards supported by stakes in a horizontal position . . . It continued to produce fruit until it lingered and died in the year 1840.' However, 'on clearing away the old wood, a portion of which is still carefully preserved near the gardener's house, a healthy young sucker was found to be growing from the root about four inches below the surface of the ground.' At the time Hogg was writing, this shoot still continued to bear fruit, and threw up suckers freely, 'so that when the present tree dies altogether', he felt, 'one of these with care would soon make a nice tree and still perpetuate the original'. In fact what started out as that little shoot lived on until 1932, so the tree had a total life span of two hundred and twenty-five years.

In the London Horticultural Society's catalogue of 1842 it was noted that the apple 'ought to be in every collection'. I wish it was – but at least I have it in mine!

TASTING AND COOKING NOTES
Before we even tested this variety I felt that it was a good omen that the Ribston Pippin has a strong parentage, in particular a direct link to the wonderful Cox's Orange Pippin.

So the expectations were high when my team of chefs and gardeners – two of whom are from Yorkshire – gathered around the testing table. To begin with, the apple looked alluring with its flashes of red, pale gold and green. Raw, it showed many of the loveable qualities of the Cox's Orange Pippin. It was crisp with a rich, clean apple flavour and a slight lemony twist; and to balance this there was a gentle delivery of natural sweetness. It also juiced well. However, when pureed it was a disappointment. The flesh was so compact that it took a long time to break down, although once it did, the flavour came through nicely.

Similarly, when baked whole it remained quite tight. However, in the Maman Blanc tarte both the textures and flavours lived up to the apple's glorious reputation; and in the tarte tatin test, of course, the density of flesh proved to be a strength as the apple halves held their shape.

Overall this was a good apple, but, for me, it was not a great one. It was missing some of the complexity and the ensemble of qualities that a great apple should have, but as I have to say again and again, it may have been picked too early to do it justice.

GROWING NOTES

The Ribston Pippin blossoms early and is a triploid variety (see page 263). It is good for gardens as it can do well on dwarf rootstock and also in pots. It grows in all parts of the world, but prefers some warmth if it is to be at its best. The trees can be prone to dropping their fruits suddenly at harvest time, but if picked carefully in October they can be stored and eaten through November. The apple will be most ripe and rich in flavour in December/January, although the texture will become more dry.

ROSEMARY RUSSET

3 trees in my English orchard
Middlesex, 1831
SEASON: *late September/early October*
APPEARANCE: *orange/red with partial russeting*
BEST FOR: *everything except puree*

I very much enjoy the mystery that surrounds an apple without any certain parentage or history. In the case of the Rosemary Russet, little is known about its genetics other than that it is an old English variety dating from at least 1831. It was first described by the Ronalds Nursery in Brentford, one of the many influential nurseries that contributed greatly to the classification and distribution of fruit through their elaborate and beautifully illustrated catalogues and books, which were full of information for anyone wanting to plant an orchard or create an ornamental fruit garden.

'Old Hugh' Ronalds founded the nursery in Brentford in 1760 and was succeeded by his son, also called Hugh. The business grew and expanded to fifty acres over six sites, and the family had a close relationship with the Royal Botanic Gardens at Kew. So much so that the director, the celebrated botanist and explorer Sir Joseph Banks, asked the Ronalds to send a selection of trees and plants out to Australia and New Zealand.

In 1831, the year that the Rosemary Russet was discovered, the younger Hugh Ronalds published *Pyrus Malus Brentfordiensis; or a Concise Description of Selected Apples*, 'with a figure of each sort drawn from nature' by his daughter, Elizabeth, known as Betsey, who was an acclaimed horticultural illustrator. In it he shared his life's work, describing some three hundred varieties and acknowledging other nurserymen with whom he had worked to introduce and improve varieties. The Rosemary Russet is listed as simply the Rosemary Apple, and he noted rather matter-of-factly that 'the fruit is firm, and of a high rich flavour. A very hardy, productive, useful sort, either for the table or kitchen use.' Robert Hogg, however, was more enthusiastic in *The Fruit Manual*, calling it: 'A most delicious and valuable dessert apple of the very first quality.'

Our local expert Marcus Roberts, who regularly holds apple identification days and workshops, tells me that this apple is a real crowd-pleaser, as it is a good introduction to the variety of flavours within the russet family, and a little more rich and pronounced in flavour than the better-known Egremont Russet (see page 105), which is an apple that I love. At the big and very popular Apple Day held by the Shenley Park Trust in Hertfordshire, with its acres of old orchard filled with heritage trees, Marcus tells me that thousands of people pass along an immense table inside a huge marquee, tasting over sixty varieties laid out alphabetically, before buying their favourites to take home. Even though the Rosemary Russet is close to the end of the table it always draws many admirers. Since this is an apple with a sharpish edge it gives me hope that, despite the big commercial growers and supermarkets telling us that we want sweet apples, we are still attracted to varieties with a little acidity and a more complex, rich flavour.

TASTING AND COOKING NOTES

When I took a bite of this apple there was a delicious burst of sweet and sour flavours and juices. This is a variety that juices well and is known to be good for cider. When pureed the apple took a long time to reach a good consistency, but it had a delightful and unusual creamy yellow colour. It kept its flavour and no sugar was needed.

Baked whole, this apple stood proud and held its shape impressively. The heat brought out a richer flavour in the creamy-coloured flesh and this was combined with wonderful aromatics.

It went on to perform well in the Maman Blanc tarte test. The apple crescents fluffed out into circles of rich gold and the complex flavours remained throughout. Remarkably the apple demonstrated its strengths again in the tarte tatin test.

It was such a special apple that I regret only planting three trees in the orchard. I must plant more!

GROWING NOTES
The Rosemary Russet grows well on dwarf rootstocks so this is a good choice for a garden, especially if you are a fan of russet apples and want to add to your collection. The trees are generally hardy, fairly vigorous, and crop moderately well, though the apples can sometimes fall early. They can be picked from late September through to early October, and then stored until March.

WORCESTER PEARMAIN

5 trees in my English orchard
Worcestershire, 1873
SEASON: *late August/early September*
APPEARANCE: *pear-shaped and bright red*
BEST FOR: *eating fresh, tarte tatin*

The Worcester Pearmain is one of those great, classic English apples that holds a sentimental attachment for anyone who has childhood memories of collecting bounteous baskets of these distinctive bright red apples straight from the tree: so sweet, crisp and easy to eat, with their faint but unusual strawberry aroma. One of its admirers is my good friend William Sibley, fruit expert and grafter, and a man whose judgement I totally trust. 'When properly tree-ripened, the Worcester Pearmain is an apple that I rate as a truly great eating experience, one that stacks up with the best in early September,' says Will.

The first Worcester Pearmain is thought to have been grown in 1872 from a pip of the Devonshire Quarrenden (see page 95) by William Hale of Swan Pool in St John's, Worcester – sadly his orchard was later destroyed to make way for a school just before the Second World War – and there is most certainly a strong family resemblance between the two varieties. William Hale initially raised two similar trees, one of which bore yellow fruit, the other red fruit, and he called them his Hale's Seedlings.

The red-fruiting trees were the ones that clearly caught the fancy of Richard Smith 'the second', at his family's St John's Nurseries nearby. His father, also Richard, had developed the nursery into one of the largest in the world, and it was of huge importance to the local community, since it covered some one hundred and fifty-seven acres, tended by a workforce of around two hundred people.

For a mere £5 or £10, depending on which story you choose, Richard Smith bought the exclusive right to take a graft from the red Hale's Seedling, and he renamed it the Worcester Pearmain. His nursery often sent new apples of interest to the great connoisseur and writer Robert Hogg to taste. Many of these, such as the King Charles Pearmain and Pigeon's Heart, are no longer heard of these days, but in 1873 Smith sent him some of the new Worcester Pearmain. Hogg was clearly charmed by this 'very handsome early apple'. In *The Herefordshire Pomona*, he wrote that 'the great beauty of the fruit, and its usefulness, both for dessert and culinary purposes, cannot fail to render it a general favourite ... When well trained, on the paradise stock, and laden with its bright red fruit, which has a peculiar rosy tint, it forms a very beautiful object.'

Smith wasted no time in introducing the Worcester Pearmain to the market the following year, and his efforts were rewarded when he received a First Class Certificate from the Royal Horticultural Society. The apple became a huge commercial success, and by 1876 Smith was seeing a great return on his bargain investment as, according to Joan Morgan in *The Book of Apples*, he was able to sell the trees for a guinea each. Not only that, but the Worcester Pearmain became one of the varieties most called into action for apple-breeding programmes.

The result of one of these programmes was the crimson Tydeman's Early Worcester, which is an apple that I like well enough to have planted six trees in the orchard. It was developed at the East Malling Research Station by the famous apple breeder Henry M. Tydeman in 1929, though the apple was not introduced until 1945.

168

Tydeman was aiming to develop a series of lucrative early apples that would fill a void early in the English apple season, and in one of his experiments he crossed the Worcester Pearmain with the McIntosh, a Canadian apple found growing on his land by John McIntosh, a Scotsman who had settled in Dundela, Ontario. The McIntosh became very famous, not only because of the popularity of the fruit in Canada, where it was often known just as the Mac, but also because back in 1979, when an employee of the Apple computer company began work on a new design, he named it after his favourite apple. Enter the Apple Macintosh (the spelling was changed slightly, possibly for legal reasons), later rebranded as simply the Apple Mac. Sadly for the fruit, while its technological counterpart became world-famous, the apple has now almost entirely disappeared from the market.

TASTING AND COOKING NOTES
At first bite the Worcester Pearmain was delicious, full of wonderful aromatics, low in sugar and with a very rich flavour. It also makes a pleasant, light, sweet juice, which can benefit from the addition of some Bramley apple juice to inject a little more acidity.

Pureeing was not this apple's vocation, however, as although it had a great flavour the flesh did not break down easily. It took 40 minutes to properly bake whole – one of the longest times of all of the apples we tested – and so inevitably a great deal of moisture was withdrawn and the texture was drier than the ideal, but the flavour remained rich and multilayered.

It made a good tarte Maman Blanc, with tight-textured slices of apple that were succulent-tasting, with a good level of acidity. However, this apple was truly destined for tarte tatin. This was a huge success. The halves of apple stood compact, tight and firm, yet still succulent, and had enough acidity to compete harmoniously with the caramel to produce a wonderfully flavoured, richly perfumed dessert.

GROWING NOTES
The trees will grow in both the south and north of England and will crop and colour well in most soils. They are fairly frost-resistant and are also supposed to be resistant to mildew, but can be prone to scab, particularly on clay soils. Some very old trees can grow surprisingly large in good situations, but they also grow very prettily on dwarf rootstocks in small gardens.

The variety is prone to tip-bearing, which means that the apples form at the ends of the branches, rather than along them (some varieties are partial tip-bearers, which do both). This means they must only be pruned gently or you risk losing fruit from the tips of the branches. The apples are picked in late August/early September and are only good for a short season, until October.

BRIGHT FUTURE

It is well known that The Prince of Wales has been a tireless ambassador for British agriculture, the environment and for organic values, and we share the same views on provenance and ethics. I had the honour of being invited to Highgrove House, to see his gardens and give a little speech, in which I congratulated him on his commitment, but also teased him that my garden at Le Manoir aux Quat'Saisons might be as lovely as his! And so I invited him to come and see for himself. A year later, just as we had completed the second phase of our orchard and also our heritage produce garden, His Royal Highness paid us a visit, hosted by James Campbell, Chief Executive of Garden Organic of which I am Vice President. As well as promoting organic gardening, their Heritage Seed Bank is hugely important in conserving the diversity of vegetable varieties in the UK.

All of our team were so excited about the visit. But when the day came the weather decided to conspire against us, and there was a huge rainstorm. It didn't dampen The Prince of Wales's enthusiasm, though, and together we visited every single garden, finishing at the orchard. I was so inspired by his knowledge and curiosity and we shared a lot of laughter and fun. Finally we celebrated this happy occasion by planting two apple trees together in the pouring rain. The variety was bred specifically for organic gardeners and its hopeful name is Bright Future.

APPLE TASTING CHART

BEST FOR:

EVERYTHING
Cheddar Cross
Cox's Orange Pippin
Red Windsor
Rosemary Russet (except puree)

JUICE
Egremont Russet
Granny Smith

PUREE
Adams' Pearmain
Blenheim Orange
Cox's Orange Pippin
Devonshire Quarrenden
Edward VII
Golden Noble
Keswick Codlin
Red Windsor

BAKING WHOLE
Adams' Pearmain
Annie Elizabeth
Chivers Delight
Claygate Pearmain
Cox's Orange Pippin
D'Arcy Spice
Golden Delicious
Red Windsor
Reine des Reinettes
Rosemary Russet

TARTS
Adams' Pearmain
Blenheim Orange
Captain Kidd
Cheddar Cross
Cox's Orange Pippin
D'Arcy Spice
Devonshire Quarrenden
Discovery
Egremont Russet
George Cave
Lord Lambourne
Orleans Reinette
Red Windsor
Reinette Grise du Canada
Rosemary Russet

TARTE TATIN
Braeburn
Chivers Delight
Cox's Orange Pippin
Devonshire Quarrenden
Granny Smith
Orleans Reinette
Red Windsor
Rosemary Russet

PEARS,
QUINCE,
FIG AND
MEDLAR

In the fruit gardens at Versailles there is a bronze statue of the genius director in the time of Louis XIV, Jean-Baptiste de La Quintinie, which was commissioned by the king. In one hand he holds a pruning knife, and in the other the branch of a pear tree. The pear was La Quintinie's favourite fruit, and pear trees featured throughout the extraordinarily elaborate and ornamental planting of the royal gardens. La Quintinie was obsessive about serving the perfectly ripe pear and was most likely one of the first to divide pears for eating fresh into those with melting, soft, buttery flesh; firmer, yet still luscious ones which he labelled '*cassante*'; and ones best for accompanying savoury dishes. He appeared to have no time for the grittier varieties that would have been found in medieval British orchards.

The history of the cultivated pear goes back to the Greeks and Romans, but like apples a pear grown from seed will not be true to the parent tree, so they have to be grafted. And in the seventeenth century France was the great centre of pear-breeding and experimentation, which is why most of the greatest of these fruits, even those that were first raised in Britain, were given French names.

By Victorian times, however, another great name in the world of pears had emerged, the Belgian Jean-Baptiste Van Mons. Originally a chemist, he raised and promoted hundreds of new varieties, which he shared with the Horticultural Society in London (now the RHS), sending over parcels every winter to be tasted.

Like apples, these pears had their different seasons: the early varieties were fresh and juicy, while later they began to develop more complex flavours and perfumes. Some demanded to be eaten straight from the tree. Others were keepers. Sadly, these days we see only a handful of the varieties that the Victorians enjoyed and valued as much for the beauty of their blossom and shape as for their fruit. This is why we have planted around thirty-five French and English varieties in our orchard for our guests to discover. And we have also created a beautiful two-hundred-metre pear wall beside the gates to Le Manoir, where over twenty varieties of trees are trained against the stone in a very lovely and intricate pattern created by Will Sibley. When our neighbours pass by in autumn, I am sure they enjoy the fruit!

BEURRE D'APREMONT

22 trees in my French orchard
Apremont, Franche-Comté, France, 1800s
SEASON: *late October*
APPEARANCE: *bronze and russeted*
BEST FOR: *everything*

It is with great pride that I can say that this wonderful pear, which is often classed as one of the world's best, comes from my region of France. It was found as a seedling growing in the forest of Apremont in Haute-Saône – only twenty-five miles away from the village of Charcenne, which is home to the world-famous family nursery of my gifted friends Xavier and Pierre-Marie Guillaume (see page 13), who have planted my French orchard at Le Manoir aux Quat'Saisons.

I wish I could say who the lucky person was who first found this seedling pear tree growing in the forest, but we simply don't know. Someone, however, sent some grafts of the original tree to the Jardin des Plantes, the botanical gardens in Paris, where the pear was called after the botanist Louis Bosc, who studied and worked there as a young man. Bosc was an interesting character. While at the botanical gardens, he met and became a friend of the intellectual writer and Girondin revolutionary Marie-Jeanne 'Manon' Roland, better known as Madame Roland, and her husband, Jean-Marie, a politician and economist. Bosc himself was a member of the more radical Jacobin Club and was forced to hide out in the forest of Montmorency, where he sheltered Madame Roland and her husband before she was arrested and sent to the guillotine. Despite Bosc's support for the Revolution, which challenged the wealth of the aristocracy and the Church and their lands, as a botanist he must have feared the destruction of important orchards, and is credited with helping to remove over two hundred fruit trees from the gardens of the convent of Chartreux de Paris, transferring them to the Jardin des Plantes for safe keeping.

Under the name of Beurre Bosc, the pear was received at the Horticultural Society of London (later the RHS) in 1820, and Robert Hogg described it as 'a dessert pear of first-rate quality'. These days it is widely grown all over the world, and although it is known by most as the Beurre Bosc, in Franche-Comté it will always be Beurre d'Apremont.

TASTING AND COOKING NOTES
This is a wonderful, elegant, juicy and perfumed pear, which can meet every culinary challenge, and it is beautiful poached (as in the recipe on page 307) or baked in a *tarte fine* (see page 301), as it retains its freshness and is not oversweet.

GROWING NOTES
This is a variety that flowers late, which can help it to avoid the frosts. It prefers a light, rich soil and if grown against a wall in a sunny position in Britain it can crop well, though it can be biennial.

BEURRE HARDY

64 trees in my English and French orchards
Boulogne, France, 1820
SEASON: *September*
APPEARANCE: *green, turning yellow, with fine*
russet and sometimes a red flush
BEST FOR: *everything, from eating fresh to poaching and roasting*

The Beurre Hardy is one of my favourite pears. I have always admired the skills of the French nurserymen, and this is a perfect example of their craftsmanship. It may not be as pretty as some varieties, but the eating experience is ambrosial. As with all varieties that have *beurre* in their name, its texture, like butter, almost melts in the mouth.

It originated from Boulogne, which had a major 'Little England' colony in the nineteenth century, and was the home for a while, of Charles Dickens (and his mistress) – however, this pear is all French. It was raised in 1820 by a fruit grower, Ernest Bonnet, who was another friend of the famous Belgian chemist, horticulturalist and pear breeder Jean-Baptiste Van Mons (see page 176). After a series of disasters robbed Van Mons of his fruit gardens, he offered scion wood – the shoots that are used for grafting – to nurserymen and friends around the country to help him save his life's work. By all accounts Ernest accepted so many of these gifts born out of adversity that, according to Joan Morgan in her *Book of Pears* (2015), 'Van Mons believed that most of his collection would be growing with Bonnet.' The Beurre Hardy, however, was one of Bonnet's own triumphs, which ten years later was taken up by the nurseryman

Jean-Laurent Jamin in Bourg-la-Reine, Paris. Jamin renamed the pear in honour of Julien-Alexandre Hardy, who was the Director of the Luxembourg Gardens in Paris from 1817 to 1859.

I am sure that Monsieur Hardy deserved this great tribute, but I feel a little sad for Monsieur Bonnet, and for all the other heroes and heroines in this book who have found or raised a special new variety, but whose names have been supplanted. As a creative person I want to own my work. If I develop a wonderful new dish, I would feel cheated to see it being celebrated under someone else's name; so I am sorry that this beautiful pear is not known as the Beurre Bonnet.

Jamin was one of two Frenchmen to exhibit varieties at the great London Pear Conference of 1885 and it is most likely that he introduced the Beurre Hardy to Britain. Here the tree, as well as the fruit, became famous for its ornamental qualities, and it was trained into pyramids and other elaborate shapes in the gardens of country houses. On the pedigree of the Beurre Hardy, Robert Hogg quotes the writer Richard Doddridge (known as R. D.) Blackmore, who was the author of the novel *Lorna Doone*. Amongst his many interests and talents he had a great passion for growing fruit and, thanks to an inheritance from his uncle in 1860, he was able to build Gomer House in Teddington and create an eleven-acre walled market garden. He loved to grow unusual varieties and specialised in pears as well as strawberries, peaches and grapes, which he sent to the Covent Garden fruit market. Blackmore – like me – was a romantic, not a businessman, and his garden never made him much money, but he became a nationally recognised expert on fruit and a fellow of the Royal Horticultural Society, so his opinion was valuable. And in his estimation, the Beurre Hardy was 'a very fine pear and very highly bred'.

Our orchard is about flavour, beauty and organic principles,
which begin with a healthy soil.

The orchard is the latest chapter in the story of our magical gardens at
Belmond Le Manoir aux Quat'Saisons.

I wanted to celebrate both
English fruit and varieties from
my region of Franche-Comté.

The beautiful *Violette de Bordeaux* fig
graces The Dovecote.

The pale sun of April creating its magic in the orchard is a sight to behold.

Heritage apples often have intriguing or amusing names.

In summer, the apricot trees fanned over the walls at the entrance to Le Manoir are heavy with fruits.

L5A1

Apple
Eynsham Dumpling
Early October

Oxford, England Heritage 1960

The simple happiness of walking amongst the trees and the blossoms, and the excitement of the harvest to come.

—— Our organic apples are grown for flavour over looks.

Doyenne du Comice   *Néflier à Gros Fruits*

Around thirty-five varieties of French and English pears mingle with apples, stone fruits and the weird, prehistoric-looking medlar.

As the orchard grew, so did the enthusiasm of our young gardeners. James Dewhurst harvesting the fruits.

I wanted to know which apples would be best for juicing, pureeing, baking whole, tarts and tarte tatin.

With Head Development Chef, Adam (*left*), and Chef Pâtissier, Benoit (*right*), the tasting began.

Of course, our gardening team must always be involved in our tastings. When chefs and gardeners understand and respect each other and the challenges they face, the result is a wonderful creative environment. Over a demanding two weeks of research we tasted, juiced and cooked over a hundred varieties in order to give our guests the ultimate apple experience.

Apple and Calvados soufflé; its own sorbet.

We did it! Thanks to my expert friends, especially Will Sibley (*left*), Xavier Guillaume and my wonderful gardening team, my orchard dream is now a reality.

During a visit from HRH The Prince of Wales, hosted by Garden Organic, we celebrated by planting two apple trees in the pouring rain.

TASTING AND COOKING NOTES

When perfectly ripe, the Beurre Hardy is in a class of its own: delicately perfumed, with a faint taste of rosewater, its flesh is buttery and juicy: true nectar. This is a pear that will poach and roast well, but you must be gentle with it as it is very delicate and susceptible to bruising.

GROWING NOTES

Beurre Hardy is now grown in many orchards in England (though it doesn't like chalk soils) and is considered to be a good variety to grow organically because it has good resistance to disease; however, I have discovered for myself that it is far better-suited to the French climate. Though the blossom will normally tolerate late frosts, this year we suffered extremely harsh frosts and hail, which hit much of the orchard hard, and so half of my sixty-four Beurre Hardy trees fruited, and half did not – thank God I don't have to depend on my orchard for survival! In good conditions, however, and preferably against a sheltered wall, you should find that the trees crop very well.

The fruit should be picked just before the point at which it will come easily off the tree, usually early to mid-September, and then ripened on a windowsill, after which the pears will keep for about a week, but not more, in the fridge, as they can bruise easily and become grainy.

BLACK WORCESTER

4 trees in my English orchard
Worcester, sixteenth century
SEASON: *October/early November*
APPEARANCE: *heavy with maroon, almost black, flush*
BEST FOR: *winter salad (and history)*

This is the ugliest pear I have ever seen: misshapen and heavy with thick, rough, dark maroon skin that can be virtually black – but the trees are elegant, and in the orchard they evoke a wonderful sense of medieval history. And they do have a lovely story to tell because, in spite of their looks, a queen fell in love with them. In 1575, when Elizabeth I visited Worcester, a tree bearing these pears was uprooted from the gardens at White Ladies and replanted by the gate through which the queen entered the city. It is said that she was so taken with the tree, heavy with its unusual fruit, that she proclaimed Worcester should add three of the pears to its coat of arms, where they appear to this day, as well as on the badges of the county cricket team and Worcester rugby club.

This is probably the earliest English pear that is still in existence, though mostly these days it is to be found only in private gardens or small nurseries. It is thought that it was introduced to Britain by the Romans, and was first recorded by the Cistercian monks at Warden Abbey in Bedfordshire, the monastery that lent its name to the most widely grown cooking pear of medieval times, the Warden, Wardon or Wardoun.

Like the Warden, the Black Worcester is quite hard and its texture gritty – this was long before the development of more modern, soft, buttery-textured varieties. These pears were meant for baking or poaching, in both sweet and savoury dishes. In Elizabethan England, they would most likely have been used in a popular recipe of the time, Warden Pie, which Shakespeare mentions in *The Winter's Tale*. In a scene in which the clown is wandering down the road in Bohemia, past the shepherds preparing for the sheep-shearing feast, he lists the ingredients he must find, reminding himself: 'I must have saffron to colour the Warden pies.'

By the 1950s, the Black Worcester was no longer being grown commercially, but it has since been championed by the Slow Food movement, and in the 1990s, Worcestershire County Council, together with Pershore College, began distributing trees around the county in order to ensure that the variety did not face extinction. To help ensure its preservation and history, we have planted four of these pear trees in our orchard.

TASTING AND COOKING NOTES
Unripe and raw, the pear is gritty and totally inedible; it is a variety that begs to be stored until at least March/April, as only then does it develop some flavour, sweetness and character. Even then it cannot seduce like the great eating pears. I have never seen a pear that is quite as dense and compact, and so the tight flesh needs long poaching in order to soften it – the best idea would be to cook it in red wine, with some blackcurrants and spice, such as cinnamon. Unfortunately, it will also need sugar, to help the flavour, and the texture will stay quite grainy, therefore it will not be a truly great gastronomic experience. So, personally, I think this pear is best used raw in a winter salad, for example with endive, Stilton and walnuts.

GROWING NOTES
The trees can be trained against a wall and are easy to grow, though they need another pear tree for pollination. They are quite moderate

bearers of fruit; however, they are hardy, resistant to scab and seem to tolerate a little shade. The great advantage of this pear is its durability. It will never bruise! Even if the pears fall off the tree while still bullet hard they can lie on the ground, unmolested by slugs and other creatures, for weeks, and can still be picked up unspoilt, to use for cooking as late as Christmas, or stored until April (if picked by mid-November). This quality no doubt made it a valuable pear in ancient times when there were few fruits to be had in the dead of winter.

CONFERENCE

25 trees in my English and French orchards
Hertfordshire, 1885
SEASON: *late September*
APPEARANCE: *green gold with partial russet*
BEST FOR: *eating with cheese or in salads*

I encountered the Conference pear for the first time when I arrived in Great Britain in the early 1970s. It was, and still is, the most popular pear in this country. Will Sibley explained to me that one of the reasons for this is that it is one of the few pears that can be eaten underripe and quite crunchy, like an apple, yet still have some flavour. He calls it a 'car pear' because you can munch it on a car journey, whereas a fully ripe juicy pear is impossibly sticky and messy!

Having grown up with the delights of the many great buttery-textured varieties of French pears, at first I thought the Conference lacking in the beautiful colours I was accustomed to, and when I tasted it I found it a little grainy, although I recognised its good crunch and texture. However, I have come to love this pear.

I was curious, though, about its functional name, which sounds more like a business meeting than a beautiful fruit. In fact it takes its name from the great National Pear Conference of 1885, at which it was first introduced. Following the success of the National Apple Congress two years earlier and with the inspirational Robert Hogg at the helm, the Royal Horticultural Society put on a repeat per-formance for pears. Gardeners and nurserymen were invited to submit over six hundred varieties of pear from all over the UK, the Channel Islands and France. Once again, the idea was to taste and properly classify the fruits, which, just like apples, were often known by a confusing number of different names. The ultimate goal was finding the best established pear varieties to champion, and the most interesting new ones to introduce. As before, this ambitious event was held in the Great Vinery of the Royal Horticultural Society at Chiswick, where over six thousand plates of fruit were laid out for tasting, accompanied by their names, details of where they were grown, on what rootstock, and in what season, and once again a shortlist of sixty top varieties was drawn up.

One of the new pears on show was introduced by the renowned Rivers Nursery in Sawbridgeworth (see page 85), where Thomas Rivers' son, T. Francis Rivers, focused on breeding pears. It was a seedling of the variety Léon Leclerc de Laval, raised by Léon Leclerc, the well-known amateur fruit grower from Laval in Mayenne, Western Loire, who also introduced the Williams' Bon Chrétien pear (see page 200) to France. In a moment of marketing genius, Rivers named the pear after the Conference, and along with Williams' Bon Chrétien and Doyenne du Comice (see page 192), the new variety emerged as one of the stars of the show, which would go on to be known all over the world.

Much later, in 1968 at East Malling, Dr F. Alston created a new Anglo-French pear, the Concorde, a cross between the Conference and Doyenne du Comice, which was named after the famous supersonic plane – also, of course, a joint project between Britain and France – and the pear was introduced into the market in 1995.

TASTING AND COOKING NOTES
The first time I tasted this pear I must say I did not find it very inviting. As well as being quite grainy, it had very low sugar and

seemed to lack a pronounced pear flavour. It was on the mean side with juice too. I think I was tasting it at what Will calls its 'car pear' stage, as I have since discovered that when truly ripe, the Conference pear can produce some delicious flavours – albeit in a more muted way than that of a Williams' Bon Chrétien.

This pear is the perfect illustration of the way that the state of ripeness in any fruit defines texture, flavour and the total eating experience. It is not a pear for juicing, but when fully ripe the graininess disappears into a melting texture and its lack of sugar gives a clean flavour that is in tune with modern gastronomy. It can bake well and can make a beautiful dessert, but for me its best role is a savoury one, with some cheese, in a salad, or to accompany game, and for this it can also work when slightly underripe and the sugars are not completely developed.

GROWING NOTES
The hardy Conference is the most widely grown variety in the UK and is one of the easiest as it will adapt to most situations and should give a good, regular crop of fruit. Don't be tempted to leave the pears on the tree too long as they rapidly become over-mature. When picked in the second half of September, they can be stored into November.

DELBARDÉLICE®

9 trees in my French orchard
Malicorne, France, 1966
SEASON: *late August/mid-September*
APPEARANCE: *yellow turning to bronze*
BEST FOR: *everything*

The Delbard family call this 'the end of holiday pear' as, like Delsanne (see page 190), it is one of the latest pears of the season; and what a handsome finale it provides, as its skin turns to bronze, with flashes of red, when it is completely ripe.

The Delbardélice® was created by the senior generation of the Delbard family, Georges, and reflects the craft and skill of this great nurseryman and rose specialist in crossing the Doyenne du Comice (see page 192) with Grand Champion, an American pear dating from 1936, which the Delbards introduced to France, and which has the Williams' Bon Chrétien (see page 200) as one of its parents. Such a glorious lineage.

We grow the trees in a double 'U' cordon in our orchard and also in the intricate patterning of our pear wall at the entrance to Le Manoir, where they welcome our guests and allow our village friends to do a little harvesting as they pass by – this year there were hundreds and hundreds.

TASTING NOTES
Once ripe, this pear offers so many surprising flavours and perfumes. I have only encountered this level of complexity in a few fruits.

First, the skin is smooth and thin so you can eat the pear straight from the tree. The creamy white flesh is layered with exquisite notes of mint, banana and faintly sub-tropical, even musky, flavours.

Needless to say, this pear will do everything in the kitchen, from juicing to poaching and baking, and it makes a lovely compote. With Benoit, my Chef Pâtissier, I often use it for a *charlotte aux poires*, served with a lime and caramel sauce.

GROWING NOTES
The pear tree is regular-cropping and has good disease tolerance. However, when harvested from late August to mid-September, the pears need to be used straight away as this is not a fruit that is meant to be stored.

DELSANNE

2 trees in my French orchard
Malicorne, France, 1986
SEASON: *late September*
APPEARANCE: *dark golden*
BEST FOR: *everything*

I only have two of these trees in my orchard so far, but they are precious, as Delsanne is one of the most remarkable of all the pears produced at the wonderful Delbard Nursery in Malicorne. The variety is sometimes known as Goldember, and in France as Delbard d'Automne®. Will Sibley believes this to be one of the best varieties in the world today, and it is the result of twelve years of dedication to the cross-breeding of the Delbias pear, also raised by Monsieur Delbard, and the much older Passe Crassane, which was raised in 1845 by Louis Boisbunel in Rouen, Normandy, and has long been one of France's favourite late varieties. Passe Crassane pears were famously presented with their stems dipped in wax as this was thought to help them retain moisture when they were stored. I know this pear quite well, as we use it in our kitchens at Le Manoir aux Quat'Saisons, and it is truly luxurious.

Delsanne's other parent, the Delbias pear, was introduced by the Delbard family in 1973 and patented as Super Comice Delbard®. It too has a glorious parentage as it is a cross between the Williams' Bon Chrétien (see page 200) and Doyenne du Comice (see page 192).

TASTING AND COOKING NOTES

If eaten straight from the tree, the Delsanne delivers a lovely fresh experience, but if you put it into a bowl it will ripen fast and be at its best within a week, when the beautiful white flesh will have developed its full perfume, texture and unctuous sweetness. I never peel pears or apples, as I am lucky enough to eat only organic ones, but in this case you may prefer to peel the pear as the texture of the skin has a little roughness to it. It can be cooked in any way you like, roasted or poached. It makes a lovely charlotte and even juices remarkably well.

GROWING NOTES

One of the reasons we have only planted two trees is that we must see how well this variety will do at Le Manoir, as it likes warmth and sunshine in order to produce a good crop of fruit following its spectacular white blossom. However, it is now being grown commercially in Kent, and we are hopeful that it will enjoy its new home in Oxfordshire. When picked in late September to early October, the fruit should store until late December.

DOYENNE DU COMICE

72 trees in my French and English orchards
Maine-et-Loire, France, 1849
SEASON: *October*
APPEARANCE: *quite heavy and dumpy;*
yellowish green with russeting
BEST FOR: *everything*

This is one of the pears that we use most in the kitchens at Le Manoir aux Quat'Saisons, since it doesn't bruise easily and once sliced you are introduced to an extraordinary palette of tastes and textures. For me, it is a true connoisseur's pear; the equivalent of the Cox's Orange Pippin (see page 84) in the world of apples. And like that fruit, it is so well known that it doesn't need its full name, and is usually just known as the Comice pear.

The original tree was raised by André Leroy, who was a nurseryman at the Garden of the Comice Horticole at Angers in Maine-et-Loire in 1849, hence the name. Leroy introduced it to America in 1852 and the following year, according to Joan Morgan in *The Book of Pears*, it was listed in Britain in the Horticultural Society of Chiswick Fruit Collection. However, it is generally accepted that it was properly introduced in 1858 by Sir Thomas Dyke Acland, politician, and a trustee of the Royal Agricultural Society.

By the 1890s it was also being grown in Washington, and Oregon – where Samuel Rosenberg of Bear Creek Orchards, having tasted the Doyenne du Comice, bought up some orchards that were growing the variety in southern Oregon. When Samuel died, his sons Harry and David took over the business and decided to rename the Comice the Royal Riviera. Ironically they marketed the newly named luxury fruit back to customers in Europe through their Harry & David food company, which introduced a mail-order service in the 1930s, sending out the pears across America. To this day, their sons still send out Royal Riviera pears, beautifully packaged in gift boxes.

Writing in *The Fruit Manual*, Robert Hogg refers to the Comice as 'A most delicious pear; in use in the end of October, and continuing throughout November. M. Andre Leroy recommends that to preserve this as long in use as possible it is necessary to gather it early and dry; and after placing it in the fruit-room to handle it as little as possible.' He also quotes R. D. Blackmore, author of the novel *Lorna Doone*, writing from the walled market garden in Teddington that he created late in life and where he specialised in pears: 'This is, to my mind, the best of all pears,' noted Blackmore, 'very healthy, a certain cropper, of beautiful growth, and surpassing flavour.'

TASTING AND COOKING NOTES
White-fleshed, juicy and melting with intense perfumes, the Comice consistently excels at everything, from juice to compote and tarts. It poaches and preserves beautifully and my Chef Pâtissier, Benoit, and myself have made many wonderful desserts with it. For the cook, and for anyone who loves a great fruit, this pear is amongst the world's best. When perfectly ripe it barely needs cooking. Just warm it in the oven for a few minutes.

GROWING NOTES
Like most of the great pears, this variety does not like chalk soils. The blossom is resistant to late frosts, but nevertheless the tree needs a warm location and will particularly benefit from a warm wall. When happy in its surroundings it will crop regularly. If picked in mid-October the fruit can be stored until mid-to-late November.

FAUVANELLE

17 trees in my French orchard
Franche-Comté, France, 1911
SEASON: late October
APPEARANCE: deep red, bronze, and russeted
BEST FOR: patisserie

I am very attached to this pear as it is thought to come from Haute-Saône in my region of Franche-Comté. Little else is known about its history, except that it was recorded in 1911 by the Pomological Society of France – M. Chasset, Secretary General of the Society, thought it to be the finest of all cooking pears – and it was introduced throughout France and into Switzerland by the Bey-Rozet Nursery in Marnay. The pears were certainly planted throughout Franche-Comté and were always popular and especially prized by pâtissiers, as the pear easily absorbs sugar and holds its shape when baked. Some say these are the best of all pears for baking.

TASTING AND COOKING NOTES
A small pear, the Fauvanelle is quite chewy – this is not a pear with a melting texture – but is still juicy with a little acidity, though not as much as other varieties and it doesn't reach the succulent heights of a pear like Beurre Hardy (see page 179). It is good poached in red wine and, as predicted, bakes phenomenally well – it is typically used in pear and almond cakes.

This variety was also traditionally put inside a bottle of pear eau de vie, which lends a great beauty and drama to the bottle when it is brought to the table. As a child I was always fascinated as to how a pear could fit through the narrow neck of a bottle, but of course later I discovered it wasn't so much of a conjuring trick, after all, as a thin branch would be fed through just as it was beginning to fruit, and the pear would continue to grow inside.

GROWING NOTES
The trees are tolerant of cold winters, and when picked in October should store until around March.

FONDANTE D'AUTOMNE

33 trees in my English and French orchards
Maubeuge, 1825
SEASON: *mid-September*
APPEARANCE: *greeny yellow with patches of russet*
BEST FOR: *everything*

Thirty-three trees might seem a lot for a single pear, but I chose to plant so many in our orchard as this is a fruit with many exceptional qualities.

It is quite a mysterious pear, with many different names and two possible birth stories, from either side of the France/Belgium border. The one, of course, that I would like to believe is that it was raised in Maubeuge, in the North of France, very close to the border, in around 1825 by a nurseryman called Monsieur Fiévée. The case for the Maubeuge connection appears to make sense because two of this pear's other names are Fondante de Maubeuge and Bergamote Fiévée.

However, the alternative claim is that the pear was raised at around the same time in Belgium, and that it was another creation of the keen amateur grower and retired general Major Pierre-Joseph Espéren, who also helped to develop the Winter Nélis (see page 204) in his home town of Mechelen, or Malines, as it was known in France.

Evidence for the Belgian claim is bolstered by another of the pear's names: Seigneur d'Espéren. Also, it seems that the variety was sent to Britain by Louis Stoffels, a nurseryman in Malines, under yet another alternative name, Belle Lucrative – by which it was also known in America, where it arrived in Salem, Massachusetts, around 1835/6.

Which nation really raised the pear first, we will probably never know. What is more certain is that the nursery which received the variety in Britain was that of John Braddick of Thames Ditton, who sent scions to the Horticultural Society of London. The variety was grown in their gardens in Chiswick in 1831, where it was described as 'another of the new Flemish pears' – so another vote for Belgium! By this time it was known as Fondante d'Automne, and it was soon held in high esteem as one of the best and most handsome of late pears.

TASTING AND COOKING NOTES

When pears have *fondante* in their name, like *beurre* the term suggests a fine pear with a soft, melting texture. I really love this pear. It is particularly sweet and juicy with no graininess to its shiny, snow-white flesh.

It is beautiful juiced, in compotes, poached, baked or in savoury dishes: a pure treat whatever recipe you choose.

GROWING NOTES

Despite its French – or Belgian – origins, this pear seems at home in the British climate, and it is quite resistant to many of the diseases that normally afflict pears, so it is a good variety for gardens. The relatively small trees can crop abundantly and in autumn the leaves turn a lovely red colour. When picked in mid-September, the pears can be eaten straight from the tree, or stored into October.

POIRE DU CURÉ

2 trees in my French orchard
Indre, France, 1760
SEASON: *October*
APPEARANCE: *greeny gold and russeted*
BEST FOR: *slow poaching in wine*

This tiny pear is a reminder of many childhood escapades of hunting and gathering in our local forest with my partner in crime, René. This was one of the largest forests in Europe, in which you could regularly get lost, so you never went alone. From searching for berries to dozens of different wild mushrooms, crab apples and wild pears, these adventures were some of the happiest of my youth, and they forged the deep connection with seasonality that is the driving force of everything we do at Le Manoir aux Quat'Saisons.

It was one autumn when the trees were turning to rust and gold that we found a particular pear tree growing in a clearing, heavy with stocky green fruit, speckled with brown – surely one of nature's loveliest presents. The pears were not for biting into – they were woody and tight – but we gathered as many as we could carry and took them home for Maman to make into the most delicious *Poire du Curé au vin rouge*. Of course, it was absolutely normal for a French child to enjoy desserts made with alcohol – my mum always assumed that when cooked, the alcohol would disappear, but this is not quite true!

We always called these pears Poire du Curé. However, we frequently had our own names for certain varieties and I cannot be sure whether the pear we found was actually a seedling of the true Poire du Curé variety, or whether we just gave it this name because our adventure in the forest mirrored the first discovery of this variety back in 1760. As always there are small variations on the story, but the gist of it is that it was found in the woods of Fromenteau in Indre by M. Leroy, who was a parish priest (*curé*) in nearby Villiers. According to Robert Hogg, the priest found the seedling 'sufficiently remarkable, to induce him to propagate it. He grafted it in a vineyard adjoining his garden, and from thence have come the innumerable trees to be found in the neighbourhood.'

The pear was known by various other names around France and eventually it was propagated in Britain by the Reverend William Lewis Rham of Winkfield, in Berkshire – another of those clergymen of the eighteenth and nineteenth centuries who was also known as an agriculturalist – and in the UK it became known as the Vicar of Winkfield.

TASTING AND COOKING NOTES

I am waiting for the first harvest of these fruits to see if they compare with 'my' Poire du Curé, which, if kept for two months, would slowly develop more of its sugar and flavour and could be eaten raw as it was no longer woody, although still firm. It poached so well, with red wine, cinnamon, black pepper and a couple of slices of lemon, and once cooled down we would put it into the fridge to eat cold. Of course, it wasn't a sophisticated pear, and perhaps the enjoyment was more related to the triumph of finding this food for free, but I await my Oxfordshire 'Priest's Pears' with interest.

GROWING NOTES

A vigorous spreading tree, this variety should crop well, but can drop its fruit before they are ready to be harvested. It is also prone to damage from the codling moth. The pears are best harvested in the second half of October and allowed to ripen slowly in storage for use from December through to January, though they will most likely be at their best at Christmas.

WILLIAMS' BON CHRÉTIEN

22 trees in my French orchard
Berkshire, around 1770
SEASON: *end of August*
APPEARANCE: *smooth-skinned and golden*
BEST FOR: *everything!*

This is a truly beautiful pear, which has the greatest qualities any such fruit can offer. Along with the Doyenne du Comice (see page 192) it is the most used variety in our kitchens at Le Manoir aux Quat'Saisons and I treasure the twenty-two Williams trees that we planted in the French orchard. I grew up in Franche-Comté knowing and loving this pear and it always made me feel so proud of the French nurserymen who created such a divine fruit – or so I thought. Then – and I could scarcely believe it – I discovered that the pear comes originally from Berkshire!

I still joke with my English friends that the story must be part of a conspiracy to steal the credit for this beautiful, golden-yellow pear, but the experts insist that it was either 'found or raised' in the garden of a schoolmaster, Mr Wheeler, at Aldermaston in or around 1770. Or, according to another account, it was a schoolmaster called John Stair who raised it – it is possible that he inherited the garden from Mr Wheeler – and that the fruit was originally known as Stair's Pear!

Mr Wheeler or Mr Stair sent some grafts to the nurseryman Richard Williams at Turnham Green, who exhibited the fruit to the Horticultural Society of London, and in 1816 it was given the name of Williams' Bon Chrétien by another William, the botanist William

Townsend (W. T.) Aiton, who had followed his father as Director of Kew Gardens.

Why, then, is this pear called by the French words for 'Good Christian'? This, of course, is its full title, which is rarely used since, like the Cox's Orange Pippin (see page 84), the pear is so famous it usually goes by the short version, Williams (although, in America, the variety is known by the completely different name of Bartlett; but more of that later). As to how the pear got its unusual name, there are many different theories. First we have to go back to Robert Hogg. In *The Fruit Manual* he lists many very old varieties with the suffix Bon Chrétien – the oldest appears to be the Bon-Chrétien d'Hiver (Winter) – so it is likely that this was a fond, generic term for a group of similar sweet, juicy pears, which according to Hogg's friend, Dominique Dupuy, Professor of Natural History at Auch, were shaped 'like a calabash, or pilgrim's gourd'.

Perhaps it was as simple as that. However, another story, suggested by Joan Morgan in her *Book of Pears*, is that Francis of Paola, who founded the Roman Catholic Order of Minims in Italy in the fifteenth century, was called to the court of Louis XI to tend to him in his last illness. It is said that he brought with him some pears from Italy, which became known as Le Bon Chrétien, after St Francis.

In another tale of saints and kings, it is said that an unnamed king of France, having tasted the fruit with St Martin, who became Bishop of Tours in around AD 375, later asked for *'des poires de ce bon Chrétien'*. A different version again, told by the physician Jean Ruel in 1536, is that this kind of pear was introduced to France from Naples by King Charles VIII 'The Affable', in 1495. And if we go back to Robert Hogg, his alternative, more obscure theory was that the term *'bon chrétien'* derived from the Greek *'panchresta'*, meaning 'all good', and referred to the fact that the fruit did not rot at the core.

And so to more confusion involving the American name for the pear: Bartlett. In 1799 the Williams was taken to America by one James Carter of Boston on behalf of Thomas Brewer, who planted it on his farm in Roxbury, Massachusetts. In 1817 the estate was bought by Enoch Bartlett, a merchant and farmer from Dorchester, Massachusetts, who decided to progatate the pear trees that were growing in his fields and introduce the fruit to the market. He didn't know the name of the variety, so he called it after himself. By the time it was discovered that this was in fact the Williams pear, it was too late, the name had stuck, and it has been known in America as the Bartlett pear ever since. Hogg, in *The Herefordshire Pomona*, noted that the variety 'attains the highest perfection in America, and is esteemed as the finest and best keeping pear of its season, it has even been brought back to England with its new name'.

I still find it hard to believe that it wasn't until 1828 that the Williams was introduced to France, by Léon Leclerc. He was a fruit grower in Laval in the Western Loire and another friend of the ubiquitous Belgian pear-breeder Jean-Baptiste Van Mons (one of Leclerc's own-bred pears is actually called Van Mons Léon Leclerc). Ironically it was the widespread cultivation of the Williams' Bon Chrétien in France that later contributed to the decline of the market for it in Britain, where the pear had reached its height of fame and popularity around the 1840s. At this time it was planted in the orchards of country houses, sold in nurseries around the country, and by barrow boys on the streets of London. It had become the standard by which all pears were judged, and was one of the varieties recommended at the great National Pear Conference of 1885 (see page 185). By the end of the eighteenth century, however, the Williams pears from France, which ripened earlier, were making it into the London markets first!

TASTING AND COOKING NOTES

Fully ripe, the pear delivers the ultimate pear experience. It is heavy and thin-skinned, with melting, aromatic and delicious flesh. It has more perfumes than any other pear I have tasted and these are supported by a delicate acidity, which gives the pear great length of flavour.

Equally it poaches, roasts and preserves well, and so with my Chef Pâtissier, Benoit, I have created many wonderful desserts using this pear. And of course it has lent its name to one of the greatest French liqueurs, Poire William.

One of the most planted pears around the world, it is also the most widely used in the canning industry, so if you buy a tin of pears they are likely to be Williams. The reason is simple: this pear has the best texture and delicious flavour, but most importantly, it has the most incredible perfumes of any of the varieties, which remain, even in a tin. I would like to suggest that you bottle some for yourself (see page 299) and keep them in the cupboard to bring out for a beautiful quick dessert to share with family and friends.

GROWING NOTES

The Williams is tolerant of late frosts and hardy enough to grow well even in the North of England, though it prefers a sunny position, and, as with other fine pears, it does not like chalk soils. I hope I can tempt you to grow this tree, even if you only have a small space. It would look so elegant grown as an espalier against the wall of your house. Imagine then watching this beautiful tree through the seasons as the stark sculptural branches of winter burst into blossom before finally rewarding you with beautiful golden fruits.

WINTER NÉLIS

4 trees in my English orchard
Belgium, early 1800s
SEASON: *mid-October*
APPEARANCE: *pale gold, ripening to cinnamon-coloured russet*
BEST FOR: *everything*

I have so much respect for the dreamers, scientists and nurserymen who embark on a journey of discovery with the single hope of giving the world a new flavour experience. In this case it was a lawyer and a retired general from Napoleon's army who came together to do just that.

Jean Charles Nélis, who gave his name to this pear, was an amateur horticulturalist and councillor at the Court in the city of Mechelen in Belgium (which at the time was also known by its French name of Malines). Major Pierre-Joseph Espéren was the retired general, who took up pear-breeding. Between them they raised two of the most famous, fine-textured, sweet and perfumed late-season pears of the era: Joséphine de Malines and Winter Nélis.

In the eighteenth century, Belgium was a huge centre for the development of pear varieties, particularly those with the sought-after 'buttery' texture, and both men were in touch with the most famous breeder and promoter of pears of the day, Jean-Baptiste Van Mons, who first named the new variety La Bonne Malinoise. Van Mons regularly sent samples of fruit, scions and trees to the Horticultural Society of London and in 1818 he presented La Bonne Malinoise to them, which was renamed the Winter Nélis.

The variety was described by Robert Hogg in *The Herefordshire Pomona* as 'one of the best in quality. It is a very general favourite, and the more so perhaps, because it is always ready to enrich the dessert table through the festivities of Christmas.'

I wouldn't say that the Winter Nélis is the greatest looker, wrapped in its shades of brown and cinnamon, with flashes of yellow when ripe. However, it is a pear with many great virtues.

TASTING AND COOKING NOTES
Heavily perfumed, with white, delicately textured, succulent flesh, this is a sumptuous pear with wonderful gradations of flavour. From juicing to poaching and roasting, the Winter Nélis is great for most desserts and it preserves very well, so you can continue to enjoy the fruit long after it has been picked (see page 299).

GROWING NOTES
The Winter Nélis does well as an espalier against a wall, and can be grown in a pot, which is useful as pear trees are usually on the large side, and there is no true dwarfing stock available as there is for apple trees. The trees are hardy, beautiful at blossom time and have deep burgundy-coloured leaves in autumn. They generally crop very well – we have planted four trees in our orchard, and each year they have produced great fruit. Again, they do not like chalk soils and though they are known to appreciate a dry, warm situation, our trees have adapted well and are able to withstand the wetter British climate. The pears are great keepers and when picked in October can be stored until January.

IN SEARCH OF THE PERFECT QUINCE

I love quince. Such extraordinary and dramatic fruits. To look at them, so heavy, rippling and muscular, covered in a fine down, they appear totally masculine, and yet when you cut through the hard, hard flesh – and believe me you have to be strong – the core and seeds are completely feminine. I find this so entrancing that at one time I asked an artist to portray the sensuality of the quince on a canvas that could be hung on a wall of the restaurant at Le Manoir, like a perfect Bonnard still life.

These ancient fruits are originally from the Caucasus Mountains of Iran and Armenia. In Victorian times every walled garden would have had a quince tree amongst the pears and apples, but although there has been a revival in the fashion for membrillo, *the beautiful quince paste for serving with cheese, few people grow quince these days.*

About ten to fifteen years ago I planted some quince trees in the gardens at Le Manoir. The variety was Vranja. Sadly they never seemed happy and didn't fruit well – so we moved them to a spot right in front of the windows of the kitchen; and there they have flourished. Every year my team and I are inspired when the trees burst into white blossom – with just a hint of pink – and invariably they present us with sixty to seventy fruits.

Now, as an experiment, we have planted in the orchard five trees of an old American variety, Champion, which dates back to 1850, and should produce big fruit that are slightly more round and even more knobbly than Vranja. I am told they should do well in Oxfordshire, but it is early days and they have yet to produce fruit.

The very best quinces I have tasted so far are the magnificent fruits grown in the long-established orchards of Waterperry Gardens, close to Le Manoir. When I first saw the tree, about six metres tall, it was breathtaking to behold, hung with huge, heavy greenish-yellow fruits. I asked if I could try them and was generously given some to take back to our kitchens. When we cooked them it was a new quince experience. Their skins seemed to me to be thinner, and the flesh much less hard and easier to cut than other varieties. Usually a quince has a harsh tartness and needs a lot of sugar to bring out its flavour, but these were different. The cooking process was shorter, the graininess disappeared as their flesh turned a deep orange, almost a rich amber; and became unctuous and sweet, but with just the right trace of tartness. The flavour was gentle, but well defined.

Imagine my astonishment when I asked what this variety was, and was told it was Vranja – the same as the trees outside our kitchen at Le Manoir. This was a huge affirmation of the influence of terroir and age on a fruit. Quince trees can live for over a hundred years, and the tree at Waterperry has stood in the orchard for around thirty years. Will Sibley tells me that, in his experience, the older the tree, the bigger the fruit, and our friends the Delbard family have an old tree in France that boasts monster quinces the size of a football. Also, says Will, 'quinces love water', and so the situation of the Waterperry orchard and nursery close to the River Thame, a tributary of the Thames, with canals running through it, must also have contributed to the outstanding size and character of the fruit. I hope that as the years pass our own Vranja will turn out to be just as fabulous; and I wait with excitement for the first of our Champion trees to bear fruit in the orchard, so that we can discover how these fruits compare. When you come to Le Manoir, we will invite you to try our classic dessert 'Autumn Still Life' in which quince will be celebrated.

VIOLETTE DE BORDEAUX (FIG)

2 trees in my French orchard
South West France, around 1680
SEASON: *August*
APPEARANCE: *small/medium, purple/black, with deep red pulp*
BEST FOR: *eating fresh, jam*

I was thirteen when I first went to Provence. It was like discovering a new and infinitely different continent, full of vivid colours, aromas, flavours and textures. A local man saw me admiring the sculptured leaves of a fig tree, which I had never seen before. From inside the foliage he twisted off a gorgeous deep purple, tear-shaped fruit, its skin lightly blistered, and told me it was the variety from Solliès, the best and possibly the world's most famous fig. The first bite revealed the inner beauty of the carmine-shaded flesh, textured with thousands of micro-seeds, rich and delicately perfumed. It was pure ambrosia.

Seven or eight years ago, remembering that moment, I asked Anne Marie and James to plant a fig tree against the sixteenth-century dovecote, which is one of the most romantic corners of Le Manoir. Of course I knew that the Figue de Solliès, more used to the sunshine of the South of France, would not be happy in Oxfordshire, but certain varieties of fig have been grown successfully in England since Victorian times, in the right location with tender, loving care. The variety we were advised was the best for our area was the Violette de Bordeaux. This is a very old French variety, sometimes called Negronne (amongst other names), which is native to the South West, and is one of the figs described in 1692 by Jean Baptiste de La Quintinie, director of Le Potager du Roi, the famous fruit and vegetable garden at Versailles under Louis XIV. Since the King was so fond of figs, La Quintinie created a hollowed-out *figuerie*. It was said that he planted some seven hundred trees of different varieties and, since the fig garden was so sheltered, it allowed him to push forward the fruiting of the trees to mid-June, which is five or six weeks earlier than their normal season – even in the cooler environs of Paris.

James planted the tree himself, and decided to grow it in a fan shape, but he found that the branches were constantly reaching for the skies and producing a heavy growth of leaves, with hardly any fruit. So the great man that is Will Sibley came to help. Will suggested training the tree differently in a series of spirals and curves, which allows smaller shoots to grow along each curve, slowing down the growth. Now, even though it is in a position where it doesn't see the sun all day, it produces plenty of sweet, fleshy, juicy figs. It was a quite ingenious and beautiful solution. Everyone stops to look at the fig tree, which has made our dovecote corner even more romantic and beautiful each season.

TASTING AND COOKING NOTES
Of course these figs are best eaten fresh and fully ripe, but they also make the best jam. When dried, we make them into an ice cream with an extraordinary texture and flavour.

GROWING NOTES
This variety can crop twice a year. It can cope with drought, has good resistance to pests and diseases and will grow in cooler conditions, though it still needs a sunny, sheltered spot, preferably against a wall. In more northerly areas it can be planted in a container and brought inside somewhere cool, away from frosts, over winter. Most figs fruit better in a rich soil with a restricted root-run to help prevent them producing foliage at the expense of fruit. Some people advocate setting some paving slabs into the ground to create a 'container' around the roots, but a big pot will achieve the same effect.

NÉFLIER À GROS FRUITS (MEDLAR)

3 trees in my French orchard
Holland, pre-1859
SEASON: *late October*
APPEARANCE: *large, yellow/orange flushed with red*
BEST FOR: *jelly*

My grandfather introduced me to the weird *néflier*, or medlar, a strange, fascinating, mystical fruit that looks like it belongs to pre-historic times. He grew them in the orchard that he tended, and in late spring to early summer the trees would be covered in pure white blossom. This was the beauty before these ugly beasts of fruits arrived in late October – they are so unattractive to look at that in the North of France they call this fruit '*le cul de chien*' (the backside of the dog)!

Medlars are too sharp to eat raw, but they can be ripened on the tree – they can even be left beyond the first frosts if possible; or they can be picked and stored, so that they ripen (not rot, or ferment as sometimes described) over two or three weeks. This process is known as 'bletting'. During this time the starches turn into sugars and the hard flesh softens and turns into brown mush.

My grandfather showed me how to squeeze the fruit and suck the squishy, sweet flesh straight into my mouth, spitting out the five large pips. But these were not fruits for a child, and I never took to their sweet, light, earthy taste until my grandmother, the kitchen magician, turned them into amazing preserves.

I have stayed fascinated by this odd fruit, which originates in ancient Persia (now Iran) and was grown by the Greeks and Romans. In

Britain the Elizabethans and Victorians were equally fascinated by medlars. They loved them, but later they fell out of favour. Now, though, there is something of a revival of interest in these oddities, and I just had to include some trees in our orchard.

TASTING AND COOKING NOTES
Although once tree-ripened or bletted it is possible to eat a raw medlar, it is an acquired taste, which some people liken to 'custard and dates'! However, these fruits really come into their own when turned into a beautiful pinkish-red jelly to eat with cheese or game.

GROWING NOTES
Xavier planted three of these ancient and intriguing fruit trees in our French orchard. Néflier à Gros Fruits simply means a large-fruited medlar, and there are various varieties – Nottingham is one commonly grown in Britain – all quite similar. Medlars will tolerate most fertile, well-drained soils, but like a warm, sheltered spot out of the wind. They are largely free of pests and diseases and give a superb show in the garden with large white flowers followed by autumn-coloured leaves, not to mention the unusual fruits. Pruning well in winter helps to produce good blossom and fruit.

STONE
FRUITS

Cherries, peaches, apricots and the wonderful plum family are at the heart of our French orchard, planted with the help of my great friends Xavier and Pierre-Marie Guillaume, and since most of these trees have been grown not twenty miles from the house where I grew up, it fills my heart with joy to see them here with me in Oxfordshire.

When I see the peaches beginning to ripen, I recall the beautiful letter I received from an English lady who had picked up a slightly unripe peach in the South of France and brought it home to let it finish ripening on her windowsill. The way she wrote about slowly anticipating the juiciness, the melting flesh, and then the sensual satisfaction of finally tasting the peach, was so seductive and hugely flirty. And then at the end she closed the letter by saying to me, 'Monsieur Blanc, I hope you will forgive me, I am an old lady of ninety years of age, who still dreams a little.' Oh, how I loved that letter! And the story tells you everything you need to know about the wonder of a ripe peach.

Most of the tender peach and apricot trees in the orchard are still young, and we try to protect them as we would babies as they blossom, swaddling them in a fine veil of cotton. Even so, sometimes we fail. Alas, this year while the trees trained against the walls at the entrance to Le Manoir were laden with fruit, the apricots in the open field of the orchard were exposed to too much frost, icy winds, rain and snow. Of course, I was distraught, but sometimes you have to accept that there is only so much you can do against the forces of nature, and sometimes nature wins, which is always humbling.

And so to cherries. How I wish we could rediscover the joy of waiting for the local season. The shires around Le Manoir used to be famous for their cherries. In Buckinghamshire the local black varieties were nicknamed 'chuggies' and as late as the 1960s the first Sunday in August was known as 'Cherry Pie Sunday' to mark the end of the harvest. Northampton, too, was notable in the eighteenth century for its acres of cherry orchards within the old town walls. At the annual cherry festival people came from miles around to eat the fruit and drink ale. And the remnants of large cherry orchards can still be discovered dotted in between the beech woods of Berkshire.

So I felt sure we could grow cherries well. The big problem is how to protect them from the birds! At one time cherry trees grew so huge that netting them involved supporting the nets with posts like ships' masts, and often small boys would be paid a pittance to patrol orchards, shaking loud rattles to scare the birds instead!

However, the good news for anyone wanting to grow a tree in the garden nowadays is that there are genuine dwarfing rootstocks available (see page 262), and especially if the tree is grown against a wall, they are much easier to net and harvest.

As I mentioned in the introduction to this book, the sorry sight of a carpet of fallen, rotting plums in the Vale of Evesham was one of the big catalysts for our orchard project. I was filming an episode for the TV series *The Great British Food Revival* in this beautiful vale, where, since 1910, plums had been the main crop. Although I did see some healthy orchards full of gorgeous fruit from the famous Victoria (see page 260) variety to golden Yellow Egg plums and Purple Pershores, I was keen to understand why so many acres of orchard had been abandoned.

I found out that during the First World War plums were still a valuable crop because plum jam was one of the staples of the British diet, as it was cheap and easy to produce. But once the war was over, there was a demand for fresh fruit again. And this was a problem for the growers because the British weather was unpredictable, and could ruin an entire crop. British plums with truly exquisite flavours, like Transparent Gage and Coe's Golden Drop, tended to be too fragile to be grown commercially; others, like the Yellow Egg and Purple Pershores, had been grown primarily for canning or for jam, and only the Victoria plum now had the commercial quality to match the cheaper fruit coming in, mainly from Europe, South Africa and California. This would arrive around three weeks ahead of the local varieties. And to add to the growers' tribulations, the railways capitalised on the new overseas markets by offering lower rates for freight trains bringing fruit from the ports to London to sell at the Covent Garden fruit market.

By the 1930s, the 'tragic stage' of the industry around Evesham was being debated in Parliament, and the middlemen were making money at the expense of consumers who had to pay high prices, while the growers received a relative pittance – a story that is still true today.

So, in my small way I felt I must restore some plum growing to my county at least. But although I wanted to champion the great British Victoria plum, I also wanted to show off the varieties that I love from my region of France and, unlike the apricots, our plums have been so successful. I was particularly proud of our Agen plums (see page 248), and when I saw our Reine Claude gages (see page 257) and Mirabelle de Metz (see page 251) ripening, I jumped for joy.

THE FIRST APRICOTS

Beyond the large cast-iron gates (which are always open) at the entrance to Le Manoir aux Quat'Saisons, four large espalier apricots, trained in a fan shape to receive as much sun as possible, adorn the old fifteenth-century yellow Oxford stone walls. I wanted to pass on a very powerful message to our guests: 'You are about to enter a magical place of beauty where food, and the growing of it, are at the heart of everything.' They were planted in 2008, long before I created the orchard, but the search for the right variety of apricot was part of the adventure, the dreaming, the planning and research aimed at proving that fruits more used to the sunshine of the South of France or Italy could be grown in Britain. And I thought I would be the first, like one of the great Victorian horticultural pioneers!

With my great friend and fruit expert William Sibley I visited many of the apricot-growing regions of France, including St-Gilles, just south of Nîmes, where the blossoms form later and are more resistant to frost, so it was thought that the varieties that flourished there could also thrive in the cooler, wetter Oxfordshire climate. William knew two, Tomcot® and Flavorcot®, that were being trialled in Nîmes, and which had been developed at Washington State University by Tom Toyama, 'a brilliant stone-fruit breeder', in around 1980, and these were the ones he recommended.

Having found our apricots, we celebrated in glorious French style, drinking a toast to the idea of this wonderful golden fruit gracing my Oxfordshire gardens. We planted the trees and lovingly trained them against the walls, so that they would be protected from frost and warmed by the sun, and they are magnificent in every season. The dramatic barren skeletons of winter are transformed by the cascading white blossoms of spring, and then the first, tiny fruit begin to appear until, in summer, the branches are heavy with a multitude of perfectly formed, orange-blushed fruit dotted with red. Tomcot® is the first to ripen, around mid-July, then Flavorcot® follows about two weeks later.

Plucked straight from the branches, the apricots are excellent, if not quite as sweet as the fruits of Provence, but when you bake them in a tart the catalyst of heat deepens the colour and flavour into a perfect harmony of acidity and sugar.

When I harvested my first apricots I was the happiest man on earth, the great trailblazer. Then I discovered that there is a village on the border of Oxfordshire and Northamptonshire called Aynho, which dates back to Saxon times and is known as 'the apricot village' because they have been growing apricots there for hundreds of years. What a lesson in humility! I had to go and see for myself with my lovely head gardener, Anne Marie, and what a blissful sight it was: almost every cottage and house had an apricot tree trained against a wall, covered in white blossoms. No one knows for sure when the apricot tradition began, but it is thought that the diplomat Thomas Cartwright, whose family bought the manor house Aynhoe Park in 1615, may have had the trees planted some time in the early eighteenth century. And it seems this wasn't the only part of Northamptonshire where apricots were grown from the early seventeenth century, as it is known that at the Paulerspury Estate, half an hour's drive away, Sir Arthur Throckmorton, brother-in-law of Sir Walter Raleigh, created an orchard and grew apricots, which were also trained in espaliers against a wall of the mansion.

Marcus Roberts unearthed a copy of the London Bicycle Club Gazette *from much later, in 1880, which recorded that on one of their rural rides through Northamptonshire, arriving at Aynho '. . . we were surprised at the number of apricot trees on the walls*

219

of the houses, and every tree loaded with fruit. Even in the streets every house had its tree, and anyone walking on the pavement could easily help himself.' According to local stories, however, delivery boys were always sternly warned not to pick the apricots!

Whatever the origins, Aynho is a great story of the importance of terroir, as the village is mostly south-facing, sits on limestone and is well irrigated with spring water, and so it has the perfect micro-climate for apricots.

BERGERON (APRICOT)

10 trees in my French orchard
Mont d'Or, France, 1920s
SEASON: *early September*
APPEARANCE: *large, yellow/orange flushed with red*
BEST FOR: *eating fresh, juice, tarts and jam*

This is considered to be one of the great classic French apricots, and is probably the variety that is most commonly grown commercially. It originates from the Rhône Valley. Although more famous for its wines, between the wars this region was planted with many orchards and, in summer, students and fruit pickers would descend on the valley for the harvest of apricots and other fruits. Here, in the 1920s, the Bergeron was found as a chance seedling by Pierre Bergeron of Saint-Cyr-au-Mont-d'Or. Originally he named it Gabrielle Bergeron, after his daughter, and it is still sometimes known by her full name.

TASTING AND COOKING NOTES
This is a variety that is often picked unripe and exported, but in order to experience its full deliciousness it must be completely ripe, and then it is extraordinary. The fruit is quite big, sweet, firm-fleshed and beautifully perfumed. Yet there is also enough acidity to produce a beautiful juice, or 'nectar' as it is known, when bottled in the region.

This is the perfect apricot for a tart, as it will hold its form with a lengthy perfume, and it features in one of my classic desserts, Cassolette d'Abricot. It is also famously made into Bergeron apricot jam.

GROWING NOTES

The beautiful pink blossom appears early and can be susceptible to frost, so this is a variety that really needs a sunny, sheltered south-facing position, although if properly protected it can cope with the British winter. In its first year at Le Manoir it produced a wonderful harvest, but this year, sadly, it failed.

POLONAIS (APRICOT)

6 trees in my French orchard
France, date unknown
SEASON: *late July/August*
APPEARANCE: *orange flushed with red*
BEST FOR: *eating fresh, juice and jam*

This is a very old French variety, which in the South East of France, where it is grown prolifically round Nyons, is called Orange de Provence. However, in my region it is known as the Polonais, or Polish apricot. It is said that the name is in tribute to the Polish King, Stanisław I Leszczyński, who became the Duke of Lorraine and Bar, and whose daughter Marie eventually married Louis XV and so became Queen of France.

Stanisław was a nobleman who was given the throne by Charles XII of Sweden after his army invaded Poland and deposed the then monarch, Augustus II. In the years that followed, Stanisław was alternately removed and reinstated, and spent one of his periods of exile in Alsace. Eventually the Peace Treaty of 1738 saw Augustus III installed as King, but Stanisław was allowed to keep his royal titles and given the provinces of Lorraine and Bar.

His court in Lorraine was known for culture and science, and it is said that he particularly loved this variety of apricot. And the King has another great claim to fame, as he is credited with the original idea for the famous dessert rum baba. Of course, as always, there are many different versions of the story: one is that the king, who had a sweet tooth, dipped some local Kugelhopf yeast cake, which was too dry for his taste, into a glass of sweet wine. Later his pastry chef, Nicolas Stohrer, who followed Queen Maria to Versailles, is said to have enhanced the idea by flavouring the cake with rum. Both rum baba and Kugelhopf have become great classics – the best Kugelhopf I ever tasted was at Christine Ferber's wonderful patisserie in Niedermorschwihr, in Alsace, where she is also famous for her artisan fruit jams.

Sadly poor Stanisław came to a very nasty end, when a spark ignited his silk clothing as he slept by the fire, and he died later of his injuries. It can be hard to separate true history from legend, but this last part, at least, is a fact!

TASTING AND COOKING NOTES
Eaten fresh, the apricots are meltingly juicy and perfumed, with enough acidity to save them from being cloyingly sweet. They make a beautiful juice for mixing with sparkling wine and they are excellent for jam (see page 312).

GROWING NOTES
When Xavier Guillaume suggested planting six of these trees, I was a little sceptical and anxious because, although it is grown in Franche-Comté, this tree is at its most prolific in the South East and South of France, where they have very mild winters, relatively little rain and, of course, lots of sunshine. However, this is a hardy variety of apricot, and it fruited soon after planting.

PRÉCOCE DE SAUMUR (APRICOT)

6 trees in my French orchard
Saumur, France, 1960s
SEASON: *mid-July*
APPEARANCE: *golden, dusted with red*
BEST FOR: *tarts*

These are the earliest heralds of the apricot season. The story is that some time in the 1960s someone (we don't know who) took down a wall and found a tree growing in a piece of ground. A neighbour replanted it in his garden, where it could be seen from the street, and it attracted the attention of a nurseryman in nearby Doué-la-Fontaine, who marketed it, and its fame spread rapidly across Maine, the Loire – around the elegant town of Saumur – and the Touraine.

TASTING AND COOKING NOTES
A big flavour with a touch of acidity at the end, this apricot has little sugar and little juice, so when eaten fresh it is a bit on the dry side, although the flesh is still soft. However, when cooked the heat lifts all the flavours, sugars and acidity, so it makes some wonderful tarts and other desserts.

GROWING NOTES
This is a productive variety that has adapted well to the climate of Central and Northern France, so I am hoping that it will also like Oxfordshire. The danger always is the threat of late frosts, which can hit the blossom hard and compromise the fruit, so again, a wall – preferably south-facing – is the best position.

ROUGE TARDIF® (APRICOT)

1 tree in my French orchard
Malicorne, France, 1971
SEASON: *August*
APPEARANCE: *medium size, orange red*
BEST FOR: *eating fresh and compote*

We were only able to find one tree to plant of this variety of juicy, perfumed apricot, the relatively recent creation of my friend Monsieur Delbard, whose family is one of the most influential growers in France and beyond. But at least it allowed us to run a trial to see how these apricots, which are a little alien to our climate, will fare.

We planted the two-year-old tree as an espalier, and in its first year it produced about twenty apricots, which were truly delicious. This was a small victory, for sure, and it was reassuring to know that it was possible to grow the fruit in an open space. Unfortunately, this year, the horrendous frost that travelled down the hill through the orchard, followed by hail and strong icy winds, all conspired to murder the beautiful white flowers, and so we had no fruit. I was so disappointed, but we are constantly learning about these more delicate beauties that have joined us from France, and next year we will be ready to protect the blossom better.

TASTING AND COOKING NOTES
These apricots are a feast eaten just as they are. The flesh is soft and juicy and intensely perfumed, but not overpowering as can be the case with some apricots.

Because of their juiciness they break down far too quickly for jams, but they make especially beautiful compotes.

GROWING NOTES
This variety grows vigorously and can give a good crop. Xavier Guillaume, who planted our French orchard, promised me that the apricots should normally do very well here as the tree has a late flowering time and so next year we hope to miss the frosts, which decimated many of our apricots this year.

BIGARREAU BURLAT (CHERRY)

2 trees in my French orchard
Loire-sur-Rhône, France, 1915–1917
SEASON: *June*
APPEARANCE: *big, dark red fruits*
BEST FOR: *eating, clafoutis and tarts*

The Bigarreau Burlat is my favourite cherry since it connects me to wonderful childhood memories of hunter-gathering. My friend René and I would sneak stealthily through the tall grass of a cherry orchard close to our family house, trying to be incognito, constantly on the watch for the owner, and with our sights set on our targets: the five beautiful trees that bore what seemed to us to be millions of rich, dark, ruby-red cherries. These were the ultimate prize.

In the mind of the child that I was, I still remember the frisson of fear of the terrible punishment that might follow if we were caught in the act of marauding, but that was part of the thrill, and well worth it as we gorged ourselves on the cherries faster than any flock of birds could devour them. We ate so many that almost our entire faces were stained black with the sweet juices.

And now, thanks to my friend the fruit magician Xavier Guillaume, I have two of my favourite trees in the French orchard at Le Manoir aux Quat'Saisons. I wonder now why I did not plant more, but of course it was because we had to see how well they would fare in our part of Oxfordshire.

I only ever knew these cherries by the name of Bigarreau; it didn't occur to me that there might be many different varieties that carry the name, as in fact it is a generic term for a group of cherries that have a plump heart shape, are normally quite big, sweet and rich in flavour, but are firm-fleshed rather than overly juicy, and the trees are known to crop prolifically. In his *Fruit Manual*, Robert Hogg classified Bigarreaux, or 'white hearts', as having 'red or light-coloured mottled skin, and hard crackling flesh', and he listed numerous varieties, some of which date back to the early nineteenth century, from all around France and beyond, many with intriguing names, such as Bigarreau Napolean, Weeping Black Bigarreau, Bohemian Black Bigarreau, or Early Bed Bigarreau.

Bigarreau Burlat was found during the First World War as a seedling growing in a hedge in the district of Gerland, near Lyon, by Léonard Burlat. Burlat was a farmer and fruit grower who, in 1915, was mobilised, at the age of forty-three, to a factory making shells in the Artillery Park of Lyon in Gerland. The story goes that one spring day he noticed the seedling in blossom and returned again in May to find it bearing fruit. He took some cuttings and experimented with them back at his farm in Loire-sur-Rhône, eventually grafting some of the wood onto a six-year-old cherry tree in 1917. The fruit that it bore exceeded all his expectations, and a stunning new variety, originally named *Hâtif (early) Burlat*, was born (in France it is still known by this name).

These were the days before refrigerated transport and so, in order to see how well the new fruit would travel, it is said that he asked François Rossignol, a shipper in the Loire whose son was an importer of fruit in London, to send some cherries on a delivery run to London and back. When they came back five or six days later they were still in perfect condition, so he knew he was on to a winner. In 1925 the cherries were presented to the French Pomological Society and in 1931 Leonard's son, André, moved the fruit farm to Pierre-Bénite in the suburbs of Lyon, and began distributing the new cherry throughout France and beyond. It was renamed the Bigarreau Burlat and, in 1937, rapidly became one of the most popular cherries in France, so famous that there is a street bearing Léonard Burlat's name in Loire-sur-Rhône, in honour of his wonderful fruit.

TASTING AND COOKING NOTES
When sliced in half the Bigarreau Burlat offers the most beautiful spectacle, with thousands of micro-threads running through the ruby flesh.

I can certainly proclaim this to be one of the best dessert cherries, and it has the advantage of keeping well, so it is a lovely cherry for the fruit bowl. It is fantastic in a tart and will make a beautiful clafoutis (see page 329 for a version with mirabelles), though make sure that the cherries are not overripe, or they will produce too much juice in the oven. With this cherry I made one of my classic desserts at Le Manoir, *Le Paquet Surprise*, a biscuit parcel, filled with lemon compote and parfait, garnished with spiced cherries.

GROWING NOTES
An early variety, the Bigarreau Burlat trees herald the start of the cherry season, bursting into white blossom, and then in mid-to-late June they produce the beautiful, big, dark purply-red glossy cherries, so deep in colour that they can appear almost black. The trees are happy in most climates, and they can grow quite big, but as pruning can weaken the tree, it is best to do this only as lightly as possible, after harvest in August or September.

CARMELITE (CHERRY)

2 trees in my French orchard
Besançon, France, date unknown
SEASON: *end June/early July*
APPEARANCE: *black with dark red flesh and black juice*
BEST FOR: *eating fresh, clafoutis, tarts and bottling*

The first of the black cherries to arrive, this big, shiny, beautifully heart-shaped variety originates from Besançon, which is the capital of my region, Franche-Comté. My village, Saône, is only six miles away, and I used to eat these fleshy and juicy cherries by the handful as a child. Besançon is famous for its Couvent des Grands Carmes, the Convent of the Great Carmelites, which dates back to 1685 and which I believe gave the cherry its name.

You could almost claim that Franche-Comté is the capital of cherries – though my friends in Alsace and Kent may disagree. The whole region is particularly known for its black cherries, which are most famously made into kirsch, and every area has its favourite variety, which, of course, the locals will tell you makes the best alcohol.

TASTING AND COOKING NOTES
These cherries are best eaten straight from the tree or the bowl. When slightly underripe they are excellent for clafoutis and tarts, but when fully ripe, if you try to pit them you will make a big juicy mess! They make beautiful dark juice, and are lovely bottled in kirsch (see page 323) to store for the winter. They also freeze well.

GROWING NOTES
This is a hardy variety, yielding a good crop of cherries.

COEUR DE PIGEON (CHERRY)

2 trees in my French orchard
Rhône, France, 1540
SEASON: *mid-June*
APPEARANCE: *large, yellow and red*
BEST FOR: *eating fresh*

So many French stone fruits are a mystery. It is as if, like spies, they have many aliases, but their true past has been erased – I wonder why so many secrets?

All I can tell you about this magnificent, pretty, yellow and red heart-shaped Bigarreau variety of cherry is that it is probably from Anjou originally and is recorded from 1540, but may have been known for much longer. It was a favourite for planting next to family homes, so that the fruit could be picked and eaten fresh, transformed into tarts, clafoutis and other desserts, and then preserved in jams or in bottles. In Britain Robert Hogg knew it as Belle de Rocmont – about which he said simply that it was 'of a sweet and excellent flavour'. And it is also sometimes known as Gros Coeuret, or 'Big Heart'.

TASTING AND COOKING NOTES
These cherries are best eaten just as they are, as when juiced or baked in a tart or clafoutis they don't have quite the full-on, deep cherry flavour of the darker varieties. But straight from the fruit bowl they are so refreshing, delicate and satisfying, thanks to their size. Their sugar level isn't too high and because of their firm flesh, they keep well.

GROWING NOTES
One of the easiest varieties to grow in a garden but, like many cherries, it needs a pollination partner (see page 263).

232

MARSOTTE (CHERRY)

2 trees in my French orchard
Doubs, France, known by 1895
SEASON: *mid-June*
APPEARANCE: *medium size, black/red*
BEST FOR: *eating fresh, tarts, clafoutis and jams*

When I was young I worked at Le Palais de la Bière in Besançon, a classy restaurant in Place Granvelle, where there is a statue of Victor Hugo, the great French writer, who was born in the town. I started as a cleaner, worked my way up to pot washer and finally became a waiter. A favourite *digestif* offered to the guests was Kirsch de la Marsotte, made with these black cherries, and it was also the first alcoholic drink I tasted – my mother's cherries bottled in kirsch or the occasional eau de vie-soaked sugar cube that my grandfather would slip to me under the dinner table didn't count! The drink tasted divine, and at 60 per cent alcohol it certainly packed a punch!

This famous kirsch used to be made in the Co-operative de la Marsotte, which dates back to 1911, in Mouthier-Haute-Pierre in the Loue Valley in Doubs, near my home. (Other similar small dark cherries, like La Grande Queue Noire and Marie Jean Diaude, are grown not far away in Fougerolles, which has its own local kirsch.)

The picturesque, mountainous old village of Mouthier-Haute-Pierre, which was founded around a Benedictine priory in the ninth century, nestles in the foothills of the cliffs of the Haute-Pierre and Monk mountains. It is an amazing place, where falcons and buzzards fly over the meadows and deer roam amongst wild orchids. It is a village that is also known for vineyards, but it is the cherries that truly made it famous. In mid-April the trees are covered in a snow of white blossom, before the luscious black cherries appear.

In the 1930s, the co-operative had around fifty members and was producing 2,400 to 9,000 litres of kirsch per year. The commercial growing of the Marsotte cherries and the production of the liqueur has dwindled, so much so that the co-operative is in danger of liquidation. If it closes it will be a sad story because it will affect so many communities. This once greatly loved local *digestif* will be no more – although knowing my French friends I am sure that the locals will carry on the tradition, albeit less legally!

The word digestif is often a misnomer by the way, as most alcohol slows down your digestion rather than helping it. Some of the exceptions are Gentian, and Chartreuse, which was first made by monks in the eighteenth century from a blend of one hundred and thirty herbs. My mother used to make her own green and yellow versions, which would miraculously settle the stomach after a typical long French lunch going into dinner!

TASTING AND COOKING NOTES
These cherries are obviously brilliant for distilling, but are also good for the fruit bowl and, of course, they are a local favourite baked in tarts and clafoutis or made into jams and other preserves.

GROWING NOTES
This is a variety that can be difficult to graft; and it doesn't like bad weather during the season, especially frost.

MONTMORENCY (CHERRY)

Soon to be replanted in my French orchard
Val-d'Oise, Paris, around the thirteenth century
SEASON: *late June/early July*
APPEARANCE: *large, light red skin with pale flesh*
BEST FOR: *tarts, clafoutis, pies, griottes and jam*

This is such a nostalgic fruit for me. When I was growing up there were three trees behind our house in the Franche-Comté, one being a Montmorency cherry tree. Eight summers ago when I was visiting my mum – who was a sprightly eighty-nine-year-old at the time – it was an excellent year and the cherry tree was weighed down with more fruit than it had ever borne before. Every branch was bending beneath the ripe clusters, like thousands of red baubles on a Christmas tree.

One morning Maman was not in the house, so I went looking for her. To my horror, I found her perched on top of a ladder. She had hooked a basket onto a branch of the tree and she was busily filling her basket with the bright, shiny cherries to make a beautiful *tarte cerise*. 'Maman, come down, it is too dangerous!' I begged her, but she ignored me completely, and there was no arguing with her. She was doing as she had always done; growing, cooking and giving food to her family, as a pure act of love. A year later the cherry tree died, along with our apple and pear tree, but my friend Xavier immediately planted new ones for her, along with a little apricot tree, which has already borne fruits.

Like the Morello, Montmorency is a sour cherry. These typically small, bright red fruits are actually a different species (*Prunus cerasus*) to sweet cherries, which are classified as *Prunus atrium*, or 'bird cherries'. These are the fruits used for glacé cherries and they are divided into two categories: amarelle, which are characterised by pale flesh and juice that is almost transparent; and griotte, or morello, cherries, which have darker red skin and flesh, giving a richer-coloured juice. The Montmorency belongs to the amarelle group, although Maman Blanc only ever called our tree *aigre* (which means 'sour'), as the fruits are too tart to eat raw – Robert Hogg thought them 'only fit for preserving' – but they are transformed by heat into delicious tarts, or by macerating in alcohol and sugar.

This cherry takes its name from the medieval 'fief', or estate, of the ancient and noble Montmorency family, who first occupied the wooden ancestral castle of Montmorency, just to the north of Paris, from the tenth century, which the English destroyed during the Hundred Years War! The village of Montmorency that grew up around the castle is now part of the Val-d'Oise suburb of Paris. The family was so powerful that Henry IV is supposed to have said that should the House of Bourbon ever fall, no European family deserved the French crown more than the House of Montmorency.

The cherries are said to have been grown there since the thirteenth century, having been introduced by the Romans, and the variety was introduced to the United States by French settlers some time around 1760, if not earlier, where it has become more famous and widely grown than in France, as it is *the* fruit for the American favourite: cherry pie.

TASTING AND COOKING NOTES
The Montmorency cherries may be quite sharp and sour from the tree, but they are the variety most used for juicing. They are wonderful for clafoutis and tarts – and at the invitation of British friends I enjoyed a brilliant cherry pie made with these cherries. They are especially good macerated for an hour with a little sugar and a

splash of kirsch, they make colourful and beautiful jams, and they are a classic accompaniment for duck and other game.

One of the greatest specialities of my region is griottes – which, of course, is really just the name for the sour cherries. My mother would always make these for Christmas. My job at home was to wash the fruits and cut the stalks shorter for Maman, who would steep them in sugar and alcohol for the whole winter. They could be served just like this with coffee, but for the griottes they would be dipped into warm fondant icing, cooled and dipped into melted dark chocolate. After this they would be kept for three to five days, during which time the icing would dissolve and merge with the alcohol, so that when you bit into them, the crunch of chocolate was followed by a burst of cherries and kirsch – they were divine.

When I mentioned these to Will Sibley, he immediately recalled that one of his tasks in his first job with the fruit farm Seabrook & Sons in Essex was to drive their crop of morello cherries to London in an old Bedford van and deliver them to Fortnum & Mason and the chocolatiers Prestat in Piccadilly, where the cherries would be steeped in barrels of brandy, and then rolled in fondant and chocolate. 'Fortnum & Mason's confectionery department,' he remembers, 'was just like Willie Wonka's Chocolate Factory, with its huge copper pans and men in aprons and tall hats, and the aroma was incredible. I have very happy memories of returning to Essex with these magnificent cherry chocolates for everyone there.'

GROWING NOTES
Sour cherry trees tend not to grow as big as sweet cherry trees can, and they are less vigorous, with a different leaf. Montmorency is a variety that normally sets well if the frosts allow, but sometimes there are small tragedies in an orchard, and our two young Montmorency trees died in the first year they were planted. They were on the outer edge, and took all of the frost, but I will plant some more and we will start again, as this cherry is very special to me.

NOIRE À TOUT FAIRE (CHERRY)

1 tree in my French orchard
Basle, Switzerland, seventeenth century
SEASON: *mid-July*
APPEARANCE: *elongated, purple turning black*
BEST FOR: *eating fresh, baking and jam*

This is another cherry whose past is shrouded in mystery. It originates from Basle some time in the seventeenth century, and was probably known by the name of Herzkirsche, which was given to many small, heart-shaped, sweet black cherries.

TASTING AND COOKING NOTES
The dark juice of this cherry is abundant, and it is a traditional cherry for kirsch, but when harvested later it is good fresh – the darker the fruit becomes in colour, the more it develops its sugars, but it also has some good balancing acidity. It is good for baking and for jam too, justifying its name, which implies it can 'do anything'.

GROWING NOTES
This is a strong variety of cherry whose trees are very tall – they can grow up to twenty feet and, like most black cherry trees, they are able to live a long time, well over seventy years (this is much longer than other varieties, and some black cherry trees have been known to live for up to two hundred and fifty years). In Franche-Comté Xavier tells me that the variety fruits generously every year, so I am hopeful for a bountiful crop at Le Manoir.

PÊCHE DE VIGNE DE ROUGE/ SANGUINE VINEUSE (PEACH)

7 trees altogether in my French orchard
Coteaux du Lyonnais, seventeenth century
SEASON: *June–August*
APPEARANCE: *red skin with orange/yellow flesh*
(Pêche de Vigne de Rouge); dull red downy skin with
bright crimson flesh (Sanguine Vineuse)
BEST FOR: *everything*

I tasted my first Pêche de Vigne in the fruit gardens of the chateau at Serres-les-Sapins, which my grandfather tended (see page 47). The orchard was heaven for a young boy to explore, filled with wondrous fruits from apples, pears, apricots and plums to the grapes in the little vineyard, where, amongst the vines, there was a long row of smaller peach trees. In early summer these would be laden with clumps of pale fruit, much smaller than the conventional Provençal peach. Unripe they would be inedible bullets, harsh and sharp, but if you were patient and waited for the sun to ripen them they would turn a dazzling deep crimson red. Each fruit would be covered in a fine down and the juicy, deep sunset-coloured flesh had a distinctive, almost exotic, flavour all of its own. What better refreshment could there be, after hours of hard work in the garden, than to help yourself to a small basketful of these delightful fruits?

How extraordinary it seemed when I learned later that these peach trees' primary role in life was not to give us wonderful fruit to eat,

239

but to protect the vines. The history of the Pêche de Vigne goes back to the Coteaux du Lyonnais over two hundred and fifty years ago, when this variety of small tree was planted in the middle of the vineyards and its job was to act as a control for powdery mildew. This would attack the peach leaves first, sending out a warning to the vignerons that it was time to protect the vines. So they are some-times known as 'wine peaches' and, when they have deep crimson skin and flesh, Sanguine Vineuse: 'blood peaches'.

Thank God someone realised that the fruit was worth so much more than the role of bodyguard.

TASTING AND COOKING NOTES

These two varieties look a little different. The Pêche de Vigne de Rouge has a red skin but an orange-coloured flesh, while the Sanguine Vineuse has the deep red colour of skin and flesh that I remember tasting with my grandfather. When fully ripe, the flesh of these peaches simply overflows with juices. Thanks to the influence of the local terroir, their flavour is entirely different to that of the bigger Provençal peaches. They are more refreshing than sweet, and their acidity is low, but their perfume is incredibly intense.

These miraculous little fruits have no limits in the kitchen. They can be simply baked in the oven and, though the stones can be difficult to extract, they will make incredible tarts. When I was growing up my mother would poach these peaches in white wine with slices of orange and lemon and whole vanilla pods: a magnificent treat enjoyed by adults and children alike. The peaches can also be grilled or barbecued, and will make a wonderful compote or sorbet. They can even contribute to a summer salad and, of course, are also made into a famous liqueur.

GROWING NOTES
The trees are relatively undemanding if planted in a sunny, sheltered position, as they are vulnerable to wind and late frosts. They need light, well-drained semi-clay or sandy soil (they don't like chalky or alkaline soils). If the soil is quite dry, it isn't a problem, as this is a variety that dislikes excess moisture.

PÊCHE PLATE (PEACH)

3 trees in my French orchard
Bordeaux, 1975
SEASON: *August*
APPEARANCE: *yellow and red and doughnut-shaped*
BEST FOR: *everything*

I was hugely excited to grow these flat peaches in England, not only because of their curious beauty, but also for their extraordinary taste. Ever since I first discovered them in the 1980s, I have roasted and poached them in various recipes for Le Manoir and also our Cookery School.

The story of this peach takes us back to China around two thousand years ago, where it first occurred as a natural mutation of the wild fruit, and it was known as *'pántáo'*, which translates as 'coiled peach'. In the nineteenth century it found its way to both France and Britain, where this 'singular peach' was described at length in the *Transactions of the Horticultural Society*. It was explained that it had been introduced by Mr Joseph Kirke, of the Brompton Nursery, from Java, under the name of the Java peach, 'to which country it had no doubt been carried from China'. The flavour and consistency of its flesh was described as 'that of a good melting peach, being sweet and juicy, with a little noyeau (almond-like) flavour, or bitter aroma'. However, in the *Practical Gardener* it was noted that: 'Its real merits will not warrant its admission into small gardens, or where fine fruit only is an object. Its singularity, however, claims a place in the collections of the curious.'

In France, too, the fruits were considered something of a curiosity, but nothing more. Then, between 1975 and 1999, scientists at the French National Institute for Agricultural Research in Bordeaux, led by René Monet, began crossing the Kiang-Si variety with an Independence nectarine, to produce a better-yielding and tasting flat peach, which was eventually called Ferjalou Jalousia® and was not overly sweet, but had more complexity of flavour. Everything about this fruit was interesting: the shape, colour, texture and taste.

In America, where the fruit was known as the 'doughnut peach', scientists at Rutgers New Jersey Agricultural Experiment Station had also been working on the genetics in the 1960s and 1970s to produce hardier, frost-resistant trees with bigger, sweeter fruit, which they called Saturn. In the late 1990s/2000 in Britain, the doughnut, flat, or Saturn peaches finally took off and were greeted as a new sensation. They were especially popular with children, as the shape of these peaches makes them easy to eat and the stone is released easily from the flesh.

TASTING AND COOKING NOTES
This beautiful flat peach is a show-off with its velvety sunset of reds and yellows. It is a delight to eat raw as the skin is quite fine and the pulp is heavenly and melting with that delectable characteristic peach flavour, although you could argue it does lack a little of the acidity of a regular peach. When cooked the flavours explode with more complex notes, including that touch of almond that the Victorians recognised. Not only does it roast and poach well, but it is good for preserving and for compotes. One of my signature desserts is a flat peach, poached in vanilla syrup, with a roasted fig filled with fig-and-port ice cream. A divine hymn to the season.

GROWING NOTES
These are hardy trees, which are easy to grow in a sunny part of the garden, even in a pot, or against a south-facing wall.

REINE DES VERGERS (PEACH)

3 trees in my French orchard
France, around 1845
SEASON: August
APPEARANCE: purple red with flashes of yellow
BEST FOR: everything

With a name that means 'queen of the orchards', how could I fail to be seduced by the charms of this glorious peach? And how could I resist the challenge laid down by the great Victorian experts who, when the variety appeared in Britain in the mid-nineteenth century, felt sure that it could not be grown successfully in this climate?

The Reine des Vergers is said to have been discovered around 1845 in Maine-et-Loire and introduced by Jean-Laurent Jamin of Paris – unfortunately, we know no more. In England, *The Gardeners' Chronicle* recorded that in the December 1847 edition of the French journal *Portefeuille des Horticulteurs*, the peach was heralded as 'one of the most important introductions of the season, in as much as it supplies the desideratum of a variety adapted for succeeding as a standard; for as such it produces abundantly, and its fruit is equal in size and flavour to the finest wall varieties'. *The Chronicle*, however, added this note of caution for anyone considering planting the new peach: 'When we take into consideration the superior climate of France compared with that of England, we will not be disappointed should this variety be found not adapted for a standard in this country; but if it maintains a superiority on an east or west aspect, or even against a south wall in situations where other varieties prove too tender, we may be satisfied with the acquisition.'

Robert Hogg also knew this peach. In *The Fruit Manual*, he wrote that although this was 'a valuable market peach from its large size and firm flesh', and 'the tree is very hardy, and is an abundant bearer', he noted that 'Mr Blackmore says it never ripens at Teddington'. Mr Blackmore, of course, was the novelist and fruit expert R. D. Blackmore, to whom Hogg regularly deferred on the subject of peaches.

It was a challenge I had to take up. Perhaps I could prove all these experts wrong and grow beautiful Reine des Vergers peaches in Oxfordshire.

TASTING AND COOKING NOTES
A delicious white-fleshed peach that is a big success both gastronomically and commercially. It is exquisite eaten fresh. However, it is only truly wonderful when truly ripe. It is then you can appreciate all its strengths: a melting quality, a concert of flavours and an abundance of juices – so much so that you need napkins on hand. It also makes wonderful compotes and ice creams, the best *pêche au vin blanc* and lovely preserves.

GROWING NOTES
Unfortunately, this year the British weather decided to be unkind and killed the blossom, preventing any fruiting. A big drama! So we will move the peach trees against one of the many beautiful, warming walls of the garden, where I am sure they will prosper and provide a good harvest for our chefs. Most peaches, apart from the Avalon Pride (see page 11), are prone to peach leaf curl in the UK due to the weather conditions, which often prevail at the flowering period, and so shelter from the rain may also be needed.

THE BEE VILLAGE AND
GYPSY CHICKEN HOUSES

Our orchard and gardens are all part of an entire integrated eco-system, based on authenticity, heritage and biodiversity, so bees are essential, because they are the pollinators. That is the serious side, but I am still a child at heart and I love to bring a sense of fantasy and fun to the gardens, so I found myself drawing pictures of a colourful village where these bees would live. It took the best part of two years of working with specialist friends and craftsmen, and especially Ian Harper, an extraordinary Irishman and a great artist, who has worked with me on so many designs at Le Manoir, but soon our village will be finished, and the queen will have her castle.

There will be twelve houses, each with a different style of archi-tecture from around the UK and France, with real windows and porches and shutters, hand-coloured with organic water-based paint. Six of them will be real hives, and a spiralling path will lead to the top of a mound where the queen bee's castle will sit, with a French flag on top. And maybe an English one too! Around the hives will be rockeries planted with herbs, heather and lavender. The village will be looked after by a wonderful local beekeeper, Mark Blanchette, who has his own school and is a great teacher. His daughter also works at Le Manoir, so we are keeping things in our 'family'! There is a serious by-product of this fantasy in that each hive should give us around sixty kilos of organic wildflower honey per hive every year to serve to our guests – though actually I am expecting much more, as the bees will have such a variety of flowers to feast on throughout our twelve gardens.

When I dreamed of our orchard I also saw chickens meandering through it, and soon they will arrive. No less than one hundred big, grey-black French Maran chickens in long runs – and maybe we will put a few British cockerels into the roost! Their houses will be Romany gypsy wagons, which can be moved around the orchard in the traditional organic/free-range system. These chickens will have some important tasks to accomplish. They will eat the aphids, provide nitrogen for the soil and, of course, deliver rich, golden-yolked eggs for our guests' breakfasts – then, at the ends of their happy lives, make a glorious poule au pot *for the Manoir team.*

AGEN (PLUM)

2 trees in my French orchard
Agen, France, twelfth century
SEASON: *mid-August*
APPEARANCE: *oval, mauve blue, with a fine white blush*
BEST FOR: *everything, except bottling*

A bowl of fresh Agen plums at the height of summer can be quite beautiful, but it is in its dried form – Pruneaux d'Agen – that this fruit is famous around the world. I know that some of my British friends have terrible memories of menacingly medicinal prunes sitting in a pool of weak custard to finish off the compulsory school dinner. But Pruneaux d'Agen are entirely different, a connoisseur's fruit: sweet and rich, with glossy dark skins and a caramel-like amber flesh around their stones, which are always left in, enhancing the flavour.

The Agen, or Ente plum as it is also known, is actually a cross between an ancient variety of plum and a damson. The first small blue plums from China found their way via the Silk Road to Europe and the Greeks and Romans planted them all around the Mediterranean where, as well as being eaten fresh, they would be laid out in the sun to dry in order to provide fruit through the winter months. However, in the twelfth century, crusaders returning from Damascus brought with them the Damask plum, now known as the damson, which Benedictine monks in the Lot Valley grafted onto the local varieties to create a new plum, known as the Prune d'Ente (the grafted plum). These beautiful, thin-skinned, mauve-blue fruits with their fine bloom took very happily to the soil and climate around

Agen and, since the town was perfectly placed on the Garonne river, the plums, once dried, would be transported by *gabarres*, traditional flat-bottomed wooden boats, to Bordeaux, where they could be loaded into ships and sent further afield. The boxes of fruit were stamped with the port of origin, and so they became known as Pruneaux d'Agen.

The precious little bundles of sweetness, fibre and nutrients were hugely important in the diet of sailors on board ships from the seventeenth century until the end of the nineteenth century. Their popularity spread all over the world and, in Britain, the Victorians cherished both the fresh plums and the prunes.

After the harsh frosts of the winter of 1709 destroyed many of the trees around Agen, some growers expanded their farms further west into the more moderate climate and limestone soils of Villeneuve-sur-Lot. And now we have extended the growing region even further, to Oxfordshire – with some success!

TASTING AND COOKING NOTES
Fresh Agen plums are delicious, smaller than a Victoria plum, and sweeter, tighter and packed with more flavour. They make fantastic tarts, pies, cakes, chutneys and compotes, although they don't bottle well as they break down too much during cooking.

In French markets in the autumn you will see new-season *mi-cuit*, or semi-dried, and elegantly wrinkled Pruneaux d'Agen, which are toffee-like in sweetness and texture. So delicious. Even fully dried they are soft and sumptuous, so I urge you to keep some always in the cupboard as they have a place in savoury dishes as well as sweet. My mother would make a wonderful Sunday dish of roast pork stuffed with prunes (see page 324) and they go well with game. You can also make beautiful, home-made appetisers to serve with a glass of wine by wrapping each prune in a thin slice of streaky bacon, and baking them on a tray in the oven. Or simply stuff each prune with some crushed walnuts or pistachios.

In France, Pruneaux d'Agen cooked in red wine, port and vanilla is part of our culture, often even for breakfast. So I transported the idea to Le Manoir, where for over thirty years our guests were offered prunes in red wine as part of the breakfast experience, until we decided to revise the menu and I realised that this was not the healthiest option. We now serve them poached in organic redbush tea, which is said to have extraordinary health benefits as well as a wonderful flavour.

GROWING NOTES
In early July I made a full survey of the orchard to understand the health of the trees and their fruit. It took six hours to look at all of the two thousand five hundred trees with my wonderful James taking notes. As we approached the two young Agen plum trees I had some anxiety, as I know full well that the best climate for them is the South West of France, where the winters are mild and the summers are hot – and this is not always true of Oxfordshire! So I had little hope that they would bear any fruit. At first I could see only green foliage but, as I looked closer, I jumped for joy as I saw one, then two, five, ten ... eventually I counted more than thirty perfectly formed green plums hidden amongst the leaves. It was not an abundance, but it was such a wonderful, important moment in the story of the orchard.

MIRABELLE DE METZ (PLUM)

3 trees in my French orchard
Lorraine, fifteenth century
SEASON: mid-August/September
APPEARANCE: tiny, golden, with red blush
BEST FOR: eating fresh, tarts and clafoutis

Of all the fruit that my grandpapa tended in the orchard he looked after in Serre-les-Sapins (see page 47), the one that has the most powerful association for me is the mirabelle. None of the other varieties of plums have the extraordinarily intense, sophisticated flavour of a perfectly ripe mirabelle, which is almost impossible to describe. You have to taste it for yourself and then you will become a disciple.

This is a very French story, of a particular time, post-war, in my beloved Franche-Comté. In the orchard there was a line of around twelve mirabelle trees which in late summer, would be dense with fruit. As kids, we would help the men with the harvest, climbing the ladders, hooking our baskets over the branches and filling them with handfuls of the tiny sienna-coloured fruit, flushed and freckled with sunset red, and no bigger than marbles. Once the men and boys had finished their jobs, the women would take over (though, of course, I was the kitchen minion, whose job it was to flick out the stones from the mound of mirabelles). My mother and grandmother would bake some of them into heavenly tarts and the rest would be made into preserves, which were stored in jars in the cellar. However, some of the fruit would be left on the trees for longer, so that their sugars intensified even more, and they would be harvested differently, by the local men only. They would spread out a tarpaulin around the base, and shake the branches so that the fruit tumbled down into it and then they would be carried down into the cellar.

I must confess, when I was about six years old I got 'drunk' for the first time. Let me explain: I could hear activity, so I crept down the mossy steps to the cellar. The big creaky doors were ajar and, in the half-light, I saw the shapes of the men gathered around what looked like a monstrous copper 'creature', in which something was bubbling, and from a tap a clear liquid was dripping slowly into a big bucket. I was mesmerised by this extraordinary alchemy and the smell was so powerful and heady that after only a few minutes I felt quite dizzy. I started to sway back up the steps. Then I saw my grandmother, who was a stocky lady, standing at the top with her hands on her hips. At that moment she appeared immense. 'You have been drinking!' she said, and I received the biggest spanking!

Of course, later I learned that this wonderful, intoxicating smell was of the mirabelle eau de vie being distilled, just as earlier in the season a glut of apples and pears would also have been fermented in big barrels and turned into alcohol: it was what everyone did in the countryside at that time. As children we were no strangers to a little eau de vie in a dessert – and sometimes, when my grandmother wasn't looking, my grandfather would dip a sugar lump into the pure alcohol and slip it to me under the table. Of all the eaux de vie, the mirabelle is the most beautiful and the one that you really must try. If you pass by my region of Franche-Comté, I hope you will stop at some hospitable bistrot where I am sure they will find you a bottle.

The name mirabelle comes from the Latin *mirabilis*, meaning 'wondrous'. The best and most famous varieties, which, along with their eaux de vie, were awarded Protected Geographical Indication status in 1996, are the Mirabelle de Metz and the Mirabelle de Nancy from Lorraine, now part of the Grand-Est region, just to the north of Franche-Comté. So many hybrids these days are being bred for colour and size, but mostly to the detriment of flavour, whereas these two varieties have the flavour I remember so vividly from my childhood. They are very similar, but the Mirabelle de Metz is the one I know best as I did my military service in the town, and it is my favourite as it is a little smaller, thinner-skinned and more delicate.

Although plum and mirabelle stones have been found in Gallo–Roman excavation sites, the more romantic story is that in the fifteenth century King René d'Anjou, who was the Duke of Lorraine and Count of Provence, returned from the crusades with some mirabelles, whose stones he planted around Metz. It is also said that in 1568 Catherine de Medici and her son King Charles IX were presented with 'mirabelles preserved in sugar, a specialty from the Metz country'.

The season there is quite short, from mid-August to September, and each August in Metz a two-week festival is held to celebrate the fruit, with markets, music, fireworks and parades, and the crowning of a Mirabelle Queen.

TASTING AND COOKING NOTES
Mirabelles are, of course, delicious straight from the tree, but they are at their most beautiful baked into a tart or a clafoutis (see page 329) as heat is the catalyst that intensifies their flavour. Clafoutis is so much a part of my French heritage and one of the simplest of desserts to make, especially if you can enlist your partner or children to help you stone the fruit! Luckily, mirabelles are much quicker to prepare than cherries as the stones flick out quite easily.

GROWING NOTES
The trees are hardy enough to grow in most parts of Britain, but they like a sunny, sheltered, south-facing spot. The Mirabelle de Metz that

we have planted in the French orchard are now about three years old, and I was so happy to see them fruiting abundantly – but the birds got to them before I could bring them into the kitchen. In an orchard there are enemies everywhere and sometimes you feel defenceless.

Also, I must pass on this beautiful suggestion from Will Sibley: 'Unlike most tree fruits, mirabelles come almost entirely true to seed, so why not plant mirabelle hedges, by buying one tree then collecting the stones and planting them in rows?'

QUETSCHE D'ALSACE and QUETSCHE BLANCHE DE LÉTRICOURT

(PLUM)

5 trees altogether in my French orchard
Alsace, 1914 (d'Alsace); France, before 1882 (Blanche de Létricourt)
SEASON: *August (d'Alsace); September (Blanche de Létricourt)*
APPEARANCE: *deep purple blue, with golden-orange flesh*
(d'Alsace); large, with very pale yellow, mottled skin and
white flesh (Blanche de Létricourt)
BEST FOR: *eating fresh, compotes, tarts, jams*

The word *quetsche* is Alsacian for the Damask plum from Damascus, which we know as damson, and these are typically grown around Alsace and Lorraine.

We have planted two very different-looking varieties. The first to fruit in August are the three Quetsche d'Alsace trees. As the name suggests, this fine-looking, big purple fruit is from Alsace, and it dates back to 1914.

Next, in September, it is the turn of the Quetsche Blanche de Létricourt. This older variety was found by M. Alix, a nurseryman in Nancy in the Meurthe-et-Moselle *département* of what used to be Lorraine, but is now part of the Grand-Est region – not far from Metz, home to some of the best mirabelles. Although this plum has 'white' in its name, it is in fact yellow and it reminds me of the Pershore Yellow Egg that I saw while filming in the Vale of Evesham. These damsons thrive in the village of Létricourt, nestled in the North East of France, which has harsh winters, often followed by hot summers.

TASTING AND COOKING NOTES

The Quetsche d'Alsace is delightful fully ripe and straight from the tree. Easy to eat, with a stone that can be removed fairly effortlessly, it will grace any fruit bowl. It is also very well suited to compotes and purees, and in tarts the fruit will hold its shape during cooking and release its impeccable perfume.

The Quetsche Blanche de Létricourt is a big fleshy fruit, which doesn't have very much moisture so, again, it will release its stone very quickly and easily. It is a variety that is traditionally used in tarts and jams. Alsace produces some magnificent Quetsche plum brandies, so if you could brush your tarts with a little of this, along with some melted butter and a small amount of sugar, they will blossom into something divine.

GROWING NOTES

Hardy and productive, these are varieties that need relatively little looking after and can survive reasonably harsh winters and fairly hot summers. They require little water, but are also able to survive a large amount of rain and at Le Manoir they have done well, giving an abundance of fruit.

REINE CLAUDE DORÉE and
REINE CLAUDE D'OULLINS (GREENGAGE)

1 of each tree in my French orchard
France, eighteenth century (Dorée) and 1850s (d'Oullins)
SEASON: *late August/September*
APPEARANCE: *medium, green ripening to gold (Dorée);*
large and yellow with pink blush (d'Oullins)
BEST FOR: *eating fresh, tarts, compotes and jams*

The gardens at Le Manoir aux Quat'Saisons have always been central to the magic and are at the very heart of the food that we serve, and so it gives me great joy to see our guests admiring these beautiful greengage plums on the tree, grown without a single chemical, and then enjoying them in an exquisite compote for breakfast.

The name 'Reine' or 'Queen' Claude refers to a delicate, juicy cultivar of plum that is smaller than its sturdier, purple-red cousins, but bigger than the mirabelle. It is derived from a wild plum found in Armenia, where the cold winters and warm, dry summers developed its delicate sweetness. The fruits, probably dried, found their way along the Silk Road to Europe, arriving in Greece and Italy, wherever a stone was planted. From Italy they reached France during the reign of King François I, who succeeded to the throne in 1515; and it is said that his consort, Queen Claude, enjoyed the plums so much that they were named after her.

In Britain the fruits are known as gages, or greengages, though some are not green, but gold, or even purple. For a long time it was thought that they were first introduced to Britain from France by

Sir Thomas Gage of the historic family, the Gages of Firle, whose history goes back to Henry VII. However, it now seems certain that the credit must go to a different branch of the family, the Gages of Hengrave, and that it was Sir William Gage, second baronet of Hengrave, who had seen the Grosse Reine Claude while in France and imported some trees to Britain in 1725. One legend has it that the labels were detached in transit, and so, as the fruit was green, William's gardener simply called them green Gage's plums, later shortened to greengages.

Robert Hogg called the greengage 'one of the richest flavoured of all the plums, ripe in the middle and end of August', but also reasoned that the fruit may actually have arrived in Britain from Italy at around the same time it appeared in France, therefore a whole century before William Gage brought over his cargo from France, though at that time it was known by its Italian name of Verdochia. Hogg quotes the botanist John Parkinson as mentioning, in 1629, a plum called 'Verdoch', which 'seems to have been not at all rare, nor even new'.

The sweet and juicy Reine Claude Dorée is one of the oldest and most famous varieties of gage, which dates from the second half of the eighteenth century in South West France; while the bigger, gold Reine Claude d'Oullins was discovered by chance and cultivated by M. Massot in the 1850s in Coligny in the Ain region, which is quite close to my home in Franche-Comté. It is thought that he called it after his home town of Oullins, near Lyon, but it is sometimes also known as the Massot.

TASTING AND COOKING NOTES
Eaten fresh and fully ripe, these gages are juicy and rich, but with a harmonious balance of gentle acidity – the Dorée is the sweeter and more perfumed of the two. Baked, lightly brushed with butter and a

sprinkling of sugar, they are absolutely delicious – especially when flambéed with mirabelle liqueur and served with ice cream. They are known for their jams and they make beautiful compotes for our guests for breakfast as they need no sugar, only a little lemon juice to prevent discoloration and to heighten the flavour and natural colour. And in tarts they are wondrous, as the acidity of the fruit comes through beautifully.

GROWING NOTES
So far I have only one tree of each of these varieties in the French orchard, and though these had a difficult year, in which they had to endure a very rough winter and an extreme hot spell, they still fruited wonderfully. The Reine Claude Dorée, which fruits a little later, was especially recommended to me by Xavier as very vigorous and productive . . . and both have made my gardeners and me very happy.

VICTORIA PLUM

To be planted in my English orchard
Sussex or Suffolk, nineteenth century
SEASON: *late August/September*
APPEARANCE: *gold, turning bright red, then purple*
BEST FOR: *tarts, pies and crumbles*

Back in 1972 on a beautiful late-summer's day, I arrived in the UK to begin working as a waiter at a charming inn, the Rose Revived, at Newbridge on the banks of the Thames, close to the old humpback bridge that gave the town its name when it was rebuilt in the thirteenth century! This was my first taste of ancient rural Oxfordshire. My second was a Victoria plum crumble, which was on the menu. I had no idea what a crumble was, but the chef kindly gave me a large spoon to delve through the crunchy crust to find the soft cooked purple fruit beneath. I was told a good helping of custard was de rigueur. What a wonderful introduction to British puddings. I only wish more of my French friends would discover this country's great heritage of desserts.

This is the best known of English plums, named after Queen Victoria, but the rest of its history is somewhat confused. Unusually, Robert Hogg's account of the plum being found in a garden in the Sussex village of Alderton – and repeated ever since – must be mistaken, for the simple reason, as pointed out by Christopher Stocks in his book *Forgotten Fruits*, that there is no village in Sussex called Alderton! Stocks suggested that Alderton may have been a misspelling of the village of Walderton. Another theory is that the village in question may be Alderton in Suffolk, not Sussex; but we may never know. Hogg also suggested that the plum was originally known as Sharp's

Emperor and was ultimately sold by a nurseryman named Denyer at Brixton, near London, as Denyer's Victoria, in 1844.

Plums have lost a little of their traditional place in British hearts thanks to imports with thicker skins that don't bruise as easily as the finer old home-grown varieties, which are difficult to promote and transport in the age of the supermarket. Plums for the supermarket are picked early and packed while still hard, again to avoid bruising, but unlike a plum picked slightly underripe from a tree, which will ripen fully in a fruit bowl, most supermarket plums will never develop their full flavour. While perhaps not as elegant as some, of all the British varieties, Victoria still holds her own better than most, and the variety has such a place in people's hearts that it has probably been the most planted fruit tree in the UK for the past fifty years. There are so many trees in gardens around the country that, Will Sibley tells me, 'If it is a good plum year, commercial sales will drop by about 40 per cent due to the sheer volume of the garden crop!' It makes me so happy to hear that.

TASTING AND COOKING NOTES
When left on the tree until properly ripe, the colour and flavour of the Victoria deepens and becomes a very juicy and sweet plum to be celebrated. It will make lovely tarts, pies and crumbles, and the flesh separates readily from the stone, so the fruit is easy to prepare.

GROWING NOTES
The tree is quite hardy and not very large. It is such a prolific fruit-bearer that the 'fruitlets' need to be thinned in order for the plums to develop properly and reduce stress on the tree. Otherwise the boughs tend to break under the weight of the fruit, and the wounds leave them susceptible to fungal infection, such as silverleaf. To reduce the risk of disease, don't prune in the dormant season, but immediately after harvest, to remove any damaged branches, and again in spring just after flowering, making as few cuts as possible.

GROW YOUR OWN TREE

Outside the brick wall of my Oxfordshire home I have two small Williams' Bon Chrétien pear trees in a single palmette shape. They don't receive much sun as they are shaded by huge neighbouring trees, but each year they give me around twenty beautiful pears, and every morning I say hello to them as they grow and ripen. These trees are so undemanding and they give me immense joy.

Anyone can grow a fruit tree. Can you grow a rose? If so, you can grow a fruit tree. It is so easy to train an espalier apple, apricot or a pear against a wall – they are not greedy for space, 70cm–100cm is all they need – or you could plant a tree on dwarf rootstock in a pot in a small garden or on a balcony.

I really want to encourage you to champion a heritage tree, one of our great old varieties that are in danger of disappearing, but do bear in mind that some can be a little unpredictable and won't necessarily give you as much fruit as a modern variety that has been bred to be more consistent and resistant to disease. I have consulted with my good friend Will Sibley and listed some of my favourite varieties that should do well in a garden (see page 266).

You can buy a fruit tree in a pot or as a bare-root plant. A pot-grown tree is the easiest to plant out. Most trees that you buy in pots from nurseries are two to three years old and will have already been pruned to grow into a bush-type tree on a medium rootstock, but you can also buy them already trained into espalier, palmette or fan shapes.

A bare-root tree will usually be cheaper and can sometimes give better results as it can adapt better to its new soil. You are also likely to be offered more choice of rootstock. Dwarf rootstocks for apples, developed by East Malling (the M before their number stands for Malling) are brilliant for small gardens as the trees can even be grown in flower borders. Choose a tree on an M27 rootstock (the smallest) or an M9 rootstock (a little larger). Your bare-root tree is also a blank canvas if you want to train it against a fence or wall.

Apple (and other fruit) trees can be self-fertile, or they often require another tree of a different variety to act as a pollinating partner. If an apple tree is described as a triploid variety, this means that it needs two or more such partners. This is not usually a problem as most apple trees grown in towns or villages will have enough local apple or crab apple trees nearby to do the job, with the help of busy bees who can detect flowers from a long way away, as they have an extraordinary sense of smell – even better than my own! Marcus Roberts told me of a moment at an Apple Day at which a local beekeeper opened some jars of honey for people to taste and within twenty minutes swarms of bees were swooping in to steal the honey. The beekeeper knew where every local hive was located and the nearest was several miles away, yet the bees could still smell the honey and make the proverbial beeline for it!

If, however, you have planted particularly early- or late-flowering varieties, they may struggle to find pollinating partners at the right time, so if your tree is tending not to fruit, you might need to consider planting another compatible tree – most nurseries offer lists of the best varieties to plant together.

Many fruit trees can be grown in containers in a small space. It is best to use a wooden or plastic pot rather than terracotta, which is porous and heats up in the direct sun. This can be more stressful to the tree and you will need to do a lot more watering. And I am afraid watering is a job that you must do regularly if you are growing a tree *in a pot: every day in hot weather. However, you could use a simple home irrigation system on a timer, which can also help to save water.*

If you are looking for an old, interesting variety, it is worth getting in touch with your local heritage or community orchard group, where you will find wonderful, knowledgeable enthusiasts who share a passion and will be only too happy to introduce you to the traditional fruits of your area. Often they will be able to put you in touch with local grafters and specialist nurseries.

Apple Days are great occasions to buy trees, or to have one grafted for you. You can even sign up to do a grafting course yourself, and can learn enough in a morning to go home with two or three trees. Brogdale Farm, home of the National Fruit Collection, offer grafting courses, and you can buy fruit trees, including ones trained in espaliers and planted in pots, directly from them at Grow at Brogdale (www.brogdaleonline.co.uk).

Here at Le Manoir I am very proud of our Raymond Blanc Gardening School, supported by the RHS, Garden Organic and Hartley Botanic, who built our beautiful greenhouse, and we offer pruning courses, if you would like to learn how to keep your trees in good shape.

Remember that most fruit trees will grow best in full sun. They can tolerate limited shade for part of the day, but the more shade, the lower the quality of fruit. So, against the warmth of a wall is the ideal place.

Planting a fruit tree is such a lovely thing to do; it will embellish your home and garden, and your children will love the magic of watching a tiny tree grow and blossom. Imagine the joy of following the story through the seasons, as the fragile petals fall and the tiny fruits begin to form and slowly emerge from the green foliage, changing their colours, growing stronger, bigger and fuller in the face of all the elements. This fruit tree is a microcosm of our own miraculous story, of life itself. No less. And so, finally, you will receive the most delicious gifts to enjoy straight from the tree or turn into juices and wonderful ice creams, tarts and, of course, the British crumble. With French vanilla cream, or English custard!

BEST FRUIT FOR GROWING
IN A GARDEN

APPLES

Adams' Pearmain
Annie Elizabeth
Beauty of Bath
Belle de Boskoop
Braeburn
Bramley's Seedling
Captain Kidd
Charles Ross
Chivers Delight
Discovery
Egremont Russet
Ellison's Orange
George Cave
Kidd's Orange Red
Orleans Reinette
Red Windsor
Reine des Reinettes
Reinette Grise du Canada
Ribston Pippin
Rosemary Russet
Worcester Pearmain

PEARS

Beurre Hardy
Concorde
Conference
Delbardélice®
Delsanne
Williams' Bon Chrétien
Winter Nélis

QUINCE

Champion
Vranja

APRICOTS

Bergeron
Flavorcot®
Tomcot®

PLUMS

Reine Claude d'Oullins
Reine Claude Dorée
Victoria

PEACH
Pêche de Vigne

CHERRY
Montmorency

RECIPES
FROM
THE LOST
ORCHARD

BIRCHER MUESLI

This is part of our delicious breakfast at Le Manoir aux Quat'Saisons, which is based on the original muesli creation of the Swiss naturopathic doctor Dr Maximilian Oskar Bircher-Benner in the early twentieth century. I make it with my favourite of all apples, the Cox's Orange Pippin, but you could also use a Granny Smith, which is low in sugar and less prone to discoloration than some other apples. Soaking the muesli rehydrates and softens all the ingredients, so that they release their nutrients more readily. You need to prepare the muesli at least half a day in advance in order to allow the flavours to develop. So, the best thing to do is make it in the evening, cover, then put it in the fridge overnight so it will be ready for breakfast.

Of course, you could replace the apple juice with pear juice and use a different milk. I prefer oat milk, which is light and has a wonderful flavour; however, you could use almond or soya milk. In winter I sometimes add a little spice, such as cinnamon or nutmeg, into the mix. This really is one of the best breakfasts you can have to set you up for the day.

SERVES: 4

20g almonds, finely sliced
20g brazil nuts, roughly
  chopped
1 teaspoon sunflower seeds
1 teaspoon linseeds
150g jumbo oats
1 teaspoon flaxseeds
1 teaspoon amaranth

8 baby figs, dried or fresh, sliced
1 tablespoon blueberries, dried
  or fresh
1 tablespoon goji berries
1 tablespoon cranberries,
  unsweetened, chopped
1 tablespoon raisins,
  unsweetened

200ml apple juice (preferably organic), unsweetened
200g whole probiotic yoghurt
200ml oat milk
juice of ¼ lemon

To serve
1 Cox's Orange Pippin apple, skin on

Preheat the oven to 180°C/160°C fan/gas 4.

Spread the almonds, brazil nuts, sunflower seeds and linseeds over a baking tray and put into the preheated oven for 6 minutes. Remove and leave to cool.

Tip the roasted nuts and seeds into a bowl, add all the rest of the ingredients and mix together. Cover with cling film and put into the fridge, preferably overnight.

When ready to serve, grate the apple straight into the muesli, stir it through and spoon into bowls.

RB'S BROWN SAUCE

As a Frenchman, I have to admit that I used to despise the idea of brown sauce, thinking it a scourge of British cuisine. However, one year I was with some friends fishing for trout. I love to go fishing, but rarely have the chance. It is so wonderful to be on the riverbank at dawn, at one with your surroundings, and just cast your line and wait. Of course, by late morning everyone is famished, so on this occasion we went back to my friends' house, where I could smell bacon cooking. 'Would you like a bacon butty?' I was asked. I didn't know what a butty was, but I was told I must try it, and with brown sauce. I thought about telling them that I hate brown sauce – as I was sure I would – but I was so hungry I said, 'OK, why not?' As I was handed this hot sandwich, made with white sliced bread, I had ruled out the possibility of any enjoyment, but then I took a bite and I was astonished: the flavour was divine. I had discovered a new English culinary delight! It was a great salutary lesson in not being prejudiced against any food, but to be willing to try anything. After that experience, I decided to make my own sauce using apples from our orchard. Now RB's Brown Sauce has become quite famous at Le Manoir aux Quat'Saisons – I really should bottle it!

This is a great recipe for using up the last of the season's fruit or any windfall apples that you find. Just remove any bruised parts of the apple first. We use an aged Cabernet Sauvignon vinegar as well as red wine vinegar, as it adds a little sweetness.

It is a low-sugar sauce, so it must be kept refrigerated and only for up to two months.

MAKES: 1 litre sauce

EQUIPMENT: airtight jars or bottles (sterilised as on page 312), blender

165g pitted dates, finely
  chopped
675g Bramley or Granny Smith
  apples, peeled
pinch of ground allspice
pinch of ground ginger

pinch of nutmeg, freshly grated
135g dark brown sugar
100ml Cabernet Sauvignon
  vinegar (sweet red wine
  vinegar)
100ml red wine vinegar

In a large heatproof bowl, add the chopped dates. Grate the peeled apples on a coarse cheese grater directly into the bowl, add the ground spices and nutmeg, mix together and leave the bowl to one side.

Put the sugar and both vinegars into a small saucepan over a high heat and bring to the boil, stirring until the sugar dissolves. Remove the pan from the heat and pour onto the dates and apple, then cover the bowl with cling film and leave to cool at room temperature for around 40 minutes until the dates and grated apple absorb some liquid and become soft.

Pour this mixture into a heavy-based saucepan and simmer over a very low heat, stirring occasionally so it doesn't catch on the base, for 1½ hours, or until soft and pulpy. Cool down until just warm.

Blend the mixture in two batches to a smooth consistency, then leave to cool completely.

Divide between the sterilised jars or bottles and refrigerate until needed or for up to two months.

APPLE CHUTNEY

I have my British friends to thank for my love of chutneys – especially Adam Johnson, my wonderful Development Chef, who is a chutney specialist! At first I was unsure about this new experience of fruit and spice, which was quite alien to me, but over the years I have become completely enamoured with the idea. This chutney has a lower amount of sugar than many traditional recipes, which will reduce the length of time that you can keep it for, but it has a cleaner, fruitier flavour and, of course, it will be better for you.

MAKES: 1.6kg chutney

EQUIPMENT: jars (sterilised as on page 312)

1 tablespoon rapeseed oil
1 large onion, peeled and diced into 1cm cubes
500ml white wine vinegar
125g muscovado sugar
1 teaspoon sea salt
1 teaspoon sweet mixed spice
1.5kg apples, such as Braeburn, peeled, cored and diced into 1cm cubes

1kg plum tomatoes, diced into 1cm cubes
75g golden sultanas
good pinch of cayenne pepper
1 large piece of fresh ginger, peeled and finely grated

Heat the oil in a large saucepan on a high heat, add the onion and cover with a tight-fitting lid. Turn down the heat to medium–low for 3 minutes to allow the onion to soften and sweeten, but not take on any colour.

Add the vinegar, sugar, salt and mixed spice, bring to the boil and reduce by half.

Add the diced apple, tomatoes and sultanas, bring back to the boil, then turn down to a simmer for 20 minutes.

Stir in the cayenne pepper and ginger and turn off the heat.

Spoon into sterilised jars and seal each with a tight-fitting lid. The chutney should keep for around six months in a cool place, but once opened keep in the fridge.

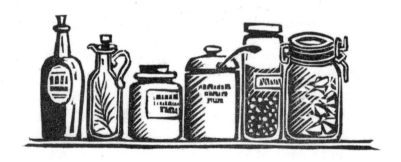

BAKED APPLES WITH CARAMEL SAUCE

This is one of the many desserts that Maman Blanc would make with apples throughout the autumn and winter, and it is truly delicious. You need a full-flavoured variety of apple with a good texture so that it won't collapse. I have found some of the best for baking to be Adams' Pearmain, Annie Elizabeth, Cox's Orange Pippin and Reine des Reinettes, but you can see the full list of the apples that excelled in our kitchen tests on page 172. I have given the baking time as 35–40 minutes, but this can vary according to the size and variety – even whether the apple is a late- or early-season one, and the length of time it has been stored. All of these can affect the apple's texture, and therefore the time it will need to become tender while still keeping its shape.

If adding the garnish, you can vary it to your taste by toasting any mixture of nuts (brazils, pecans, walnuts, hazelnuts), along with some seeds (sunflower, pumpkin or sesame). You can also add some dried fruits (such as cranberries, blueberries, raisins and/or golden sultanas) and a pinch of ground spice (cinnamon, nutmeg, allspice).

If you like, you can par-bake the apples three-quarters of the way through in advance and finish them in the oven when ready to serve. The apples are also lovely on their own or with custard or ice cream.

SERVES: 4

For the baked apples
4 large apples
60g unsalted butter, melted
60g caster sugar

For the caramel sauce
1 tablespoon water
50g caster sugar
80ml apple juice
½ teaspoon arrowroot, mixed with a little cold water
1 tablespoon Calvados or cider (optional)

For the garnish (optional)
15g pistachio nuts
10g almond flakes
15g bread, diced
15g icing sugar

To prepare the baked apples, preheat the oven to 170°C/gas 3. It is best not to use a fan as the power can be too much for the apples, causing the skins to split.

Wash the apples and pat dry. Using a small knife, trim a slice off the base of each apple so that it will sit upright. Now make a small incision through one side of each apple, slightly above and beyond the core. Push the apple corer up through the base of the apple as far as the incision and then twist it to release the core. (Alternatively, you could leave the apples whole.)

Brush the apples with some of the melted butter and roll in enough caster sugar to coat all over.

Brush a baking dish with the rest of the butter and sprinkle with the rest of the sugar, then stand the apples in the dish. Bake for around 35–40 minutes until the apples are tender but still holding their shape. Set to one side.

To prepare the garnish, if using, toss the pistachios, almond flakes and bread cubes in the icing sugar and scatter on a small baking tray. Toast in the oven for 8–10 minutes until lightly caramelised.

To make the caramel sauce, while the apples are in the oven put the water into a large saucepan, spoon the sugar evenly over and let it absorb the water for 1–2 minutes. Now bring to the boil and cook for 2–4 minutes to a dark golden caramel – the colour is important as the caramel will have a deep rich flavour. If it is too light, it will be too sweet and ruin the dish.

Add the apple juice very carefully as it will splutter violently and is hot enough to cause burns. Bring back to the boil, thicken with the arrowroot, then remove from the heat and stir in the Calvados or cider, if using.

To serve, place a baked apple on each warmed plate and pour on the caramel sauce. Scatter the garnish, if using, around.

APPLE SORBET WITH APPLE CRISPS

If you have an ice-cream maker at home, this is a wonderful, fresh and easy sorbet that you can make in 10 minutes. As you can see, tangy Granny Smith apples are the best for this. As well as its flavour, this apple has the advantage of not oxidising as quickly as some apples, so it will not turn brown too quickly after slicing. There is little sugar in this sorbet so it will harden quickly and is best eaten just a few hours after it has been made. You can decorate your sorbet with a lovely apple crisp.

SERVES: 4

EQUIPMENT: blender, ice-cream maker, mandoline

For the apple sorbet	For the apple crisps
600g (4) Granny Smith apples	1 Granny Smith apple
30ml lemon juice	100ml water
100g crab apple jelly	50g caster sugar
50g caster sugar	1 small lemon wedge
20ml Calvados (optional)	pinch of vitamin C powder

Leave the peel on the apples and just cut them in half, remove the cores, then chop into 1cm cubes. Put into a blender with all the other sorbet ingredients and blend until smooth.

Pass the puree through a fine sieve, then put into the bowl of your ice-cream maker and churn for 9–10 minutes. Transfer to the freezer.

For the apple crisps, preheat the oven to 100°C/80°C fan/gas ¼ and have ready a non-stick baking tray.

Halve the whole apple, then using a mandoline set to 1mm, cut six slices vertically through each half.

In a small pan bring the water, sugar, a squeeze of lemon juice and a pinch of vitamin C powder to the boil to form a light syrup, then turn off the heat and dip the apple slices in the syrup for 1 minute (the vitamin C will prevent the apple from oxidising). Lift out with a slotted spoon, shaking off any excess syrup, and lay the slices on the non-stick tray.

Put into the preheated oven to dry out for about 30 minutes. The slices will be quite firm, but will continue to crisp up and become brittle as they cool.

Once frozen, scoop three balls of sorbet into each of four bowls and top each with an apple crisp.

SPICED APPLE TURNOVERS

These spiced apple triangles are delicious and so quick to assemble. They are perfect for a quick treat or for a dinner party dessert. I suggest two pieces per person, served warm with a scoop of vanilla ice cream or a spoonful of crème fraîche.

SERVES: 4 (8 pieces)

EQUIPMENT: pastry brush

110g caster sugar
50g unsalted butter
2 apples, peeled and diced
50g golden sultanas
1 teaspoon ground cinnamon
4 sheets of ready-made filo pastry
4 tablespoons unsalted butter, melted

For the spiced sugar topping
2 tablespoons golden caster sugar
1 teaspoon ground cinnamon
1 teaspoon ground ginger
2 teaspoons sesame seeds

Preheat the oven to 210°C/190°C fan/gas 6.

In a medium frying pan on a medium heat, cook the caster sugar to a blond caramel. Remove from the heat, carefully add the 50g butter and swirl the pan so the butter emulsifies with the caramel. This will stop further caramelisation.

Place the pan back onto a medium heat. Carefully add the diced apple pieces and cook for 1 minute, stirring occasionally.

Remove the pan from the heat, add the golden sultanas and cinnamon, stir and leave to cool.

Meanwhile, lay out one sheet of filo pastry and cut it in half lengthways to give you two long rectangles.

Lay one of the rectangles horizontally in front of you and brush with a little of the melted butter. Spoon 2 generous tablespoons of the cooled apple mixture onto the left side, making sure you leave a margin of half a centimetre to the edge of the pastry.

Take the top left-hand corner and fold to the bottom to form a triangle. Fold twice more into triangles. There will be surplus pastry, so fold this over to secure your turnover.

Brush the turnover all over with more of the melted butter and place on a baking tray.

Repeat with the remaining pastry and apple mixture so that you have eight evenly sized triangular parcels.

In a small bowl, mix together the golden caster sugar, cinnamon, ginger and sesame seeds and sprinkle some over the top of each parcel.

Bake in the oven for 10 minutes, then leave to cool slightly before serving.

APPLE BEIGNETS

I have fond memories of Mardi Gras, when the children of our village would dress up and visit every home, where we would receive a 'penny' and the fluffiest, delicious beignet. My mother made her own version with the Reinette Grise du Canada apples that grew behind our house, and I still remember the beautiful contrast between the crisp, light batter and the soft, intense apple filling. The beignets are especially good served with chocolate sauce, ice cream, or a lovely English custard.

MAKES: 24 fritters

1 medium egg
240ml whole milk
1 teaspoon vegetable oil
100g caster sugar, plus 30g
pinch of salt
150g plain flour

1 teaspoon baking powder
400ml vegetable oil, for frying
4 apples, cored and cut into
  1cm rings
1 teaspoon ground cinnamon

In a large bowl, whisk together the egg, milk, oil, 100g of sugar and salt.

Into a separate bowl, sift together the flour and baking powder, then sieve this again into the egg and milk mixture. Whisk together until you have a smooth batter. Have a tray lined with kitchen paper ready.

In a shallow frying pan, carefully heat the oil to 180°C.

Cook the fritters in batches, dipping each apple ring into the batter and then carefully lowering into the hot oil. Fry on each side for 1–2 minutes until golden brown, then, using a slotted spoon, lift out and lay on the kitchen paper to soak up any excess oil.

Mix the 30g of sugar and cinnamon together in a shallow bowl or tray, then, while still warm, toss each fritter in the mixture, coating them evenly. Serve immediately.

TARTE MAMAN BLANC

You know by now that, for me, Maman Blanc makes the best apple tart in the world. When I was growing up she would make it regularly during the apple season, and she always made it look so simple: just some shortcrust pastry, rolled out with some apples from the garden sliced in concentric circles on top, a few dots of butter and a sprinkling of sugar, and then into the oven it would go, where the apples slices would fluff up and caramelise beautifully, yet still hold their shape. Sometimes, just before it was ready, she would take out the tart, pour over a beautiful custard and then put it back into the oven to finish off. If you want to do this, just whisk 1 medium egg with 50g caster sugar and 100ml whipping cream – you can add a splash of Calvados if you like! Then 10 minutes before the end of the cooking time, pour in the custard.

I can still remember coming home from school, or from helping my father in the garden, or my grandfather in his orchard, and when I opened the door of our house it would be filled with the exquisite aromas of the tart baking. Of course, simplicity is deceptive, because Maman was a great cook and she made the best pastry, but she also had wonderful Reinette Grise du Canada apples from our tree. We put one hundred and twelve apples to the Maman Blanc tarte test to see how well other varieties would do, and the two most outstanding turned out to be Lord Lambourne and Captain Kidd, slightly ahead of Blenheim Orange, Devonshire Quarrenden, George Cave, Orleans Reinette and Red Windsor, which of course are not easy to find in shops these days. But equally outstanding was the Cox's Orange Pippin, while Braeburn will also make a beautiful tart.

You can use this recipe with plums, apricots and cherries in season too.

The method below is for making the pastry by hand, but you could make the pastry in a food processor, using the pulse button to bring the dough together.

A common problem with tarts is that the base stays undercooked and soggy. The reason for this is insufficient heat beneath. As you will see in this method, I use a combination of a bottomless tart ring and a baking stone or tray that has been preheated in the oven, as this creates an instant transfer of heat from the hot stone or tray to the pastry base so that it will be lovely and crisp when it is baked.

SERVES: 6
EQUIPMENT: 18cm bottomless tart ring, baking stone (optional)

For the shortcrust pastry
100g unsalted butter, diced, at room temperature
200g plain flour
pinch of sea salt
1 medium egg (preferably organic or free-range)
1 tablespoon cold water

For the apple filling and glaze
3 dessert apples, such as Cox's Orange Pippin
15g unsalted butter
15g caster sugar
1½ teaspoons lemon juice
2 teaspoons Calvados (optional)
icing sugar, for dusting

To make the shortcrust pastry, have the butter at room temperature so that you can distribute it evenly within the flour – this is what gives the pastry its flakiness.

In a large bowl, rub together the flour, butter and salt gently with your fingertips until the mixture is crumbly and has a sandy texture.

Make a well in the centre. Add the egg and water and work them in with your fingertips, moving them in little concentric circles. Flours differ in their absorbency, so if the dough feels too wet add a little flour; if too dry add a little water.

At the last moment when the egg has been absorbed, bring the dough together and press into a ball.

Turn out the dough onto a lightly floured work surface and knead gently with the palms of your hands for 10–20 seconds until you have a homogeneous dough, but be careful not to overwork it or it will lose some of its flakiness and retract during baking.

Break off 20–30g of the dough, wrap it in cling film and put into the fridge to chill. Wrap the remaining dough in some more cling film and flatten it until it is about 2cm thick – this will help it to chill more quickly. Put this into the fridge, too, and leave it to rest for 20–30 minutes. This is important because you have worked the gluten in the flour, and so the dough will be elastic at this stage. Resting it in the fridge makes it more pliable, easier to roll and will help minimise shrinkage in the oven.

When the dough has chilled, lay another sheet of cling film – about 40cm square – on your work surface. Unwrap the large piece of dough, place it in the centre and cover with another sheet of cling film of similar dimensions. This allows you to roll out the dough without adding extra flour in order to stop it sticking to your work surface.

Roll out the dough to a circle, 2–3mm thick.

Have ready a flat baking tray lined with greaseproof paper and place the tart ring on top.

Lift off the top layer of cling film from the pastry and discard it, then lift the dough by the lower cling film and drape it over the tart ring. Remove the remaining cling film and ease the dough into the ring. Now take your little ball of dough from the fridge and, still in its cling film, use it to press the dough gently into the shape of the ring.

Trim the pastry by running a rolling pin over the edges of the ring.

Now, press between your index finger and thumb all around the edge of the tart ring just to raise the edge of the pastry 2mm above the ring, to compensate for the slight retraction of the pastry during cooking.

With a fork, prick the bottom of the pastry case. This will help the even distribution of heat when the tart is in the oven. Put into the fridge again for about 20 minutes to relax the pastry.

Preheat the oven to 220°C/200°C fan/gas 8 and put a baking stone, or another baking tray, onto the middle shelf to heat up.

Peel and core the apples and cut each one into 10 segments. Arrange these close together in overlapping circles in the base of the tart case.

In a small pan, melt the butter and sugar, then take the pan from the heat and mix in the lemon juice and Calvados, if using. Brush this mixture over the apple slices and dust liberally with icing sugar.

Slide the tart from your tray directly onto the preheated baking stone or tray in the oven and cook for 10 minutes, then turn down the temperature to 200°C/180°C fan/gas 6 and bake for a further 20 minutes until the pastry is light golden and the apples are beautifully caramelised. (If you are adding custard, pour this in 10 minutes before the end of cooking time.)

Remove from the oven and leave to stand for about 30 minutes before serving as the tarte will be at its best when barely warm. Remove the ring and slide the tart onto a large, flat plate. Dust with a little more icing sugar to serve.

TARTE TATIN

This is a book of stories, and the story of the Tatin sisters, Caroline and Stéphanie, is one of the most famous of them all. In the late nineteenth century the sisters unquestionably made this glorious, sensuous tarte famous at their hotel just north of Lamotte-Beuvron in the historic region of Sologne – though it has long been debated whether it really was, as legend has it, the result of a happy accident after Stéphanie left some apples for a pie for too long and rescued the situation by draping them in pastry and baking them anyway. The sisters may not even have truly invented the concept, as rustic upside-down tarts, or cobblers, were said to be known in the Sologne region, but they almost certainly perfected the seductive combination of sweet caramel, sharp apples and crisp pastry that is still one of the best-loved of all desserts. Of course the choice of apples is crucial, as you need a variety that will hold its shape and have enough character and acidity to counteract the sweetness of the caramel. Our tasting tests showed us that the very best apples are the Cox's Orange Pippin, Chivers Delight, Devonshire Quarrenden and Red Windsor, and I also like to use Granny Smiths.

Serve the tarte with crème fraîche or a scoop of good-quality vanilla ice cream.

SERVES: 6

EQUIPMENT: 20cm deep flameproof tarte tatin dish or a deep oven-proof frying pan

300g all-butter puff
  pastry

For the filling
40ml water
100g caster sugar

6 apples (approx. 900g),
  such as Braeburn or Cox's
  Orange Pippin
90g unsalted butter (60g chilled
  and diced, 30g melted)

On a lightly floured surface roll out the pastry to 3mm thick and cut out a 24cm circle, using a plate as a guide. Lightly prick all over with a fork, wrap in cling film and put into the freezer until ready to use.

Preheat the oven to 180°C/160°C fan/gas 4.

Pour the water into the tatin dish or pan, spoon in the sugar evenly and let it absorb the water for 1–2 minutes.

Meanwhile, peel, halve vertically and core your apples. Cut a tiny piece from the base of each half to help it to stand upright.

Place the tatin dish or pan over a medium–high heat and cook until you have a dark amber caramel, then take off the heat, stir in the 60g of chilled, diced butter and put to one side to cool slightly.

Arrange the apple halves upright on top, in concentric circles, packing them in as tightly as you can like spoons and trimming them as necessary so that there are no gaps. Brush the fruit with the melted butter.

Bake in the preheated oven for 30 minutes, then take out the dish or pan. Remove the sheet of puff pastry from the freezer and lay on top. It will defrost very quickly and allow you to tuck in the edges all the way around.

With a knife, prick a few holes in the pastry to allow steam to escape. Return the dish or pan to the oven for a further 30 minutes until the puff pastry is golden brown and crisp.

Allow the tarte tatin to cool at room temperature for about 1–2 hours, to allow the pectin to thicken the juices, then simply run a knife around the edge of the dish and invert onto a large, deep serving plate.

APPLE CRUMBLE COOKIES

Granny Smiths are good for this recipe. I have suggested rolling out the dough to make round biscuits, but if you want a chunkier, rustic-looking cookie, just divide the mixture into thirty equal pieces, flatten them very slightly and then bake them as below.

MAKES: approx. 30 cookies

EQUIPMENT: 5cm pastry cutter

200g self-raising flour
1 teaspoon bicarbonate of soda
160g rolled oats
100g demerara sugar
1 apple, such as Granny Smith,
    Bramley or Red Windsor,
    grated

60g dried cranberries
120g unsalted butter
30g maple syrup

Preheat the oven to 180°C/160°C fan/gas 4.

In a medium bowl, sift together the flour and bicarbonate of soda. Add the oats, sugar and grated apple and stir until evenly distributed. Remove 4 tablespoons of the mixture and set aside. This will be used to top the cookies and give a crumble effect.

Stir the cranberries into the mixture in the bowl.

In a small saucepan on a medium heat, melt the butter with the maple syrup. Add this to the flour and fruit in the bowl, mixing well until it comes together in a crumbly dough.

Lay a large piece of greaseproof paper on a flat surface and spoon the mixture onto it. Lay a second sheet of greaseproof paper on top and then, with a rolling pin, roll over the top until the mixture has flattened to 1cm in thickness.

Transfer to the fridge to chill for 10 minutes.

Using a 5cm pastry cutter, cut out circles of the dough and arrange on two baking trays lined with greaseproof paper, leaving a gap of about 5mm between each one. Sprinkle each cookie with some of the reserved crumble mixture and bake in the preheated oven for 10–12 minutes until lightly golden.

Once the cookies are baked, remove from the oven and cool on a wire rack.

Once cool, you can store them in an airtight container.

BUCKWHEAT PANCAKES
WITH APPLE COMPOTE

Buckwheat pancakes are popular in Northern France, often filled with chopped ham, tomato or Comté cheese from my region of Franche-Comté, but they are equally beautiful with a delicious apple compote and a big spoonful of crème fraîche. I like to use Braeburn apples because they have a good balance of sweetness and acidity, which results in a compote with a perfect texture, not too watery and with a big apple flavour.

MAKES: 16 pancakes

EQUIPMENT: medium (30cm) non-stick frying pan

For the pancake mixture
500ml whole milk
3 medium eggs (preferably
　organic or free-range)
pinch of sea salt
200g buckwheat flour
80g butter, melted, plus
　extra butter, for cooking
　the pancakes

For the apple compote
4 Braeburn apples, cored, peeled
　and cut into 3cm pieces
2 tablespoons water
juice of ¼ lemon, to taste
crème fraîche, to serve

In a large jug, whisk together the milk, eggs and salt.

To a large bowl, add the buckwheat flour, make a well in the middle and gently pour in the milk and egg mixture, whisking as you go until you have a smooth batter. Whisk in the melted butter, then leave to rest in the fridge for 30 minutes.

In a non-stick 30cm diameter frying pan on a medium heat, melt ½ teaspoon of butter until foaming, then pour in enough pancake mixture to cover the base of the pan with a thin film (this should be about 60ml). Cook for 15–20 seconds until golden, then flip over using a broad spatula and continue to cook for a further 15 seconds on the other side. Slide onto a warm plate and continue with the remaining mixture until you have 16 pancakes.

For the compote, in a medium saucepan on a medium heat bring the apples and water to a simmer with the lid on. Make sure this is tightfitting so that you retain all the moisture otherwise the pan will boil dry and the apples will caramelise. Cook for 10–12 minutes until the apples break down and become soft. Add a little more water if necessary.

Add a squeeze of lemon juice, stir and serve with your buckwheat pancakes and a big spoon of crème fraîche.

OONAGH FAWKES'S APPLE CRUMBLE

This recipe is based on the one kindly given to me by Clare Scheckter of Laverstoke Park after I tasted the crumble when I visited the farm. This was her mother Oonagh's recipe, which was so delightful that it convinced me to reconsider Bramley apples, as that was the variety she had used, but here I have suggested a mixture of Cox or Braeburn and Bramleys. Clare and her husband Jody, the former Formula One World Champion, farm buffalo at Laverstoke Park. We are kindred spirits as they farm organically and biodynamically, as we do at Le Manoir aux Quat'Saisons, and since they are famous for their buffalo milk which goes to make beautiful mozzarella and ice cream, they serve this crumble with home-made buffalo-milk custard! I always like to pre-cook the crumble mixture by spreading it over a baking tray for 15 minutes or so first, so that you keep it light and crisp and avoid that slightly gluey, stodgy layer just below the crunchy surface, which is caused by the steam rising from the fruit underneath.

SERVES: 4–6

8 apples, a mix of Cox's
   Orange Pippin or Braeburn
   and Bramley
100ml fresh apple juice

caster sugar, to taste
290g self-raising flour
290g demerara sugar
175g butter, cut into chunks

Preheat the oven to 180°C/160°C fan/gas 4.

Peel, core and quarter the apples, then cut each quarter into chunks and put into a pan. Pour the apple juice over the chunks.

Cook gently for 8–10 minutes until the apples are almost soft, but be careful not to let them become mushy. Taste and, if necessary, add a little caster sugar.

With a slotted spoon, lift half of the apples from the juice into a pie dish. Gently press with the back of a spoon.

Use the slotted spoon to lift out the remaining chunks of apple from the pan and scatter over the mixture in the dish. Pour the juices over the top.

To make the crumble, in a bowl mix the flour and demerara sugar, and rub in the butter gently between your fingertips, as if making pastry. When the butter is incorporated and the mixture resembles breadcrumbs, squeeze clumps of it gently again with your fingertips, so that it becomes quite lumpy and sticky.

Spoon the crumble over the fruit, but don't press it down, then put into the preheated oven for about 40 minutes or until lightly browned. Serve hot with custard.

MINCE PIES

Of course I am biased, but I think that Le Manoir mince pies are the best in the world! The mince pie is one of those British traditions that I so completely love, but I cannot resist trying to improve on a classic, and the making of the mincemeat, ready to encase in the finest, crumbliest pâte sablée is all part of the Christmas ritual at Le Manoir aux Quat'Saisons, which our guests love – and my family in France, too.

Every year when I go home for the big celebrations, I take boxes of the mince pies with me (though they are quite fragile, and don't always arrive in one piece!), as well as two Christmas puddings, and almost the first thing my mother will say to me is, 'Raymond, *mon fils*, did you bring the mince pies and the puddings?' Every year the ritual is that I do a reading in the local church, which I write myself, and one year my reading was inspired by the puddings and pies!

I prefer to use much less sugar than you will find in many mincemeat recipes, as the sweetness of the currants and peel is enough to counteract the sourness of the Bramley apple. The mincemeat may be made one month in advance. The pies may be made and frozen, then cooked when needed. Or, once cooked, they will keep in an airtight tin for five days; just pass them through the oven to freshen the pastry before serving.

MAKES: about 30 pies

EQUIPMENT: 30 non-stick tartlet moulds, pastry cutters

For the mincemeat

225g (1 large) Bramley apple, peeled, cored and finely diced

110g suet

110g currants

175g mixed peel, chopped

110g dark brown or muscovado sugar

1 teaspoon sweet mixed spice

pinch of nutmeg, freshly grated

zest and juice of 1 lemon

zest and juice of 1 orange

2 tablespoons Cognac

For the sweet shortcrust pastry

125g unsalted butter

60g icing sugar

1 medium egg

250g plain flour

To finish

1 egg, beaten

icing sugar

To make the mincemeat, in a large bowl mix all the ingredients together, and stir well. Store in an airtight container in the fridge for four days before using (you can keep the mincemeat in the fridge for up to a month).

To make the pastry, mix together the butter and icing sugar until they are completely blended. Add the egg and finally the flour. Knead until you have a smooth dough. Leave to rest for at least 1 hour before using.

Preheat the oven to 190°C/170°C fan/gas 5.

Roll the pastry out to a little less than 5mm thick. Cut out thirty rounds just a little larger than your tartlet moulds and thirty rounds with a pastry cutter two sizes down.

Line the tartlet moulds with the large rounds of pastry. Fill them with the mincemeat to level with the sides.

Now, brush a little beaten egg around the edges of the smaller rounds and stick them on top of the mince pies. Brush with a little more beaten egg, then bake for 25 minutes until golden brown.

Transfer from the moulds to a wire rack and leave to cool. Sprinkle generously with icing sugar.

BAKED CARAMELISED CRAB APPLES

I have created these beautiful autumnal petits fours as a celebration of the season. The apples are simply baked, then coated in caramel that is infused with a little ginger and lime, and encrusted in nuts. Chilled first to set the caramel, then served at room temperature, they are delightful little treats to serve to your friends at the end of dinner.

MAKES: 12 petits fours

12 small crab apples
  (approx. 20g each), washed
50g caster sugar
25g unsalted butter, cubed

25ml lime juice
pinch of salt
½ teaspoon finely grated fresh
  ginger

For the garnish
1 teaspoon pistachio nuts, roughly chopped
1 teaspoon nibbed almonds

Preheat the oven to 175°C/160°C fan/gas 4.

Arrange the crab apples upright in a heavy-based oven tray. Place in the preheated oven for 25 minutes until the apples are cooked through and soft, but still hold their shape.

In a medium saucepan on a medium heat, bring the caster sugar to a blond caramel.

Remove from the heat, carefully add the butter and move the pan to allow the liquid to swirl around and cool down, to prevent it from caramelising further.

Add the lime juice, salt and ginger, return the pan to the heat and simmer until you have a thick caramel that will coat the back of a spoon. Take off the heat and allow to cool slightly.

Line a clean tray with baking parchment.

Holding each of the crab apples by its stalk, dip into the caramel sauce, and place on the lined tray.

Sprinkle with the chopped pistachios and nibbed almonds and put into the fridge for 30 minutes.

Remove from the fridge and allow the apples to come back to room temperature before serving.

HOME-PRESERVED PEARS

When I was growing up, the preserving, bottling and labelling of fruit was a wonderful and constant ritual. It is very satisfying to prepare, peel, cook and preserve your favourite pears, such as Williams' Bon Chrétien or Doyenne du Comice, to be enjoyed throughout the winter as an easy dessert. These are not for children, though, as the alcohol will not completely disappear. Serve them with some Chantilly cream or crumbled ginger biscuits and a simple chocolate sauce (see page 307) for a true winter feast.

MAKES: enough for 2 x 1-litre jars

EQUIPMENT: kilner jars (sterilised, see page 312)

8–10 pears (not too ripe)
juice of 1 lemon, plus 1 litre
  water
200g caster sugar

1.5 litres water
2 whole vanilla pods
150ml Poire William eau de vie

Peel, core and quarter the pears and put immediately into a bowl containing the lemon juice and water. This is to prevent them from oxidising and turning brown.

In a large saucepan on a high heat, bring the sugar and 1.5 litres water to the boil. Transfer the pear quarters from the bowl into the hot syrup and add the vanilla pods. Bring back to the boil, then turn down to a gentle simmer for 7–10 minutes, depending on how ripe the pears are, until they just begin to turn soft.

Using a slotted spoon, transfer the pears into the sterilised kilner jars.

Divide the eau de vie equally between the kilner jars and then add the hot cooking liquor. Include a vanilla pod in each jar.

With a clean cloth, wipe the jars clean of any spilt cooking liquor, especially around the rims. Seal the lids and leave to cool.

The pears can be kept for up to 2 months in a cool place.

Alternatively, if you want to store them for a lot longer, place a small round wire rack, upturned plate or cloth in the bottom of a large stockpot. Place the jars on top, so they are not in direct contact with the pan (this will prevent them from shattering). Completely submerge in cold water (starting from cold water will also prevent shattering) and bring to a simmer (96°C) for 30 minutes.

Carefully remove the jars from the water and leave to cool down completely at room temperature. The jars can be kept in a cool place for many months.

TARTES FINES AUX POIRES

Traditionally *tartes fines* are made with apples, but I think the thin, crisp golden pastry is the perfect foil for a ripe, juicy pear like Doyenne du Comice, which will hold its shape once cooked, and have just enough acidity to balance the sweetness of the dessert. These individual tarts can be made a few hours in advance and baked at the last minute.

MAKES: 4 tarts

EQUIPMENT: 15cm pastry cutter, mandoline

For the tarts

400g all-butter puff pastry, refrigerated

50g unsalted butter, at room temperature

50g caster sugar

50g ground almonds

1 medium egg (preferably organic or free-range)

2 medium pears, cores removed

icing sugar, for dusting

For the glaze

45g unsalted butter

2 tablespoons caster sugar

1 teaspoon lemon juice

2 teaspoons Poire William eau de vie (optional)

Two hours in advance, roll out the cold puff pastry to 1.5mm (it is important that it is thin, in order to achieve the finest crust). Leave to rest in the fridge. This will make it easier to work with and will help prevent it from shrinking.

Preheat the oven to 220°C/200°C fan/gas 8.

301

Take the puff pastry out of the fridge and either use a pastry cutter or cut around a small plate to give four discs, 15cm in diameter. Lay these on a baking tray, cover with greaseproof paper and put back in the fridge while you make the almond cream.

In a large bowl, combine the butter, sugar, almonds and egg, and mix until well blended.

Remove the tray from the fridge and prick the pastry discs with a fork, leaving a 1cm border around the edge. The area that you have pricked will not rise so much and will crisp in the oven, leaving the border to puff up around the outside. Spread the almond cream equally over each pastry disc as far as this border.

Using a mandoline, cut each pear lengthways into 2mm slices. Fan the slices on the top of the almond cream, again keeping within the border.

To make the glaze, in a small pan melt the butter, then add the sugar, lemon juice and Poire William eau de vie, if using, and brush most of this all over the tarts, including the border. Keep back the remainder to reglaze the tarts when they come out of the oven.

Put the tray into the preheated oven for about 15 minutes until the pastry is golden brown and crisp at the base and the border has puffed up.

Allow to cool a little, but while still warm brush the tarts once again with the glaze and then sprinkle with a little icing sugar.

PEAR FRANGIPANE TARTELETTES

These tartelettes are a variation on the previous recipe, made with bottled or tinned pears and no pastry. If you prefer, instead of making individual ones, you can use a large ring (16cm) – bake it for the same length of time – and then cut the tarte into slices. And you can add your own flourish to the flavour palette by mixing a little orange or lemon zest, some chopped nuts or dried fruits into the frangipane mixture.

MAKES: 10–12 tartelettes

EQUIPMENT: 12 x 7cm tartelette rings, 4cm pastry cutter

50g unsalted butter, at room
   temperature
50g caster sugar
50g ground almonds
1 medium egg (preferably
   organic or free-range)

12 pear quarters, bottled (see
   page 299) or tinned
10g flaked almonds
icing sugar, for dusting

Preheat the oven to 175°C/155°C fan/gas 3.

To make the frangipane, in a large bowl combine the butter, sugar, ground almonds and egg and mix until well blended.

Place the tartelette rings on a baking tray lined with greaseproof paper and spoon the mixture evenly into each one so that it comes a third of the way up the ring.

Drain the pear quarters. Lay on a chopping board and, using the pastry cutter, cut out a circle from the widest part of each one and set aside. Chop the trimmings of each pear and distribute amongst the tartelettes, then top with a reserved circle of pear. Scatter with the flaked almonds.

Bake the tartelettes in the middle of the preheated oven for 20–25 minutes until the frangipane is golden in colour. Leave to cool before sliding off the rings (if necessary, run a knife around the edge to release them).

Dust with icing sugar and serve.

PEAR AND GINGER STEAMED PUDDING

You might not expect a French chef to love a steamed pudding, but I do! When I first arrived in Britain all those years ago, I understood that ginger was a traditional ingredient in English baking, but as a ground spice. Then I discovered root ginger in an Asian supermarket and I was completely seduced by this new flavour and the possibilities that it opened up. In this celebration of a traditional English dessert, the warm spiciness of the ginger works beautifully with the sweetness of the pear and the slow, gentle steaming of the pudding leaves you with a light, delicate sponge, which has soaked up all the aromatic juices from the pears and caramel. Serve it with ice cream, clotted cream, crème fraîche or crème anglaise.

SERVES: 6–8

EQUIPMENT: pastry brush, 2-litre pudding basin, foil, string, large saucepan with a lid and a trivet, food mixer

To prepare the pudding basin
60g unsalted butter, at room temperature
60g caster sugar

To caramelise the pears
100g caster sugar
4 pears, peeled, cored and quartered
125ml dessert wine
1 teaspoon finely grated fresh ginger
zest and juice of 2 limes

For the sponge
150g unsalted butter
150g caster sugar
2 medium eggs (preferably organic or free-range)
2 teaspoons ground ginger
2 tablespoons crystallised ginger, finely chopped
2 tablespoons syrup from the crystallised ginger
300g self-raising flour
250g crème fraîche

To prepare the pudding basin, using a pastry brush lightly coat the inside of the pudding basin with butter and pour in the caster sugar. Roll the bowl around in order to coat the inside of the bowl with a thin layer of the sugar. Set to one side while you prepare the rest of the filling.

To caramelise the pears, in a medium saucepan on a high heat, bring the sugar to a golden caramel. Put in the quarters of pear, reduce the heat to medium and gently caramelise the pears for 5 minutes on each side.

Add the dessert wine, ginger and lime zest and juice. Bring to the boil, then reduce for a further 5 minutes until you have a thick glaze.

Transfer the caramelised pears to your prepared pudding basin and set to one side while you prepare the sponge mixture.

In a food mixer fitted with the paddle attachment, cream together the butter and sugar until light and fluffy, then add the eggs, ground ginger and crystallised ginger and syrup and beat until all the ingredients are evenly incorporated. Now add the flour and crème fraîche and continue to beat until you have a smooth batter.

Spoon the mixture over the pears, cover the top of the basin with a double layer of foil and secure with string.

Place the basin in a large saucepan on a trivet and pour in enough boiling water to come halfway up the outsides. Cover with a lid, bring to the boil over a medium–high heat, then reduce to a simmer and cook for 2 hours 45 minutes, topping up with extra boiling water when necessary. When cooked the pudding will be firm but springy to the touch.

Carefully place a large plate on top of the basin and turn the pudding out onto the plate.

POACHED PEAR WITH GINGER BISCUITS AND CHOCOLATE SAUCE

Poire belle Hélène – pear in chocolate sauce – is a classic French dessert, created in 1864 by the great chef Auguste Escoffier. He named it after the Offenbach operetta *La Belle Hélène*, which is a parody of the famous story of Helen of Troy. This dish was the inspiration for my own dessert. Texture is very important, and so for my interpretation I use soft poached or preserved pears (see page 299), which contrast with the crunchiness of home-made ginger biscuits, unified by a simple but rich chocolate sauce. If you have a jar of pears in your cupboard you are halfway there, and your family and friends will love you for the extra effort of making the gently spiced biscuits.

SERVES: 4

4 pears, poached or
    preserved as on page 299

For the ginger biscuits
200g plain flour
2 teaspoons bicarbonate of soda
2 teaspoons baking powder
100g unsalted butter, diced, at
    room temperature
80g golden caster sugar

1 teaspoon mixed spice
1 teaspoon ground ginger
1 teaspoon ground cinnamon
40g golden syrup

For the chocolate sauce
2 tablespoons whole milk
90ml whipping cream
80g dark chocolate (70 per cent
    cocoa solids), chopped

To make the ginger biscuits, sift the flour, bicarbonate of soda and baking powder together into a large bowl.

Add the diced butter, sugar and spices and rub in evenly.

Have a sheet of greaseproof paper ready on a large baking tray.

In a small pan on a high heat, bring the golden syrup to the boil, then pour slowly into the biscuit mix, stirring with a wooden spoon until all the ingredients are combined and you have a smooth but slightly sticky dough.

Spoon the mixture onto the sheet of greaseproof paper and press it down so that it is approximately 2cm thick. Cover with another sheet of greaseproof and then put the tray into the fridge to rest for a few minutes. This will allow the butter to firm up slightly so that the mixture will be easier to handle.

Preheat the oven to 180°C/160°C fan/gas 4.

Line two more baking trays with greaseproof paper. Take the biscuit mixture from the fridge and divide the dough into golf-ball-sized pieces.

Flatten each one slightly and lay on the lined trays.

Bake in the preheated oven for 10 minutes, then reduce the temperature to 150°C/130°C fan/gas 1 and continue to bake for 5 more minutes.

Meanwhile, make the chocolate sauce. In a medium pan, bring the milk and cream to the boil, then take off the heat and add the chocolate, stirring continuously until it has melted and you have a smooth sauce.

To serve, gently crumble some of the biscuits into the centre of each of four plates. Top with the poached or preserved pear and pour the chocolate sauce over and around.

ROAST APRICOT COUSCOUS

This is delicious and quick to make. It can be served on its own but is also lovely with slow-roasted shoulder of lamb. Couscous recipes often use dried apricots, but by roasting fresh apricots you win all the way. All the juices become concentrated as the fruits roast in the oven and when they are lightly tossed through the couscous you have a vibrant and colourful dish. You can make the couscous up to four hours in advance.

SERVES: 4 as a starter or 6 as a side dish

To roast the apricots
4 apricots, stoned and quartered
½ teaspoon ras-el-hanout (Moroccan spice mix)
15g clear honey

For the seed and nut mix
20g sunflower seeds
20g pumpkin seeds
15g flaked almonds
½ teaspoon coriander seeds
½ teaspoon cumin seeds
½ teaspoon fennel seeds

For the couscous
125g couscous
30ml olive oil, plus a little extra to serve
2 pinches of sea salt
pinch of saffron powder
200ml boiling water
¼ bunch of fresh coriander
¼ bunch of fresh parsley
¼ bunch of fresh mint
juice of ½ lemon
2 spring onions, finely sliced
1 red chilli, deseeded and finely sliced

Preheat the oven to 180°C/160°C fan/gas 4.

In a bowl mix together the apricots, ras-el-hanout and honey until all the apricots are coated. Transfer to a baking tray lined with baking parchment and roast in the preheated oven for 8 minutes. Remove and allow to cool.

For the seed and nut mix, spread the sunflower seeds, pumpkin seeds and flaked almonds over a baking tray and put into the oven for 7 minutes until golden. Remove and allow to cool.

In a medium frying pan over a medium heat, toast the coriander, cumin and fennel seeds for 2–3 minutes until they start to pop and release their aromas. Remove from the pan and allow to cool. Mix with the toasted nuts and seeds and keep to one side.

In a large bowl, mix the couscous, olive oil, salt and saffron. Pour the boiling water over the top and cover tightly with cling film. Allow to stand for 5 minutes before fluffing up the couscous with a fork.

Roughly chop the fresh herbs and add two-thirds to the couscous together with the lemon juice and seed mix. Combine all together, taste and adjust the salt if necessary.

Top the couscous with the roasted apricots and sprinkle over the rest of the freshly chopped herbs together with the sliced spring onions and chilli. Drizzle with a little olive oil and serve.

APRICOT CHUTNEY

This chutney is delicious with any cheese, but my favourite is an aged Comté cheese from my region in France, whose delicate, nutty flavour is beautiful with the sweet and sour apricot chutney and a glass of Vin Jaune – although my French ancestors might turn in their graves at the idea of serving an English chutney with one of our greatest French cheeses. The chutney will only keep for around four weeks in the fridge in a sealed container, and for a week after opening.

MAKES: 700g chutney

EQUIPMENT: food processor, muslin bag, sealed container

500g dried apricots
1 tablespoon white wine
   vinegar
500ml dry white wine
60g caster sugar

1 star anise, ½ cinnamon stick
   (crushed) and 8 black pepper-
   corns, in a muslin bag
1 tablespoon vanilla extract
juice of ½ lemon, to taste

In a large food processor using the pulse button, chop the dried apricots four times for 20 seconds each time, until you have a fine dice.

In a medium pan over a high heat, bring the vinegar, wine and sugar to the boil for 2 minutes. Add the remaining ingredients and simmer for another 2 minutes.

Take off the heat and leave to cool at room temperature, covered with cling film.

Once cool, taste and add a little more lemon juice if necessary to balance the sweetness. Keep in the sealed container in the fridge.

LOW-SUGAR APRICOT JAM

Traditionally, most jams are made with an equal part of sugar to fruit. Sugar is the magical ingredient loved by pâtissiers because it preserves as well as adding flavour and density to a jam, but I am someone who believes that good cooking, nutrition and good health must go together and so, many years ago, I cut down the sugar used in the kitchen and the patisserie. Not only is there a point where sugar actually overpowers the flavour of the fruit rather than enhancing it, but we are all now becoming aware of the health challenges that we face as a society that is collectively eating too much salt and sugar.

Yes, if you put less sugar into a jam, you won't be able to make a massive batch from one fruit and keep it for years, but think of it as a chance to reconnect with the seasons and make smaller quantities from whatever fruit is in abundance at a particular moment. At first my pâtissiers were unhappy at my war on sugar, but now they embrace these values, and are happy to make wonderful, less-sweet jam with a succession of fruits throughout the year. This particular recipe is beautiful made with the Tomcot® or Flavorcot® apricots, which we grow in abundance.

I have found that apple pectin is the best for jam-making, as it has a stronger binding than any other I've tried.

You need to sterilise your jars ready to receive the jam, so put them into a large pan, cover them completely with water, bring to the boil and then continue to boil over a high heat for 10 minutes. Remove with tongs and allow the jars to drip-dry upside down on a clean wire rack. Fill them while both the jars and the jam are still hot.

MAKES: 1kg jam

EQUIPMENT: airtight glass jars (sterilised, see previous page)

970g apricots, stoned and quartered (not peeled)	10g pectin
	4 tablespoons water
230g caster sugar	4 teaspoons lemon juice
To make the jam	**To seal the jars**
20g caster sugar	80ml kirsch liqueur

To prepare the jam, in a large bowl macerate the apricots in the 230g of caster sugar for 15 minutes. The sugar will permeate the fruit, providing better texture and increasing the flavour.

In a large, heavy-based saucepan over a medium heat, bring the macerated apricots to a gentle simmer. Skim off any froth that rises to the surface and cook for a few minutes until broken down (the riper the fruit, the quicker this will happen).

In a small bowl, mix together the 20g of sugar, pectin and water until smooth and lump-free. Leave to one side for 15 minutes for the sugar to absorb the water and form a paste. Stir the paste into the simmering apricots and bring to the boil for 3 minutes.

To test if the jam is the right consistency, pour a tablespoon onto a plate and put into the fridge for 10 minutes. Turn off the heat under the jam. The jam is set if it wrinkles when you push your finger into it. If the jam isn't quite setting, bring it back to the boil for 5 minutes and repeat the test. Once at a setting consistency, stir in the lemon juice and allow to cool slightly before pouring into sterilised jars.

To create an airtight seal, gently warm a small pan with the kirsch and, using a long match or lighter, set it alight, then carefully pour a layer over the jam. Quickly screw on each lid and leave to cool. This will create a bacteria-free vacuum inside the jar. Unopened, you can store the jam in a cool, dark place for up to two months. Once open, keep refrigerated and use within two weeks.

ROAST APRICOTS
WITH COCONUT RICE

This Thai-style dessert is all about the apricots, so you need really ripe fruit. The rice needs to be soaked for a minimum of four hours and preferably overnight. If you like you can add a dash of kirsch or apricot liqueur to the apricots as they roast in the oven. You could also make this with nectarines or white peaches.

SERVES: 4

For the coconut rice

50g glutinous rice

300ml coconut milk

20g palm sugar

juice of 2 limes

pinch of cayenne pepper

For the apricots

6 large apricots, cut in half and stoned

15g unsalted butter, melted

20g light brown sugar

zest and juice of 1 lime

juice of 1 orange

To serve

1 tablespoon crushed pistachios

Soak the rice in water for a minimum of 4 hours (preferably overnight), then drain.

Preheat the oven to 180°C/160°C fan/gas 4.

In a large saucepan on a high heat, bring the drained rice, coconut milk and palm sugar to the boil, then turn down to a simmer for 15 minutes, stirring frequently, until the rice is cooked but still keeps its shape.

Remove from the heat. Stir in the lime juice and cayenne pepper and set aside. At this point the rice will look a little 'soupy', but as it cools it will thicken up and absorb all of the coconut milk.

Meanwhile, lay the apricots on a baking tray, cut-side up, and, with a pastry brush, brush the top of each apricot with the melted butter. Scatter over the brown sugar and finish with the grated lime zest. Pour the lime and orange juice into the bottom of the tray.

Roast the apricots in the preheated oven for 15–20 minutes until the apricots are slightly golden on top.

Divide the coconut rice into four bowls, top with the apricot halves, then sprinkle with the crushed pistachios and any apricot juice left in the baking tray.

PAN-FRIED APRICOTS
WITH PAIN PERDU

A French tradition based on the simple principle that leftover bread should never be wasted. In our house it was kept in an earthenware pot and, when the pot was full, Maman Blanc would soak slices of the bread in beaten egg, milk and vanilla and bake them in the oven. Brioche just makes the pain perdu even more luxurious. Nowadays you can buy very good-quality brioche, so this recipe is relatively simple to make.

SERVES: 4

For the pan-fried apricots
700g apricots, cut in half and stoned

For the pain perdu
2 medium eggs (preferably organic or free-range)
50g caster sugar
100ml whole milk
2 teaspoons kirsch, rum or Cognac (optional)

To serve
crème fraîche

40g caster sugar
1 tablespoon lemon juice
2 tablespoons unsalted butter

1 teaspoon vanilla extract or vanilla syrup
4 slices of brioche, 2cm thick, crusts removed and halved or quartered diagonally
40g unsalted butter

In a large bowl, macerate the apricots in the caster sugar and lemon juice for 30 minutes. This will help them to release their juices, enhancing their flavour.

316

Preheat the oven to 120°C/100°C fan/gas ½.

In a separate large bowl, using a whisk beat the eggs and sugar together, then whisk in the milk, alcohol, if using, and vanilla.

Put in the brioche slices and leave for 4–5 minutes to allow them to absorb the egg mixture. With a large, wide spatula, carefully lift the brioche slices from the bowl and reserve on a plate or tray.

Melt the butter in a large frying pan over a medium heat. When it is foaming, fry the brioche slices, in batches if necessary, for 2–3 minutes on each side until they turn a rich golden brown.

Lift the brioche slices from the pan with the wide spatula and place on a baking tray, then transfer the tray to the preheated oven for 5 minutes.

Meanwhile, to pan-fry the apricots, in a large frying pan on a high heat, add 1 tablespoon of the butter and cook until it starts to turn a golden brown, then add half the apricots. Pan-fry for up to 1 minute, depending on their ripeness, until they start to soften and begin to caramelise. Transfer the apricots to a shallow dish and leave to cool slightly while you repeat the process for the remaining butter and apricots.

To serve, remove the hot brioche slices from the oven and divide onto four warmed plates. Spoon the warm apricots onto the brioche and serve with a bowl of crème fraîche on the side.

APRICOT CHEESECAKE

This recipe is a little different and slightly more elaborate than many cheesecakes. It looks long, but I promise you it is worth the effort as it is one of the tastiest and most good-looking desserts.

SERVES: 10

EQUIPMENT: 18cm x 4cm mousse ring, sugar thermometer, food mixer

For the roast apricots
8 apricots, stoned and quartered
30g caster sugar

For the cheesecake mixture
300g cream cheese
130g crème fraîche
1 tablespoon vanilla extract
juice of ½ lemon (keep back
  1 drop for the egg whites)

2 gelatine leaves
5 teaspoons water
100g caster sugar
4 egg whites

For the apricot compote
500g apricots, cut in half
  and stoned

50g caster sugar

To serve
30 amaretti biscuits, crushed

For the roast apricots, preheat the oven to 180°C/160°C fan/gas 4.

Place the mousse ring on a flat baking tray and line tightly with cling film, making sure there are no holes.

On a flat non-stick baking tray, arrange the quartered apricots, skin-side down, and sprinkle with the caster sugar. Put into the preheated oven for 10 minutes.

Remove, allow to cool, and then roughly chop and keep to one side.

For the cheesecake mixture, in a large bowl mix the cream cheese, crème fraîche, vanilla extract and lemon juice together.

Put the gelatine leaves in a small saucepan with 2 teaspoons of the water and place over a gentle heat until the gelatine melts. Take off the heat, allow to cool slightly and then briskly whisk into the cream mixture.

In another small pan, heat the sugar in the rest of the water until it dissolves. Bring to the boil and continue to heat to 121°C (check the temperature using a sugar thermometer). Remove from the heat, and get ready a large bowl of iced water.

Now you are going to make an Italian meringue. In a food mixer fitted with the whisk attachment, whisk the egg whites, adding just a single drop of lemon juice at the beginning, until they form soft peaks.

Turn the whisk to a medium speed and pour the hot sugar syrup down the side of the bowl in a single thread as you continue to whisk on a medium speed for a further 5 minutes until the mixture is glossy – the hot syrup will partially cook the egg white, making it stable.

Remove the mixing bowl from its stand and rest the base in the bowl of iced water. Continue to whisk by hand until the mixture is completely cool.

Add half of the meringue to the cheesecake mixture and briskly beat with a whisk until smooth, then fold in the remaining meringue, followed by the reserved chopped roasted apricots.

Spoon the filling into the ring and level the surface with a palette knife or the back of a spoon. Put into the fridge for 2 hours to allow the mixture to firm up before serving.

For the apricot compote, put the apricot halves into a bowl with the sugar and leave to macerate for 15 minutes. Transfer to a medium saucepan on a medium heat and cook for 10 minutes with a lid on, so that the apricots bubble gently. Stir from time to time to prevent the compote from catching on the bottom of the pan.

Remove from the heat and allow to cool completely, taste and adjust the consistency with a splash of water if necessary, and if the flavour is too sharp, add a little sugar.

To serve, place a plate over the top of the cheesecake and invert it onto a serving plate. Carefully lift off the cling film and run a hot, thin palette knife around the inside of the ring to release the cheese-cake. Lift off the ring.

Sprinkle the crushed amaretti biscuits onto the cheesecake and serve with the compote alongside.

KIRSCH BABA WITH WARM CHERRIES

There is a lovely story about the origins of the baba (see page 223) – one of the celebrated French classics. The original was made with rum, but in our family we always used kirsch, from my region.

SERVES: 8

EQUIPMENT: cherry stoner, 16cm x 16cm container, a blender

For the cherries
50 black cherries
100ml water
20ml kirsch liqueur
2 tablespoons caster sugar
squeeze of lemon juice
pinch of ground black pepper
pinch of ground cloves
pinch of ground cinnamon

For the soaked brioches
8 individual brioches, or a loaf
   sliced into 2cm pieces
400ml water
100g caster sugar
3 tablespoons kirsch

For the vanilla cream
150ml whipping cream
1 teaspoon vanilla extract

To make the vanilla cream, in a medium bowl, with a hand whisk whip the cream to soft peaks, then whisk in the vanilla extract. Reserve in the fridge.

Remove the stones from the cherries and discard along with the stalks.

Using a sharp knife, slice each individual brioche in half from top to bottom, or into 2cm pieces if using a loaf.

In a medium pan over a medium heat, bring the 400ml water, 100g caster sugar and 3 tablespoons kirsch to the boil for a few seconds, then remove from the heat and leave to cool slightly.

Place the halved brioches in the container, pour the hot syrup over them, then cover with cling film and leave to soak for about 6–10 minutes before serving. The brioche will swell.

Meanwhile, blend half the cherries with 100ml water, then pass through a fine sieve into a saucepan on a medium heat. Add the rest of the ingredients, cover with a lid and simmer for about 3 minutes.

Take off the lid and cook for a further 5 minutes, then remove from the heat.

To serve, place two halves of soaked brioche, cut-side down, on each plate, top with some of the warm cherries and serve with the vanilla cream.

CHERRIES IN KIRSCH

Some of my earliest memories are of the wondrous Aladdin's cave that was the cellar beneath our house, filled with bottles and jars of home-made preserves, including the Montmorency cherries from the tree in our garden, which were bottled in local kirsch or the cherry alcohol my grandfather made. The drunken cherries (picked in June) would appear at Christmas. They are delicious straight out of the jar with a cup of good coffee, and once you have finished the cherries the juice can be drunk as a liqueur, or used to soak a sponge cake.

MAKES: enough for 1 x 2-litre jar

EQUIPMENT: kilner jar (sterilised, see page 312)

2kg sweet black cherries, such as Morello or Montmorency, stalks removed
200g caster sugar
1 vanilla pod, sliced in half lengthways
750ml kirsch

Wash the cherries in cold water and allow them to dry in a colander over the sink for 5 minutes.

Place the cherries in a sterilised jar, add the sugar, vanilla pod and kirsch. Seal the jar and store in a dark place for a minimum of two months. This maceration process is essential to enable the alcohol to permeate the flesh of the cherries.

PORK WITH PRUNES

This is a true home classic, which we teach to our students at the Cookery School at Le Manoir aux Quat'Saisons and everyone loves it.

My mum hardly ever used stocks, only water in dishes like this, as she believed that the meat or vegetables had enough flavour of their own to lend character and definition to a dish. Given that the vegetables came straight from our own garden, and the pork was wonderful and local, I think she was probably right.

These timings should give you pork that is golden brown on the outside and just 'blushed' on the inside so that the meat retains all of its juices and stays succulent. If you have a temperature probe, when the pork comes out of the oven the internal temperature should be 60°C. This will continue to rise as the meat rests and so the final temperature should be a minimum of 65°C.

The pork is beautiful served very simply with pomme puree and cabbage.

SERVES: 2

EQUIPMENT: ovenproof frying pan, cooking thermometer

6 Pruneaux d'Agen, cut in half and stoned

3 tablespoons Cognac

30ml sunflower oil

2 loin pork chops (500g), bone in, skin on and French-trimmed (ask your butcher to do this for you, but keep all trimmings)

pinch of rock salt

30g unsalted butter

150g pork trimmings

200ml water or chicken stock

1 garlic clove, peeled and crushed

1 fresh thyme sprig

2 fresh sage leaves

50ml Madeira wine

Soak the prunes in the Cognac for at least 12 hours or overnight.

Preheat the oven to 120°C/100°C fan/gas ½.

In a medium ovenproof frying pan over a low–medium heat, add the oil, season the chops with salt and place, skin-side down, in the pan for 10 minutes. Start with one edge for 5 minutes, then turn onto the other edge of the skin for a further 5 minutes, ensuring the whole skin is evenly browned and crispy.

Remove the pork from the pan and discard the oil.

Add half the butter to the pan and, on a medium heat, bring it to a light hazelnut colour. Return the pork to the pan on its flesh side, reduce the heat a little and pan-fry for 5 minutes. Do not move the pork, just allow it to sizzle gently so that the juices run out and create a beautiful residue on the bottom of the pan.

When the pork is golden brown underneath, turn it over to cook on the other side for another 5 minutes, basting the chops with the foaming butter.

Meanwhile, in a separate small frying pan on a medium heat, heat the remaining butter and the pork trimmings. Brown for 5 minutes, but do not stir. Add 50ml of the water or stock and scrape the bottom of the pan with a spoon to deglaze it.

Transfer the trimmings and all the juices to the pan of pork, lifting the chops on top of the trimmings. They will act as a trivet, keeping the meat away from direct heat and allowing the heat to circulate for the rest of the cooking time.

Add the garlic, thyme and sage and transfer the pan to the preheated oven for 30 minutes, basting occasionally.

Remove the pork from the pan (but retain this) and leave to rest on a plate for 15 minutes, covered with foil. As the meat rests it will continue to cook and, as mentioned above, if you have a meat probe, the temperature will rise to 65–66°C.

Return the frying pan to a medium heat, add the pork juices from the resting plate and the Madeira. Boil up for a few seconds to deglaze the pan, then add the remaining 150ml of water or stock and, using a spatula, stir thoroughly to incorporate all the residue created during the roasting. Taste and correct the seasoning if necessary.

Carefully strain the juices through a fine sieve into a bowl and then return to the pan.

Add the soaked prunes and simmer gently for 3–5 minutes. Spoon the sauce and prunes over the pork chop and serve.

PLUM AND GINGER CHUTNEY

When I first discovered the British love of chutney, everyone I spoke to seemed to have a special recipe passed down through the generations, which was often a closely guarded secret. Over the years, my Development Chef, Adam has shared many of his own secrets. I find chutney-making so absorbing that I am proud to be a Frenchman making my own little chapter of chutney history.

MAKES: 800g chutney

EQUIPMENT: kilner jars (sterilised, see page 312)

500g Victoria plums, stoned and quartered

150g white onion, chopped

1 garlic clove, peeled and crushed

10g fresh ginger, finely chopped

½ red chilli, deseeded and finely sliced

1 bay leaf

1 fresh thyme sprig

1 teaspoon sea salt

150g dark brown sugar

150ml cider vinegar

Bring all the ingredients to the boil in a medium pan, then reduce the heat and simmer for 20 minutes until the mixture has reduced.

Spoon into sterilised kilner jars and store in a cool, dark place for up to a year.

PLUM COMPOTE

Sometimes recipes don't need to be complicated. This simple compote gives a delicious burst of fruit to elevate anything from your morning porridge or yoghurt granola to a grilled pork chop or other meats or game. It is important that the plums are ripe so they will release a lot of juice. If they are very sweet and ripe, you can reduce the sugar to 40g. The compote is best made and served on the same day, or it will lose some of its freshness.

MAKES: 400g compote

EQUIPMENT: sealed container

50ml water
70g caster sugar
10g unsalted butter
400g plums, such as Yellow Pershores or Victoria, stoned and halved

In a medium saucepan let the water absorb the sugar. On a medium heat, bring to the boil, until you have a blond caramel. Carefully add the butter, which will emulsify into a golden syrup.

Add the plums and cook slowly, covered, for 20 minutes, stirring once at the beginning. Remove from the heat and allow to cool.

Cool completely in the fridge.

MIRABELLE CLAFOUTIS

This famous and very easy dessert is a French national treasure more usually made with cherries, but packed tight with mirabelles it is heavenly. However, you can also make it with other varieties of plums and greengages, apricots or peaches. Although I have said in the recipe that mirabelle eau de vie is optional, I am tempted to say it should be compulsory! The combination of lemon juice and mirabelle alcohol really enhances the flavour of the fruit – the children can still enjoy it as the alcohol will evaporate (mostly!) during cooking. However, it is also perfect *au naturel* if you have the best, small Mirabelle de Metz. The clafoutis mixture can be prepared a day in advance.

SERVES: 4

EQUIPMENT: 20cm wide and 5cm deep round ceramic or cast-iron baking dish, cherry stoner

For the mirabelles
450g mirabelles (preferably best-quality ripe Mirabelle de Metz), stoned
60g caster sugar
juice of ½ lemon
3 tablespoons mirabelle eau de vie (optional)

For preparing the dish
10g unsalted butter, melted
30g caster sugar, plus extra to finish

For the clafoutis batter

2 medium eggs (preferably organic or free-range)

45g caster sugar

½ teaspoon vanilla extract or vanilla syrup

20g unsalted butter

20g plain flour

50ml whole milk

75ml whipping cream

pinch of sea salt

In a large bowl gently mix the mirabelles, sugar, lemon juice and eau de vie, if using, in a bowl. Cover and leave to macerate for 2 hours for the sugar to slowly permeate the fruit and intensify the taste.

Preheat the oven to 180°C/160°C fan/gas 4.

To prepare the dish, brush the inside with the melted butter. Add the sugar and tilt the dish to coat the sides and base evenly, then shake out the excess.

To make the clafoutis batter, in a large bowl whisk the eggs, caster sugar and vanilla together by hand until creamy.

Meanwhile, in a small saucepan on a medium heat, melt the butter and cook until it foams and turns a hazelnut colour, making a *beurre noisette*. This butter will lend a wonderful roundness and nutty flavour to the clafoutis. Remove from the heat and pour into a small cold bowl to prevent it from burning.

Add the flour to the egg and sugar mixture and whisk until smooth, then slowly incorporate the milk, cream, salt and *beurre noisette*. Stir in the mirabelles with their juices and then pour into the prepared baking dish.

Bake the clafoutis for 30–35 minutes until it is lightly risen and a knife inserted into the middle comes out clean. The centre is always the last part to cook, so you must test it. Note that a dip in the middle suggests the clafoutis is undercooked.

Leave to stand for about 10 minutes. Sprinkle with caster sugar, if using, and serve just warm.

ACKNOWLEDGEMENTS

I would like to thank my friends and organisations and institutions who devoted a huge amount of their time to helping the creation of our heritage orchard, and also this beautiful little book.

Much gratitude to Will Sibley, fruit tree nurseryman and grafter, Dr David Pennell, former director of the National Fruit Collection at Brogdale, and his wife, Mary, Marcus Roberts, founder of the Mid-Shires Orchard Group, Xavier Guillaume, Vignobles Guillaume Earl, Pierre-Marie Guillaume, Pépinières Viticoles Guillaume, Brigitte Reard, Dr Barrie Juniper, and the RHS, especially Director General Sue Biggs, CBE, for her friendship and expertise. She never fails to support me and everything we do at Le Manoir. The RHS Garden at Wisley, NIAB EMR, particularly Operations Director Ross Newham, Grow at Brogdale, James Campbell, Chief Executive of Garden Organic, Ryton, and The Soil Association, especially Helen Browning and Ben Raskin; The Sustainable Restaurant Association, which is now celebrating its 10th year – I am proud to be Honorary President! Hundred Hills Vineyard and Winery, Waterperry Gardens, Arnaud Delbard, Pépinières et Roseraies Georges Delbard; Janice Hook and the Communications Team for HRH The Prince of Wales.

To the gardening team at Belmond Le Manoir aux Quat'Saisons, especially Anne Marie who never fails to support my vision, and James Dewhurst who regularly comes to maintain our orchard. Much gratitude to Hartley Botanic, who provided the wonderful greenhouse around which the Raymond Blanc Gardening School is centred – the first gardening school in the world to be based at a hotel or restaurant.

Adam Johnson, my Head Development Chef, and Daniel Fitzhugh, Assistant Development Chef, who have worked alongside me in creating these delicious recipes; Gary Jones, my Executive Head Chef, Benoit Blin, Chef Pâtissier, and everyone at the Raymond Blanc Cookery School. And thank you to Clare Scheckter from Laverstoke Park Farm who shared her family's crumble recipe.

My longer-suffering marshalls, Chloe Knight and Leanda Pearman; Lydia Shevell, my Business Director; Charlie Brotherstone, my literary agent; and, of course, Sheila Keating who has been the backbone of this book. I cannot thank her enough.

To Belmond Le Manoir aux Quat'Saisons for having supported me in the creation of this wonderful orchard project.

Enormous thanks to all of the talented team at Headline, especially Publishing Director Lindsey Evans and Senior Editor Kate Miles. To Copy Editor Kay Halsey, Senior Designer Siobhan Hooper, Publicity Director Louise Swannell, Head of Marketing Vicky Abbott, and Production Manager Louise Rothwell. And thank you to Clare Melinsky for her beautiful illustrations and Paul Wilkinson and Mark Lord for their wonderful photographs.

My loving sons, Olivier and Sebastien, for their helpful research. And last but not least, the support from my partner, Natalia Traxel, MD, PG DIP Nutrition, and teacher at The Raymond Blanc Cookery School, who wrote the 'An Apple A Day' section and her daughter, the brilliant Tata, who so patiently spent many hours with me taking dictation.

And, of course, Maman Blanc, who is at the heart of everything. The whole Blanc family celebrated her ninety-seventh birthday with her just as this book was published.

For all these friends – and family – a huge thank you.

Merci and much love.

RECIPES INDEX

INDEX